Gifts Galore

♥ ♥ ♥ ♥ ♥

Other books available from Chilton

Robbie Fanning, Series Editor

Contemporary Quilting Series

Contemporary Quilting Techniques, by Patricia Cairns

Fast Patch: A Treasury of Strip-Quilt Projects, by Anita Hallock

Fourteen Easy Baby Quilts, by Margaret Dittman

Machine-Quilted Jackets, Vests, and Coats, by Nancy Moore

Precision-Pieced Quilts Using the Foundation Method, by Jane Hall and Dixie Haywood

Putting on the Glitz, by Anne Boyce and Sandra L. Hatch

The Quilter's Guide to Rotary Cutting, by Donna Poster

Quilts by the Slice, by Beckie Olson

Scrap Quilts Using Fast Patch, by Anita Hallock

Speed-Cut Quilts, by Donna Poster

Teach Yourself Machine Piecing and Quilting, by Debra Wagner

Creative Machine Arts Series

ABCs of Serging, by Tammy Young and Lori Bottom

The Button Lover's Book, by Marilyn Green

Claire Shaeffer's Fabric Sewing Guide

The Complete Book of Machine Embroidery, by Robbie and Tony Fanning

Creative Nurseries Illustrated, by Debra Terry and Juli Plooster

Creative Serging Illustrated, by Pati Palmer, Gail Brown, and Sue Green

Distinctive Serger Gifts and Crafts, by Naomi Baker and Tammy Young

The Expectant Mother's Wardrobe Planner, by Rebecca Dumlao

The Fabric Lover's Scrapbook, by Margaret Dittman

Friendship Quilts by Hand and Machine, by Carolyn Vosburg Hall

How to Make Soft Jewelry, by Jackie Dodson

Innovative Sewing, by Gail Brown and Tammy Young

Innovative Serging, by Gail Brown and Tammy Young

Owner's Guide to Sewing Machines, Sergers, and Knitting Machines, by Gale Grigg Hazen

Petite Pizzazz, by Barb Griffin

Sew, Serge, Press, by Jan Saunders

Sewing and Collecting Vintage Fashions, by Eileen MacIntosh

Simply Serge Any Fabric, by Naomi Baker and Tammy Young

Twenty Easy Machine-Made Rugs, by Jackie Dodson

Know Your Sewing Machine Series, by Jackie Dodson

Know Your Bernina, second edition

Know Your Brother, with Jane Warnick

Know Your Elna, with Carol Ahles

Know Your New Home, with Judi Cull and Vicki Lyn Hastings

Know Your Pfaff, with Audrey Griese

Know Your Sewing Machine

Know Your Singer

Know Your Viking, with Jan Saunders

Know Your Serger Series, by Tammy Young and Naomi Baker

Know Your baby lock

Know Your Pfaff Hobbylock

Know Your White Superlock

Know Your Serger

Teach Yourself to Sew Better Series, by Jan Saunders

A Step-by-Step Guide to Your Bernina

A Step-by-Step Guide to Your New Home

A Step-by-Step Guide to Your Sewing Machine

A Step-by-Step Guide to Your Viking

Gifts Galore

♥ ♥ ♥ ♥ ♥

Jane Warnick and Jackie Dodson

Chilton Book Company
Radnor, Pennsylvania

Copyright © 1992 by Jane Warnick and
Jackie Dodson

All Rights Reserved

Published in Radnor, Pennsylvania 19089,
by Chilton Book Company

Designed by Martha Vercoutere
Charts by Jane Warnick
Illustrations by Jackie Dodson

Manufactured in the United States of
America

Library of Congress Cataloging in
Publication Data
Warnick, Jane
   Gifts Galore /Jane Warnick and Jackie
   Dodson; illustrations by Jackie Dodson
   p. cm. — (Creative machine arts series)
   Includes bibliographical references
   and index.
   1. Handicraft. 2. Gifts.
   I. Dodson, Jackie. II. Title. III. Series.
TT157.W3565 1992   91-58295
745'.5—dc20   CIP

ISBN 0-8019-8236-7 (pb)

1 2 3 4 5 6 7 8 9 0   1 0 9 8 7 6 5 4 3 2

Dedications

♥ ♥ ♥ ♥ ♥

This book is dedicated to my aunt, Ella Schuhmann Spacek, and all the other unsung heroines and heros who give lovingly of their time and talents to raise money for their schools, churches, hospitals, and favorite charities.

JW

And to the generations in my family who discovered, then passed down to me, the joy of making things by hand.

JD

Contents

Acknowledgments

Thank you:

♥ To Jackie Dodson, who knows everything about making gifts, putting on bazaars, and writing books, for being the world's greatest co-author and buddy through good times and bad.

♥ To Robbie Fanning for making sure that all our "i's" are dotted and "t's" are crossed.

♥ To Dawsie Crain for teaching me how to transform an eight-foot table into an attractive booth with no more than a station wagon full of tricks, but mostly for her friendship.

♥ To Debbie Casteel of Aardvark Adventures for sharing supplies, ideas, and experience.

♥ To my children, Shannon, Philip, Alyson, and Mary, for their support, enthusiasm, and help. And to the next generation, Lisa and Collin Hegemeyer, for another reason to create toys and baby quilts.

♥ To my father, Dr. Dan Schuhmann, who taught me through his example that giving is the greatest joy, and to my mother, Dorothy, who has sewn, knit, crocheted, needle-pointed, and crafted throughout my life.

Jane Warnick

Thank you:

♥ To Bernina of America, for the loan of its 1230 sewing machine; and to baby lock, for its serger. Both machines made the construction of my gifts easy and the results beautiful.

♥ To the women—and men—in my classes who let me try out new creations on them and in turn gave me dozens of new ideas and different slants on my old ones.

♥ To Jane Warnick, who is brimming with creativity and is probably the most needle-work-knowledgeable person in the world (not a bad combination for a book like this). And to Robbie Fanning who always makes sentences and me sound better.

♥ And to the countless others who shared their talents and imaginations with me—needlework people are indeed the most giving people in the world.

Jackie Dodson

Introduction

Our book title, *Gifts Galore*, tells it all: Inside, you'll find more than sixty-five projects to make for gifts or for sale at your next bazaar. This is the book to consult when you need a quick hostess gift or an instant gift for Aunt Sally when she arrives unexpectedly on Christmas Day. It's the book to search for a project that will take some time, but not much movement, when you have a sprained ankle and you're not supposed to run around for several weeks. It's the book to scrutinize when your best friend has her first child or grandchild. It's the book to explore when you need fifty favors for a particular event. And especially, it's the book to save your sanity when you have to supervise a bazaar.

It's the book we're sure you will return to year after year whenever a gift-giving occasion arises, whether it's for stocking stuffers or a masterpiece commemorating a once-in-a-lifetime occasion.

Each project is fully self-contained. Starting with a description of the gift, you'll find the supplies needed, along with complete directions. Sometimes we've suggested other projects for which you can use the same techniques.

Usually one idea leads to another, and variations of the original idea are born. We've included these, too. Because this is a book on how to make gifts by the ones or hundreds, there are production methods included at the end of some projects if they can be made in quantity.

We wanted a book with simple patterns, so we opted for geometric shapes (e.g., circle: sewing bag; square: totes; rectangle: make-up bag; triangle: angel pins; parallelogram manicure kit).

The few organic shapes used are also simple. And most of the gifts are easy to make, yet sophisticated, classic, and timeless—gifts we love to give and receive.

Be sure to write down your thoughts, the instructions you worked differently, the recipient of the gift you made, the colors and/or fabrics used, the cost to make—whatever you wish that will make this book yours.

In Chapter 1, "Beginnings," we suggest what tools are important and what supplies you need to make the projects. If you can't find supplies locally, look in "Sources of Supplies" at the end of this book.

Chapters that follow, from 2 through 8, are organized as bazaar booths. In Chapter 2, "It's in the Bag" booth shows you how to construct containers—bags to make and use in place of the throwaway bags polluting the environment. Chapter 3, "Special Delivery," includes stationery and gift wrap ideas. Chapter 4, called "Knit One," is a knitting booth full of everything from a small coaster to a baby blanket—using one magic knitting formula. In Chapter 5, "Grandma's Corner," we've included gifts anyone will enjoy making for children; Chapter 6, "A Woman's Touch," contains gifts that range from a nostalgic collage of yesterday's treasures to Quick Glitz Earrings for today. "M is for Male," Chapter 7, includes gifts that are exciting to make and fun for men to use.

Bazaars are more often held just before Christmas, when churches, friends and neighbors, craft clubs, schools, and community centers display and sell the gifts, stocking stuffers, and decorations made throughout the year. In Chapter 8, "The Christmas Exchange," we've included enough Christmas decorations and ornaments to keep you crafting for years.

Chapter 9, "Bazaars and Fundraisers," will give you the confidence to volunteer, not be coerced, into chairing the next fundraising function at your church, school, or guild.

If you've just become the chairman of a bazaar and this is your first experience—or even if you've had the job for years—you may want to read Chapter 9 first.

The preceding paragraphs are some of the things this book is. Now, here are a few words about what this book is *not*. This book is not a "learn to," but a "how to" book. We assume that you know your sewing machine, knitting machine, or serger. The knit, crochet, and needlepoint projects—while not difficult—also presume a basic knowledge of the techniques themselves. If there is a craft you have yet to master, our projects will tempt you.

Check the "Index" for projects that are technique-specific. For example, if you want to do needlepoint, look under that heading to find all the needlepoint projects. Do the same for sewing machine, crochet, knitting, etc.

We also can't tell you how to do business in your subdivision, town, city, county, or state, whether you're interested in selling what you make on your own—through or to a shop—or whether you're involved with a fundraiser for a nonprofit institution. We don't cover topics such as liability, insurance, sales taxes, permits, etc.—all information that you will need. We don't tell you what prices to charge; it depends not only on the cost of goods, but on what people in your area will pay. We don't know whether or not raffles are legal where you live. (Check with local authorities for any ordinances involving charitable events.) Purchase the current edition of *Starting and Operating a Business in (Your State)*, by Michael D. Jenkins with co-authors from each of the states. (See "Sources of Supplies" if you're interested in selling the gifts you make.)

When our children were in school, we worked on bazaars, school fairs, boutiques, auctions, whatever the current fundraiser. We've made countless ornaments and wreaths, aprons and potholders, sewing kits and bonnets, purses and totes, beads and earrings and pins. We've made one-of-a-kind, state-of-the-art gifts and favors for scores of women at large luncheons.

So when we first started talking about writing this gift and bazaar book, we knew we had a lot of experience to bring to it; ideas that we hadn't had room to use in other books, grandchildren who needed entertaining, a planet in danger from too much pollution, causes and questions, a knowledge of craft fairs gained from participation as contributors and purchasers, a love of making the gifts we give.

We want to share with you what's worked and what hasn't; how we convinced our friends, children, husbands, mothers, fathers, aunts, uncles, and anyone else we could corral to help us put the finishing touches on a hundred patchwork ornaments that had to be ready the next day.

Mostly, we want to give you a book that didn't exist for us when we said, "Sure, we'll chair the Spring Fair. How hard could that be? Everybody will help, won't they?"

We have a great deal in common—we love to make and give handmade gifts. When we give a gift that we've made, we give our greatest gift, a piece of our allotted time on earth. Consequently we had two prerequisites when choosing the gifts for this book: They had to be something *you* want—something that fits into your life and interests—and *we* had to enjoy making them. We feel we've succeeded in including something for everyone, and yes, we had fun doing it.

By the way, after you receive a handmade gift from us, we hope when you see it or wear it or use it, you remember us. (And in case you might forget, we always sign and date our work.) Welcome, and merry creating to all.

Chapter 1

Beginnings

Fig. 1.1 Supplies

Supplies Needed

The world has been experiencing unbelievable technological advancements. Traditional methods of doing almost everything are being replaced so quickly by faster and simpler procedures, we often haven't grasped one new way before it's replaced with another! As it is in the world at large, so it is in the world of sewing. Every day new products are coming on the market that change the way in which we sewers and crafters work. Decorative stitches on sewing machines get larger and larger, making them more appropriate as decoration on sewing and craft projects than the weak lines produced on the older machines' 4mm zigzag widths.

The majority of the projects in this book are made on a sewing machine. You can construct all of them on a simple zigzag machine and most of them on a straight-stitch machine. Some projects call for spe-

♥ *A T-square is suggested in several projects for making perfectly square shapes. If you don't have one, place your large ruler along one edge and another ruler on top and perpendicular to it.*

cific presser feet, only because they make the stitching easier (though a *Teflon* foot is a must for sewing on plastic).

If you have an old straight-stitch machine, substitute hand embroidery where we've used decorative machine stitching; turn hems, and straight stitch where we've used satin stitch edges. If you have a serger, we've suggested where its use is most appropriate, but it's not a necessity for any project in this book.

We suggest and use the following tools: First, if you don't own a rotary cutter (Fig. 1.2), mat, and a large plastic ruler with clearly delineated markings every 1/8" (3mm), put them on your want list now.

Fig. 1.2 *Rotary cutter*

Pages would be needed to tell you how these simple tools have not only reduced cutting time, but have made cutting much more accurate, since the fabric is not lifted from the cutting surface as it is with scissors.

Use a hemostat (Fig. 1.3) for turning small

Fig. 1.3 *Hemostat*

items, or use the collar point and tube turner that looks like a pair of old-fashioned ice tongs (Fig. 1.4).

Use vanishing markers to draw designs on

Fig. 1.4 *Collar point and tube turner*

fabric and a white opaque permanent marker (available at office supply stores with typing supplies) to draw on water-soluble stabilizer (another staple in our studios).

Owning several sizes of scissors for trimming threads and clipping curves makes cutting tasks more convenient.

It doesn't matter whether you own a hot or

low-temp glue gun, but using one or the other often saves time. *Household Goop* is our glue of choice for most projects, but we also use thick white tacky glue on occasion. Whenever possible, use *Wonder-Under, Transfuse,* or *Aleene's Fusible* to bond fabric to fabric or fabric to paper.

There are several implements on the market for turning tubes; add one to your bag of tricks today (Fig. 1.5).

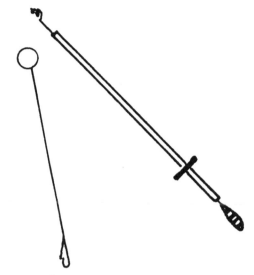

Fig. 1.5 *Two kinds of tube turners*

Wooden chopsticks or skewers make excellent stuffing tools. Use eyelet pliers to apply eyelets to the sewing bag and to set grommets in the totes. If you're making only one or two of these items, make machine-made eyelets; if you're going to produce a plurality, buy the pliers.

Work needlepoint and cross stitch on a frame of some sort so blocking is reduced to simple steaming or is completely eliminated (Fig. 1.6). Also, the needlepoint is easier to

Fig. 1.6 *To prevent distortion, use a hoop when stitching needlework.*

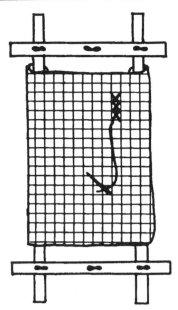

Fig. 1.7 *Stretch needlework on a frame to keep it straight.*

work with both hands if the piece is framed (Fig. 1.7), but that's a personal preference.

Both of us choose circular knitting needles over straight ones because they're lighter and don't extend beyond the body (something to consider when knitting in a crowded waiting room).

You'll find some special notions explained in several of the projects. The notions used are generally available at your local fabric, crafts, or quilt stores. If you're house-bound or live far away from stores, everything is available through the mail. (See "Sources of Supplies.")

Buying and Storing Supplies

Once you've purchased your tools and supplies, and your closets, basement, garage, and dining room table overflow with your hoard, how can you cut the clutter and get organized for the bazaar or just for yourself?

First of all, we understand clutter and can't imagine a house without it. Because we are constantly asked questions like "Where do you put all that stuff?", "When do you buy your treasures?", and "Why are you stockpiling everything?", we've decided to reveal our secrets.

Although we live hundreds of miles from each other, we find that we buy and store our purchases much the same way. And we feel we are experts at organizing (and sometimes hiding) "things."

We both have ideas gathered from our lifetimes of what Jane calls "gleaning." Yes, we buy a lot of things, and not just when we need them. We have plastic sweater boxes full of water-soluble stabilizer, for example. Instead of buying one package, we'll buy ten when the price is right. We know we'll use this item, and the purchase may save us a trip someday when we need it again.

We make lists of things so that when we do get away from our sewing machines and computers, we remember what we need now and what we'll need in the future (Fig. 1.8).

Fig. 1.8 *Keep running lists of items you need to buy at craft and fabric stores.*

If we see something else along the way that sparks an idea, that goes in the shopping cart, too. Then we can try the idea at our leisure. We are always looking. We want to know what's new and we want to see everything available. We always wonder how to use those things in new and different ways.

It's true, we don't look at fabric, paper, markers, threads, beads, and other supplies the same way as those who make only one gift a year. And it's true that those who buy gifts don't understand us at all, which sometimes includes our own families.

Once Jane's husband wandered into her fabric closet (some might call it a warehouse). It contained her harvest: the results of gleaning the best from sale tables, discount fabric stores, factory outlets, and yes, a trip or two to Britex Fabrics in San Francisco. It wasn't a small closet and there were shelves on both sides. Fabric was everywhere, yards and yards of fabric. Her husband came downstairs and looked at her with puzzlement. "What on earth are you going to do with all that cloth?"

Jane looked as confused as he, because when she looked in that closet she didn't see fabric. She saw aprons, blouses, stuffed animals, dresses, bibs, purses, quilts, curtains, appliqués, doll clothes, Christmas ornaments—all the gifts you'll find in these pages, plus many more.

Harvesting isn't limited to fabrics. We also plow through office supply stores, hardware stores, thrift shops, after-Christmas sales anywhere we find them, crafts stores, big discount warehouses, and—a life-long favorite—mail order.

The wire ornaments found at an after-Christmas sale and used in the ornaments on page 113 are an example of some great gleanings. Jane took one look at the white metal angels and immediately saw the wings and skirt filled with sewing machine-made lace. She bought all the angels she could find in the basket, and now that she's "filled" them, they'll find their way onto friends' trees this year.

Jane's greatest secret (and if they only knew, she would be the envy of fishing enthusiasts everywhere) is that she owns more tackle boxes than even the most avid fly and lure collector. She got the idea the day Debbie Casteel of Aardvark Adventures in Handicrafts walked into a machine-embroidery class and opened up what looked like a mundane tool box of some sort. When the lids were pulled back, and tray after tray of *Natesh* thread in every color imaginable slowly came into view, Jane was hooked! She now owns tiny tackle boxes (for bobbins and needles); medium-sized boxes (plasticene clay in one, rubber stamps and special stamp pads in another, stuffing and ornament finishing supplies in a third); and large boxes (which hold beads and jewelry findings, machine-embroidery teaching supplies, as well as buttons and related closings).

Over the years we've both accumulated quite a treasure trove of raw materials—from tiny seed beads to king-sized quilt batts with absolutely everything in between. Consequently storage is a sizable problem. We need barns; every good harvester should have one. But alas, no barns. Here's a clue to where most of the fruits of Jane's collecting presently dwell: Her car hasn't lived in the garage since it was acquired. Jane's fabric is washed and stored in boxes: long, narrow, under-the-bed boxes, as well as office file ones.

Jackie has a similar storage problem, but it's her basement that's jammed with cardboard storage boxes packed full of fabric, yarn, and lace. Jackie's fabric is stored according to type (velveteen, corduroy, lining, etc.) and sometimes according to color (red, white, and blue cotton or black and white prints). In an upstairs sewing room closet is the fabric she needs today.

She also uses plastic boxes of every size and description. The boxes are stacked in bookcases and contain beads, buttons, fabric paints, stabilizers, interfacings, stamps and stamp pads, doll supplies, templates, presser feet, sewing machine needles, and knitting needles. Cardboard storage boxes hold patterns, handmade paper supplies, and teaching supplies (stored according to class).

Jackie uses small, tabletop cabinets with drawers that hold jewelry findings and other small items. Markers, pencils, pens, stencil knives, crochet hooks, and short rulers stand up in a six-cup plastic rug yarn holder (Fig. 1.9). A divided cutlery tray holds jewelry-making tools, a small hand drill, pliers, etc.

Fig. 1.9 Six-cup plastic rug yarn holders keep pens, pencils, brushes, and hooks handy.

Jackie has a metal cabinet with twenty-seven drawers, which would probably be more at home in a basement workshop, that holds thread (according to color), zippers, *Velcro*, ribbon, etc. Another smaller cabinet contains drawing supplies. A desk is made from two sets of double files and an *Elnapress* is on the desk. Triple hanging baskets fill the corners of the room (Fig. 1.10), and are full of assembled project

Fig. 1.11 Expanding files store ideas, while various boxes and notebooks organize other project supplies.

Fig. 1.10 Triple hanging baskets hold supplies most often used.

pieces not yet started or those items she doesn't want to get lost (basic patterns often used for the Victorian stocking, skirts, dolls, bags and purses). Two boards with angled pegs hold still more sewing thread.

Pegboards hold sewing notions, glues, and small plastic baskets for direction sheets on using the glues, paints, and notions. Bulletin boards cover doors in the sewing room so works in progress or finished projects can be tacked up and analyzed.

We both use cardboard file boxes, moving boxes, clothes baskets, and every kind of storage bin we find on sale. Also we both have lots and lots of tote bags (each one holding a separate project).

Ideas are stored in expanding files (Fig. 1.11), cardboard boxes, notebooks, and sketchbooks. These are our greatest sources of inspiration. We believe there is truly little new under the sun. (We won't say "nothing new," though it's what we believe.) Instead, we constantly reinvent by discovering a craft that is new to us and making what seems a stupendous discovery—only to find that someone's been there before. We don't let this discourage us at all. In fact, many of the projects in the book contain new needlepoint stitch variations and crocheted cords that have come out of creative play. They aren't discoveries along the line of a new world; they're related to building on the past. Just because we haven't been able to document them doesn't mean they haven't been done before; they are simply new to us.

Record your own creativity through any means you wish. A good idea you have today may not be realized for many years, but it won't be lost if recorded somewhere accessible. We've started idea files on our computers: word-processing files in which we enter quotations, ideas, anything that tickles our imaginations. We also impale things all over our walls, trap cards and pictures to our refrigerators, and make piles on any horizontal surface.

Now is the time to get organized! Gather your supplies, and have a wonderful time making gifts galore.

Chapter 2

It's in the Bag
Tote Bags and Purses

Projects:

- ♥ *Grocery Sack Totes*
- ♥ *The "Knit One" Tote*
- ♥ *Fanny Packs*
- ♥ *Metamorphosis Purse*

When we stop and think about the waste that's generated every day in our neighborhoods alone, we wonder how the earth keeps spinning. We recycle newspapers, cans, and glass, but nobody wants our old telephone books. Our paperback books are traded for different ones at the used bookstores; some magazines go to area hospitals; unwanted clothes go to organizations for distribution to the homeless. Yet with all that recycling, we still have several bags of throwaways every pickup day.

> ♥ *When painting glue on the back of paper or pictures, place the paper right side down on the pages of your old telephone book while applying the glue. When finished, tear off the telephone page, and use a new one for each application of glue.*

Because of our concern for the environment, we've designed many of the projects in this book to use up the bits of flotsam and jetsam collected over the years. In this chapter, we have bags for you to make that will eliminate at least one type of throwaway from your life.

Included are directions for several styles of totes, lined and unlined. You can make any size you want by changing the dimensions of the body piece and scaling the other pieces up or down as needed. It's not possible to have too many totes (use them to store projects or any item you don't know where else to hide).

In this chapter you'll find directions for a purse that can grow from a coin-sized bag to a suitcase. Make purses to match every outfit; make them for gifts, for sale, or for yourself. Personalize them with pockets to hold specific items.

Also included is a quick decorating project for a purchased fanny pack. These bags leave your hands free to carry home your purchases in whatever bag you choose.

Grocery Sack Totes

Fig. 2.1 "Eat at Mom's" grocery sack

What better fundraiser could an organization have than selling tote bags for carrying home groceries? If you're a member of a school organization, talk with the art teacher about having students silk-screen a design on the front of the bag. Run a contest among the students for a design or slogan for the front of the tote: "Buy a bag, save a tree." "Packs for Provisions." "Grocery Grip." Or use the school or club emblem for the front design.

Wash the fabric, cut out the bags, mark the area to be decorated, and give the patterns to the art department. When the silk-screening is complete, construct the bags.

Tulip Paints has begun marketing an iron-on heat transfer called *Happy Chalk,* on which you can write with chalk. Bond one to the front of your tote bag (see Color Plate 6), and write your grocery list on it. On the back of the tote, add a pocket for the chalk and eraser that comes with the transfer.

Brown paper grocery sacks don't come with pockets, but we put two on the inside of this bag. One to hold the grocery coupons we hope to use on the current shopping trip, and the other to hold car keys. You may want to add a zippered pocket for your driver's license and checkbook—then you can leave your purse at home.

The bags are 11" x 7" x 17" (28cm x 18cm x 43cm), which was the size of the sack we measured. These are constructed the same way as the old-fashioned brown sack with a center back seam and a square reinforced bottom. The addition of the handles, however, means that you can carry several sacks at a time, and get from the car to the kitchen counter without dropping one of them.

The totes are constructed with the lengthwise grain running around the sack rather than up and down, which makes better use of the fabric. If you prefer to have the lengthwise grain run up and down, you will need 3/4 yard (69cm) for each sack.

Denim, our fabric of choice, often comes in a 60" (1.5m) width. Cut any pockets from this extra width. Use both sides of the denim, depending on whether you want a light or dark bag. Cut appliqués from the denim and use the reverse side as shown (see Color Plate 6).

You Will Need:

(makes two sacks)

1 yard (.9m) of 44" (112cm) heavyweight denim, duck, or canvas
2 yards (1.8m) 1" (2.5cm) webbing
Denim sewing machine needle
Thread to match denim
Wonder-Under (optional)
Stop Fraying

1. Cut the fabric in half on the fold (two pieces 22" x 36" [56cm x 0.9m]). Turn under one long edge (top), press, and stitch 1/2" (1.5cm) from the edge. Turn and press an additional 1" (2.5cm) along this edge. Open out again. Put right sides together, and stitch the center back seam using a 1/2" (1.5cm) seam allowance. Overcast these two edges together with a zigzag stitch. Press this seam to one side and topstitch 1/16" (1.5mm) from the cut edges. Turn the 1" (2.5cm) pressed hem at the top to the inside and stitch in place 1/8" (3mm) from the edge. Stitch another line 1/4" (6mm) away.

2. Cut the webbing into four 18" (46cm) pieces. (Reserve two for the second bag.) Put *Stop Fraying* or clear nail polish along the cut ends. At the top edge of the bag, on both sides, make a mark 3" (7.5cm) away from the center back seam. Fold the bag in half to find the center front. Then make corresponding marks on the front of the sack. Place the cut ends of the webbing on the inside, one strap on either side of the center back seam and one strap on either side of the center front seam. Make ends even with the bottom of

♥ *To make a comfortable carrying handle: In the center of the webbing bring the sides of the webbing together in the middle. Overlap them, and stitch along the edge, beginning 6" (15cm) from one end and continuing for 6" (15cm). Remove the presser foot and guide the stitching by placing a hand behind and in front of the webbing and easing the fabric through the machine.*

Overlap the handle webbing and stitch in place.

the hem, and place them so the inner side of the webbing aligns with the marks you made. Be sure the webbing is placed so the **soft** side of the doubled edge is inside (Fig. 2.2). Stitch the webbing in place by stitching the pattern shown (Fig. 2.3).

Fig. 2.2 *Place handle's cut ends at the bottom of the hem.*

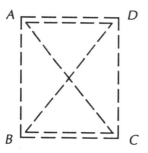

Fig. 2.3 *Stitch around from A to A. Then continue stitching to C, B, D, and finally, back to A to attach the handles.*

♥ *When bonding two fabrics together with an adhesive webbing such as Wonder-Under or Transfuse, use your iron to heat the area where the appliqué will be bonded. Place the fabric right side up on your ironing board, and run the iron back and forth across the area for at least one minute. This will heat the ironing board, as well as the fabric, and makes for a stronger and quicker bond.*

3. Bottom: With right sides together, fold the bag in half so the center back seam is at one side. Stitch the bottom seam. Press the seam open and zigzag both raw edges. Fold the bottom so the seam is in the middle as shown in Figure 2.4. The base of the triangle

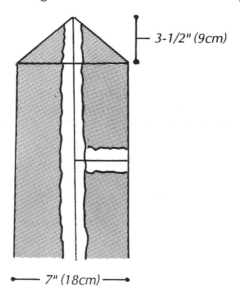

3-1/2" (9cm)

7" (18cm)

Fig. 2.4 *Fold bag as shown; then stitch across to create the bottom.*

measures 7" (18cm). Be sure the 3-1/2" (9cm) mark on the ruler is at the center of the bottom seam. Draw a line perpendicular to the bottom seam on the 7" mark. Stitch on the line you drew. This boxes the bottom of the bag. Repeat for the other side. Fold the two points to the bottom seam. Stitch each triangle 1/8" (3mm) from the folded edges, plus across the base of the triangle. Turn the bag to the right side.

4. Finishing: Press fold lines at the sides from the bottom to the top. Stitch 1/16" (1.5mm) away from each creased edge. Fold the bag along the bottom and stitch 1/16" (1.5mm) away from the edge along the bottom front and back. The finished bag is strong and durable, yet folds flat for storage.

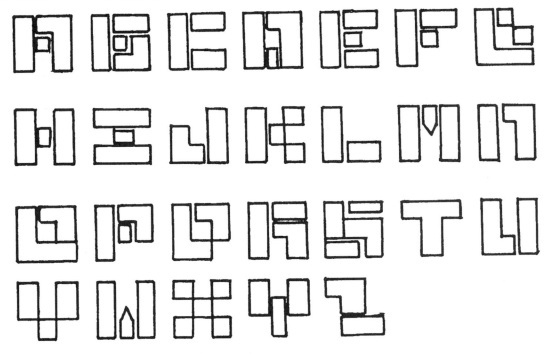

Fig. 2.5 *An alphabet based on squares and rectangles*

Variations:

A. The alphabet (Fig. 2.5) that's used on the tote (Fig. 2.1) is one Jane developed as a satin stitch alphabet for a needlepoint project. To interpret it in appliqué, bond an 8" x 12" (20.5cm x 30.5cm) piece of *Wonder-Under* to a scrap of the denim. With your rotary cutter and ruler, cut this into eight 1" x 12" (2.5cm x 30.5cm) strips. Cut the 12" (30.5cm) strips into 1" x 3" (2.5cm x 7.5cm) strips. You will need to cut some of these into 1" x 2" (2.5cm x 5cm) and 1" (2.5cm) square pieces. Use these strips to form letters. Bond the letters to the front of the bag. Straight or zigzag stitch around the letters or outline with dimensional glitter paint after the construction is complete.

B. Paint or stencil a design.

Production:

To produce these totes in quantity, do step 1 on all the bags, then steps 2, 3, and 4. Decorations, whatever decided on, should be completed after the bags have been cut out and before any seams are sewn.

♥ *Add any pockets before the bag is sewn together. The pockets may be sewn on the inside or the outside, with or without flaps or zippers. To make the pockets: Double the fabric by folding in half, right sides together. Press under 1/2" (1cm) on both sides of the bottom edge. Stitch the side seams and turn to the right side. When you stitch the pocket in place 1/8" (3mm) from the edge, the bottom opening of the pocket will be closed.*

Fold ↴

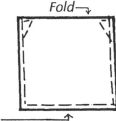

This end open with seam turned inside ⟶

Fold pocket piece in half (right sides together), stitch, turn right side out, and fold up bottom. Attach to bag.

The "Knit One" Tote

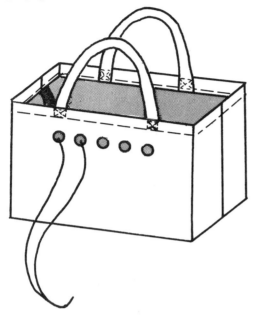

Fig. 2.6 *Grommet holes on knitting tote keep yarn from tangling.*

If you're like us, you prefer knitting with large needles so the job goes faster. However, if you have only fine yarn, or you want to combine yarns for special effects, you may have to knit with several strands of yarn held together. It's a hassle keeping these threads from tangling. Remember when we used to put separate balls in cutoff bleach bottles and feed the yarns through the handles? Or do you put severals balls of yarn in a box and cut slots for each?

One day, as Jane was removing her current project from one of the tote bags, cogs turned, lights flashed, and she had a great moment of inspiration: Why not put large grommets in the side of a tote bag and feed each strand of yarn through a separate hole? (See Color Plate 6.)

You won't need any additional paraphernalia and the yarns won't tangle. Maybe it's not a better mousetrap, but it's made our knitting neater and more compact.

Two separate events prefaced the idea of stitching one end of a measuring tape into the hem. (1) Jane's Aunt Ella, from Dime Box, TX, had a small sewing bag with a tape

attached; and (2) the local discount store had tapes on sale for thirty-three cents each. Since most hand-knitting patterns instruct "knit until piece measures however many inches from the starting row," and since one can never find a tape measure when it's needed, stitching a tape into the hem is a time-saver.

When we talked about this chapter, we decided to make all the totes of denim because of its durability and accessibility nationwide. We knew there was a choice between light and dark blue, pre-washed light blue, streaky, and black. But little did we expect the wonderful range of denims at local chain fabric stores. Not only do they have white denim that we can dye any color our hearts desire, but they have fabulous prints as well!

When you want a tote to stand alone, line it with purchased quilted fabric. We advise against lining totes that you intend to use as shopping bags; the extra bulk makes them cumbersome to carry around until they're needed.

Unlike the previous tote, this one has a fold at the bottom, not a seam.

You Will Need:

1/2 yard (46cm) printed 44" (112cm) denim (tote)
1/2 yard (46cm) quilted 44" (112cm) fabric (lining)
1 yard (0.9m) webbing
5 large grommets and kit for setting
Cloth tape measure
1/2" (1cm) seam allowance included throughout

1. Even up the cut ends of the denim and lining fabric. Your fabrics should measure about 18" x 44" (46cm x 112cm). Cut 6" (15cm) (pocket) off one end of the denim (18" x 38" [46cm x 96.5cm] remains), and 8" (20.5cm) (pocket for lining) off one end of the lining fabric (18" x 36" [46cm x 91.5cm] remains).

2. Tote Pocket: Turn 1/2" (1.5cm) to the wrong side on both short ends, and press. Fold the pocket in half with right sides together, and stitch the sides. Turn to the right side. Place the pocket on the center of the front on the top side of the tote fabric, 6" (15cm) down from the top. Stitch the pocket in place (1/8" [3mm] from the edge). This pocket is perfect for tucking in glasses, a pencil, a ruler, or straight knitting needles.

> ♥ *If you use circular needles, coil them and store in the top-loading polyester sheet protectors found at office supply stores, and note the size on a gummed label. Stitch the sheets together in the margins (or place in a notebook).*

3. Tote: Fold the bag in half with right sides together, matching the short ends, and stitch the side seams. Fold to create the bottom as shown in Figure 2.4, measuring 2-1/2" (6.5cm) down from the point (5" [12.5cm] across). (Remember, however, the bottom of this tote is on the fold and not a seam.) Draw a line across, and stitch along it. Stitch the resultant points to the bottom of the bag as you did on page 8.

4. Lining: Construct the lining pocket and the lining as you did the tote. Make the following label to stitch to the outside of the lining pocket before it's attached to the tote: "If found, please call (fill in telephone number)" and stitch it into place. You can type on some fusible interfacings, write on muslin, or stitch using the alphabet on your sewing machine.

5. Finishing: With the tote bag wrong side out and the lining right side out, place the lining inside the tote bag with the pockets on opposite sides. Stitch the two layers around the top, leaving 6" open along one side for turning. Turn to the right side and push the lining into place, which will cause a hem to be formed at the top since the lining's shorter than the tote. Place about 1/2" (1cm) of the 60" (1.5cm) end of the tape measure under the hem at the opening. Stitch 1/8" (3mm) from the edge of the tote fabric hem all the way around, closing the opening and catching in the tape measure at the same time (Fig. 2.7). Stitch the lining 1/4" (6mm)

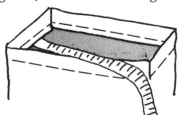

Fig. 2.7 *Stitch a tape measure under the top hem of the tote bag.*

away from the stitching line on the tote. Attach the five grommets 1" (2.5cm) apart in the center of one side, 2" (5cm) down from the top. Cut the webbing in half (two 18" [46cm] pieces). Seal the cut edges with clear nail polish or *Stop Fraying*. Stitch them in place as shown in Figures 2.2 and 2.3.

Variations:

A. "The Crochet Too Tote": We crochet and knit a lot of small projects, some of which you'll find among these pages (see "Index"). If you don't need a tote as large as the previous one for your projects, then make a smaller version of the knitting tote, complete with tape measure.

Use a piece of denim 12" x 24" (30.5cm x 61cm) for the tote and 12" x 22" (30.5cm x 56cm) for the lining. Cut pockets out of scraps. Attach five large grommets.

Make a crochet hook holder from a see-through sheet protector made of polyester (available at office supply stores) as follows: Carefully cut a line halfway down horizontally from edge to edge on only one side of the protector. This allows you to slip crochet hooks inside half way down. Stitch pockets 3/8" (1cm) to 3/4" (2cm) wide (depends on the size of your hooks) from the slit to the bottom. Stitch a 24" (61cm) piece of narrow ribbon in the margin between the bottom two holes. Slip your hooks in the pockets, turn the top edge down, roll up, and tie with the ribbon. Make it glitzy by sewing the top edges together, filling the top part with stuff, and sewing it closed right above the center slit.

B. You may reinforce the bottom by cutting an additional 18" x 11" (46cm x 28cm) piece out of the same or contrasting fabric. Turn under 1/2" (1.5cm) on each 18" (46cm) side, and stitch in place at the center of the body piece (13" [33cm] down) before proceeding with step 2. This reinforces the bottom and partway up the sides.

Fanny Packs

Fig. 2.8 *Decorate a ready-made fanny pack.*

Fanny packs are one of those things you refer to when you say, "Why didn't I think of that?" After years of slinging heavy purses and tote bags over our shoulders, we can now sigh, "Free at last." Mothers with small children are wearing them because it's like suddenly discovering an extra hand.

There are many different styles available in fabrics ranging from tapestry to suede and leather. Some contain zippered compartments, others have slots for credit cards. Patterns are available for these popular fanny packs, but the following idea is for someone who doesn't have time to make the pack from ground zero. And this ready-made leather bag, found at a discount store, costs less than if you started making the bag from scratch.

The black leather bag ($5.99) is a perfect background for leather and *Ultrasuede* scraps. Not only are you halfway to the end, the boring part is eliminated.

You Will Need:

Fanny pack
Ultrasuede and leather scraps
Shells
Assorted beads
Feathers
Heavy duty (carpet) thread
Silver cones (available at craft stores)
Scissors
Household Goop
Needle-nosed pliers

1. To decorate the pack, we pulled out *Ultrasuede* and leather scraps of black, grays, dark fuchsia, grayed orchid, lavender, blues, purple, as well as a piece of embosssed leather that reminded us of snake skin painted with all the leather colors. Use sharp scissors to cut the leather, and *Household Goop* adhesive to attach it on the bag.

2. First cut a strip of black *Ultrasuede* (5" x 3" [13cm x 7.5cm]) and fringe it by cutting into the strip at least 4" (10cm) and 1/8" (3mm) apart. Glue this strip of fringe to the center front bottom of the bag with fringes protruding down beyond the bag. Trim the fringe to follow the curve of the fanny pack. Next cut light blue *Ultrasuede* into a triangle with a 4" (10cm) base and height 2-1/2" (6.5cm). Curve the base of the triangle, and place the fringe on top of the black strip at the center front of the bag (Fig. 2.9). (Be sure you can see the black fringe underneath.)

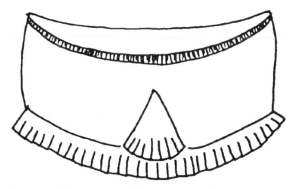

Fig. 2.9 *Glue a strip of fringe across bottom of pack and a fringed triangle above it.*

Next cut three long feather shapes from the same black *Ultrasuede*, each 5" (12.5cm) long and approximately 1-1/2" (4cm) at the middle widest point. Clip down the side of one feather making fringe on only that one side. On the second one, fringe the opposite side. On the third shape, cut fringes down both sides of the feather (Fig. 2.10). Arrange these in the center of the pack (Fig. 2.11).

Fig. 2.10 *Cut out* Ultrasuede *feather shapes and fringe them.*

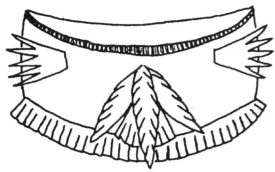

Fig. 2.11 Overlap and glue feathers in center of pack.

Cut gray leather (tanned carp skin) into two triangles 3" (7.5cm) wide at the base and 3" (7.5cm) high. Each was fringed at the bottom; the fringe clipped to a point. The point of the triangle was clipped off. Glue one of these to each side under the zipper (Fig 2.12).

Fig. 2.12 Cut off points of two triangles, then clip fringes into points.

Cut two feather shapes from two other colors (four feathers), but **don't** fringe them. Glue them at both sides of the center, one overlapping the other. Then glue another fringed feather shape of lavender blue suede above and between them. At the center front, glue a dark royal purple fringe feather (Fig. 2.13).

Fig. 2.13 Glue feather and triangle shapes to the pack.

Now that all the feathers are in place, cut 1/8" (3mm) strips of each color from your scraps. Fold in loops if long enough, and glue a lump of a dozen strips across the center front of the bag below the zipper. On top of this glue a strip of the embossed leather to hide the raw edges of all the strips and feathers.

Cut eight free-hand triangles of the tiny scraps left from the colors used. Glue these to the embossed leather across the front of the bag.

3. Then stitch square shards of shells or appropriate beads on top of the triangles. Through the center holes of the shells, stitch beads to hold the shards in place (Fig. 2.14). If you use beads only, this may not be necessary. The beads chosen are black, white, and lavender blue, and look like irregularly shaped small pony beads.

Fig. 2.14 String beads, and add feathers along with loops of leather under the zipper. Attach squares and triangles of leather with shells and beads.

Thread a needle with black polyester carpet thread or black waxed linen. Knot the end of the thread, and poke the needle through the bag at top center front. String the same beads on the thread, add a decorative clay bead at the end, and poke the needle back up through all the beads (except the clay bead). Stitch through to the inside of the bag and anchor your thread. Use needle-nosed pliers to help you pull the needle through the leather. Add another string of beads in the same manner next to the first.

4. On two of the leather strips glued to the pack, string a large clay bead at the end and tie a knot in the strip to keep the bead in place. String three other strips through silver cones. Stuff small feathers into the large ends of the cones (after covering the ends of them with *Household Goop*).

5. As a final precaution, go back and add adhesive under any leather pieces you feel need more glue. Then fill in with more strings of black and gray clay beads and long triangle shell shards like the square shards sewed to the top area.

This is only one idea to show you how to take an ordinary black fanny pack and make it extraordinary. Go to your bead, button, and trinket stashes, and put together your own original.

Variations:

A. Blank fanny packs of white or colored fabric to paint, appliqué, or embroider are also on the market. But don't limit yourself to fanny packs, consider decorating the blank tote bags, satchels, and purses found at craft and discount stores.

B. Purchase a bag of small flat wooden shapes at a craft shop, and build pins and earrings by gluing the bits of leftover leather scraps, beads, shells, etc. to the shapes. If you'd rather start from ground zero, check out the patterns in the craft and accessory sections of the pattern books at your favorite fabric store. Or see "Sources of Supplies."

Metamorphosis Purse

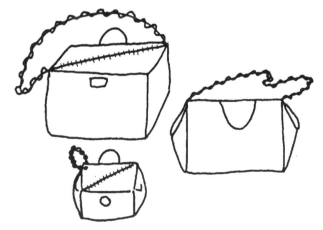

Fig. 2.15 *Coin bags and purses made from the same pattern.*

Several months ago a friend pulled out a coin purse that was intriguing because its closed shape was completely different from its open one. The purse was constructed of four rectangles, and in our minds' eyes we saw it going through a steady metamorphosis from a tiny coin purse all the way up to a carry-on for the airplane.

The sides are each squares, the body is a long rectangle, and the top is a rectangle that is divided diagonally into two triangles. It's a favorite bag to produce because of the ease of construction, its versatility, and the long rectangle that lets us showcase any technique that strikes our fancy. (See Color Plate 6.)

As you can see, the bag has a flap closure that can be any shape or size. We wanted a curved flap so we did as our grandmothers used to do when they needed a circle: We took several glasses, cups, and plates from the cupboard until we found the size we wanted. We drew the flap on heavy paper, and added a 1/2" (1.5cm) seam allowance at the top. Then we cut it out without adding any seam allowance around the shape.

The 5" x 7" (12.5cm x 18cm) is a favorite size for daytime; large enough to hold the essentials (wallet, checkbook, makeup, comb, sewing kit, day book), not quite big enough for the kitchen sink. The bag is also pickpocket proof, an important factor for us city folks.

The body portion of this bag must be interfaced with heavyweight interfacing. Interface both the body pieces and those of the lining if using lightweight fabric, and only the lining if the outer fabric is substantial. The body lining fabric may be quilted *before it is interfaced* to give added support if necessary. Nothing screams "homemade" louder than a bag that sags as soon as anything is placed inside it. If, after all your efforts, you still find that some sagging takes place, cut several pieces of plastic needle-point canvas a little smaller than the top, make a pocket of the lining fabric, slip the canvas inside, and close the end with a close satin stitch. Place this in the bottom of the bag for added support.

Make your first one of these bags with pre-quilted fabric inside and out. You'll have a bag within an hour or two, and will have learned the construction. The variations listed after the instructions will only be a start for your imagination. Leave off the flap and you have the square variation.

You Will Need:

- 18" x 22" (46cm x 56cm) (fat quarter) pre-quilted outer fabric
- 18" x 22" (46cm x 56cm) (fat quarter) pre-quilted lining fabric
- 18" x 22" (46cm x 56cm) fusible heavy-weight interfacing
- 7" (18cm) zipper
- Double-link handbag chain
- Two 11mm jump rings
- 18" x 22" (46cm x 56cm) *Wonder-Under*
- Scrap of 1/8" (3mm) grosgrain ribbon
- One magnetic French snap or *Velcro*
- Sewing machine
- Eyelets (optional)
- 1/4" (6mm) seam allowance included throughout

1. Cut the following pieces out of the outer fabric and the lining. Sides: two 5-1/2" (14cm) squares; Top: 5-7/8" x 8" (15cm x 20.5cm) (cut along the diagonal into two triangles); Body: 7-1/2" x 15-1/2" (19cm x 39.5cm). Reserve the scraps of the outer fabric for the flap and the scraps of the lining for the inner pocket.

2. Cut pieces of fusible interfacing as follows: two 5" (12.5cm) squares, one 5" x 7" (12.5cm x 18cm) piece (cut along diagonal into two triangles), one 7" x 15" (18cm x 38cm) piece. Bond to the lining, leaving the 1/4" (6mm) seam allowances free all the way around each piece. With the *Wonder-Under*, bond the interfaced lining pieces to the outer stitched pieces.

3. Inner Pocket: Cut a piece of lining 6-1/4" x 4-1/2" (16cm x 11.5cm) and a piece of interfacing 4" x 6" (10cm x 15cm). Bond interfacing to the wrong side of lining fabric. Press 1/4" (6mm) seam allowance along each 4-1/4" (11cm) edge to wrong side. Fold pocket in half with right sides together and stitch side seams. Turn, and with the folded edge of the pocket as the top, stitch in place 1-1/2" (4cm) down in the center of the body lining.

4. Top: Overcast the diagonal cut edge with a

zigzag stitch. Stitch these triangles together along the diagonal for about 1" (2.5cm) at each end using a 1/4" (6mm) seam allowance. Press seam open along the entire edge. Stitch the zipper in place (Fig. 2.16).

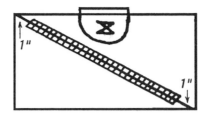

Fig. 2.16 *Stitch zipper in place beginning 1" (2.5cm) from each end. Stitch* Velcro *on flap toward zipper.*

5. Flap: Place two scraps of outer fabric with right sides together, and draw around with the flap pattern (Fig. 2.17). Stitch around the curved edge. Trim, turn to right side, and press. Topstitch 1/8" (3mm) from the edge all around. Stitch the hook side of the *Velcro* in place on one side of the flap. Stitch the flap to the center of one side of the back of the zippered piece with the *Velcro* underneath. (See Figure 2.16.)

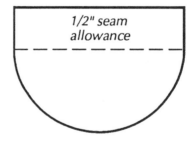

1/2" seam allowance

Fig. 2.17 *Flap pattern*

> ♥ *Using small straight stitches, stitch* Velcro *in a Z and return to the starting point. Buy* Velcro *by the yard in 3/4" (2cm) width. Keep the two sides pressed together. Using a penny as your template, cut as many circles as you need. This procedure is much less expensive than purchasing the pre-cut closures.*

6. Body (long rectangle): Stitch the loop side of the *Velcro* closure to the center of one short end of the body rectangle (Fig. 2.18).

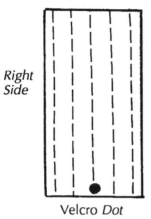

Right Side

Velcro *Dot*

Fig. 2.18 *Stitch one piece of* Velcro *to center bottom edge.*

Place marks 5-1/4" (13.5cm) from each short edge on both sides. Clip in 1/4" (6mm) at these marks. Place the right side of the body to the right side of one of the side squares (be sure the quilting lines are running up and down the same as the body) (Fig. 2.19).

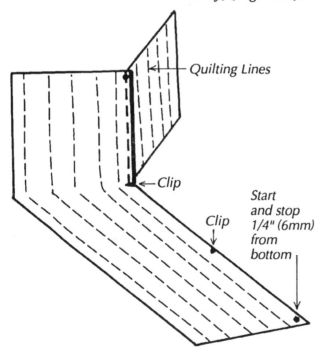

— Quilting Lines

—Clip

Clip

Start and stop 1/4" (6mm) from bottom

Fig. 2.19 *Stitch end piece to long rectangle. Turn at clip, and stitch bottom. Then turn, and stitch other side.*

With the body on top and beginning 1/4" (6mm) down, stitch to the first clipped point (Fig. 2.19). Leave the needle in the fabric and turn, pulling the body into place along the next side of the square. Again, stop at the clipped point and pivot with the needle in the fabric.

Stitch along the remaining side, ending 1/4" (6mm) from the body edge. Repeat for second side square. Zigzag the seams together.

7. Finishing: Open the zipper. Cut two 2" (5cm) pieces of the grosgrain ribbon. Fold in half, making a loop, and stitch to the top at opposite corners (Fig. 2.20). Pin the body of

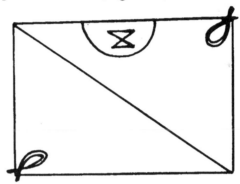

Fig. 2.20 *Attach narrow ribbon loops at opposite corners.*

the bag to the top, being sure the eyelets are on the same side. With the body on top, stitch in place, stopping and starting at each corner. Turn to the right side through the zipper. Hand stitch a decorative button on the flap if desired. Attach jump rings to the chain, then attach the jump rings to the grosgrain loops. Check out the crocheted cords in Chapter 6, page 57, for substitutes for the metal chain.

Variations:

A. To make the square bag, eliminate the flap and *Velcro* closures. Attach a grosgrain ribbon loop to the center of the two short sides of the top. Then attach the chain to the loops.

B. Needlepoint the long rectangle, and use *Ultrasuede* for the side squares, flap, and top. Bond fleece or iron-on interfacing to the suede for added support.

C. Quilt a piece of fabric before you cut out the purse by stitching with a 2mm twin needle. Instead of quilting lines: (1) stitch lines of decorative stitching either with one needle or two; (2) couch narrow ribbon in place along the marked lines; (3) work lines of hand embroidery through all layers with #5 or #8 pearl cotton; or, (4) outline quilt the motif on printed fabric.

D. Use any technique (Seminole, string-piece, cross stitch, crazy quilt) on the long rectangle.

E. Here are some suggested sizes for the tops from a coin purse to an overnight bag: 3" x 4" (7.5cm x 10cm), 4" x 5-1/2" (10cm x 14cm), 5" x 7" (12.5cm x 18cm), 6" x 8-1/2" (15cm x 22cm), 7" x 9" (18cm x 23cm), 8" x 10-1/2" (20.5cm x 27cm), 9" x 12" (23cm x 30.5cm), 10" x 13-1/2" (25.5cm x 34.5cm), 11" x 15" (28cm x 38cm), 12" x 16-1/2" (30.5cm x 42cm), 13" x 18" (33cm x 46cm).

Here's an example of how to figure out the dimensions of the pieces: Consider the first dimension of 3" x 4" (7.5cm x 10cm).

For the top, add 7/8" (2.5cm) to the dimension of the finished shorter top side (3" [7.5cm]), and 1" (2.5cm) to the dimension of the finished longer side (4" [10cm]) of the top rectangle (3-7/8" x 5" [10cm x 12.5cm]).

The side squares are the smaller of the dimensions (3" [7.5cm]).

The long side of the body rectangle is the sum of three sides of the side square plus seam allowance (3"+3"+3"+1/2"=9-1/2" [24cm]).

Use the long side (4" [10cm]) of the top piece plus seam allowance (1/2" [1.5cm]) as the other dimension of the rectangle (4-1/2" [11.5cm]). In other words, the body rectangle is 9-1/2" x 4-1/2" (24cm x 11.5cm).

F. If you don't want to quilt the purse, substitute heavyweight iron-on interfacing for the batting.

Chapter 3 will show you many other ways to recycle: Create one-of-a-kind art to use for note cards and envelopes; stamp your own wrapping paper; and personalize plastic bows for gifts by filling them with memorabilia or junk— from scraps of yarn to odd buttons. It's all so much fun, you may never buy anything new again!

Special Delivery
Stationery, Cards, and Gift Wrap

Projects:

- ♥ *Postcards*
- ♥ *Fabric-Covered Stationery*
- ♥ *Embroidered Cards*
- ♥ *Envelopes*
- ♥ *Make-It and Take-It Booth*
- ♥ *Filled Plastic Bows*

When we were children in school, just before Mother's Day, we made Mother's Day cards by drawing a toothbrush loaded with paint across a window screen. There was a cutout on the card to block the spatters in that area. What magic! We've been making cards ever since. (Purchased cards? We collect those in a design file.)

When we made these glitzy postcards, we were doing what we like to do best—creating and recycling. No two cards are ever alike, and once we made the first card, we couldn't stop. It lead to another and another.

You'll find stationery items in this chapter as well as collages for framing or sending. And if you're in charge of this year's bazaar, have we got a booth for you!

Postcards

Fig. 3.1 *Sprinkle glitter, threads, ribbon, and fabric scraps over index cards. Then cover with clear plastic and stitch in place.*

How do we know you'll love receiving one of these cards? Because we would. The following directions are also useful for Christmas ornaments, belts, purses, even raincoats.

Start now to save every snippet of fabric, every thread picked off your dark sweaters or the floor, scraps of rick-rack and ribbons, lace, newspaper clippings or comic pages, poems, ads, wrapping paper, fortunes from cookies, and sequins.

Also consider razzles (shiny colored metallic hearts, stars, snowflakes, squares) and colored glitter. Card shops offer packages of metallic ribbon in great colors.

You Will Need:

Some or all of the above
Glue stick
Teflon presser foot for sewing machine
Large index cards (4" x 6" [10cm x 15cm])
   or Strathmore Series 300 Art Paper
Clear plastic or acetate (the one for use in copiers can often be found at your local discount office supply stores)
"Postcard" rubber stamp (optional)
#80 or #90 sewing machine needles, "sharps" or "jeans"

1. Use the index cards or cut your own from the art paper (a heavy, beautiful paper that comes in several sizes and colors). According to the post office, the card must be a minimum 3-1/2" x 5" (9cm x 12.5cm) and a

maximum of 4-1/4"x 6" (11cm x 15cm) to qualify for the postcard rate. If you make a larger postcard, it will require more postage than the postcard rate. (If in doubt, contact your local post office.) Cut the acetate or plastic slightly larger than the art paper postcard. Use a rotary cutter and mat to cut both the paper and the plastic.

2. You may want to begin by making a generic card. Cut out an interesting newspaper column or piece of fabric, dab the back with glue stick, and place it on the postcard. If you have other cutouts, glue those down too. Then add snips of ribbon, rick-rack, cord, yarn, and sprinkles of sequins, glitter, and a few razzles. Don't glue down these items as you want them to move around. Place a piece of clear plastic over the postcard collage.

Set your sewing machine on a longer than normal length (use 2-1/2 to 3mm—8 to 10 stitches per inch) and a sharp #80 (#12) needle. Sharps are also called "jeans" needles. Choose a thread color that goes well with the colors in your card. If you sew with metallics, then use a #90 (#14) needle to make a larger hole in the card, which helps keep the thread from fraying.

Place the presser foot on top of the postcard edge. If possible, change the needle position on your machine to far right. Stitch the postcard, beginning at a short side. Continue across the long side and up the second short side. Now is your last chance to change the placement of any of the collage ingredients. Do this with a long darning needle or slim scissors. Remember that the smaller pieces will move, slip, and slide when completed, but move the larger pieces at this time to uncover any part of the background you wish to see. Continue stitching to the end, sewing a few stitches over the beginning ones—in the same holes if possible. Clip threads close to the card. When finished, use the rotary cutter and ruler (or a paper cutter if one is available) to clean up the edges. Turn the postcard over and use a rubber stamp labeled "Postcard," if you have one. (If you don't have a rubber stamp, see "Sources of Supplies" at the back of this book.)

3. Generic cards are all you see in art galleries and craft shows, but we like to make cards for special occasions and special people.

A. Birthday: Find an old birthday card or wrapping paper with "Happy Birthday" on it. Cut out the greeting and place it on the card. Add confetti, razzles, ribbons, a small balloon, and whatever else is appropriate. Use foreign stamps in a card for someone who loves to travel, or the daily horoscope item for a "New Age" friend. Make a party invitation beginning with a photo of the honoree, perhaps a baby photo for a fortieth or fiftieth birthday, adding whatever glitz and glitter you have on hand.

B. Patriotic: Add tiny paper flags (cut them off toothpicks or buy stickers). Cut out a few pictures from magazines such as Uncle Sam, firecrackers, and stars. Add razzle stars, ribbon, gold rick-rack, and glitter.

C. Forget-Me-Not: Cut out the front picture from a seed packet of the tiny blue flower and add old 1930s bridge tallies, for example. (You can find bridge tallies at garage sales and flea markets.) The paintings of flowers on the tallies are fitting. Add ribbons and lace or silk threads before shaking glitter over the whole card.

D. Christmas: For this one, make a collection of old poinsettia sticker packages, red and green ribbons, gold rick-rack, a Christmas poem, and a tally of Christmas candles.

E. Rose: Collect and dry rose petals from your garden. Place them on a background of a magazine photo of roses placed on rose-colored art paper. Add a quotation about gathering rosebuds, some confetti, old tiny embroidered rose appliqués, a bit of old lace, and some clippings of glittery thread.

F. Sewing: These are for friends who sew. Cut labels off rick-rack packages or mending tape, and add a cardboard of tiny hooks and eyes. Then add a needle threader, threads, rick-rack, ribbons, and the usual razzles and sequins. Be careful you don't get too much bulk on these cards.

Variations:

A. Make large sheets of collage, using either fabric or plastic as a backing. Cut out simple purse patterns or belts from them. Judy

Murphy of Atlanta, GA, made a raincoat using this technique. She incorporated buttons into her plastic fabric and straight stitched freely over the coat to hold the threads, buttons, and junk together.

B. Jane Hill from Boca Raton, FL, added a string of tiny Christmas lights and a battery pack in her blinking plastic collage purse—which brought down the house when she spoke on wearable art at a luncheon Jackie attended.

C. Catch glitzy Christmas ribbons and glitter between two pieces of clear plastic. With a marker, draw around a shape (use Christmas cookie cutters, or draw and cut out simple shapes of cardboard for patterns). Use the type that is water-soluble, yet marks on plastic (the ones used for marking transparencies for overhead projectors). Stitch around inside the marker lines. Cut out the shapes with pinking shears or scissors. Use a paper punch to cut a hole for hanging the ornament and thread a cord through (Fig. 3.2).

Fig. 3.2 Sprinkle glitz between two pieces of clear plastic, stitch into Christmas ornament shapes, and cut out.

Production:

Personal cards are special gifts, but this is also a craft that makes up quickly and works beautifully for bazaars. To make these cards quickly, production-line style, use index cards. First cover the table with newspaper, which happens to make cleanup up easier. Then lay out the entire package of cards in rows on the table. Travel from one row to the next, adding newspaper clippings, magazine pictures, or fabric scraps. Glue in place for a

> ♥ *Start with baseball, football, or Barbie trading cards—available at toy stores everywhere. Add doll-sized hangers to the appropriate cards.*

background. Metallic papers are also effective. Different colored tissue paper cut in tiny pieces works well; when overlapped, the pieces resemble watercolors.

> ♥ *If you're a long-time watercolor painter, cut unsuccessful paintings into card-sized pieces and proceed. If you're just learning to paint, use your practice works for cards.*

Cut up ribbons and rick-rack and place them in piles in front of you. Do the same with glitzy fabric, threads, yarn, and cord. Don't rule out garment labels, tickets, sales slips, lace, old photos, poems, phrases cut from magazines, anything. These cards may be the ultimate in using the most recyclable material in one project. Open packages of razzles, sequins, glitter, and such, placing them in separate saucers. With all your ingredients in front of you, travel from one card to the next, adding a bit of collage material to each card. Place a piece of plastic on each, and you're ready to sew.

Several members of your production company can stitch what one or two others put together. It's extremely fast, and so much fun you won't want to stop making postcards. Unless, of course, you start making note cards. To do this, stitch on top of one side of a single-fold blank card, or slip a small collage into a double-fold card. Then stitch around the card's round or square opening.

Fabric-covered Stationery

Fig. 3.3 *Cover plain note cards with fabric.*

It's pretty clear that we love rummaging in thrift shops. We've been known to buy old cotton aprons that look like comfortable grandmas wore them all day. Many are faded, while some are patched and darned. (Do you understand this?) Other people collect stamps; we collect fabric. When we planned the greeting card booth, we thought of the fabric-covered cards we make with new fabric. Why hadn't we used the apron collection before this? Our friends will love cards with one-of-a-kind fabric on them, and we know that quilters, sewing enthusiasts, mothers, and grandmothers will relish them.

You Will Need:

Wonder-Under
Blank note cards or art paper
Rotary cutter and mat
Old fabrics

1. First cut the aprons into squares or rectangles by cutting or tearing off any curves, ruffles, the ties and pockets (but don't throw them away—there's always tomorrow's ideas). Press the fabric (we washed the aprons when we brought them home), and iron a fusible such as *Aleene's* or *Wonder-Under* to the back of the fabric.

2. Cut the fabric (use a rotary cutter, mat, and large plastic see-through ruler) to match your blank note cards (we cover the entire card, front and back). You can also cut out the fabric to cover an index card or heavy art paper that you've cut into postcard size.

3. Iron the fabric onto the card. Go back and trim the edges with the rotary cutter and fold the note card if desired. Score the fold line with your ruler and a table knife by drawing the knife down the line. After you've folded the card lightly, draw the knife along the crease to set.

Variations:

Use this technique to make gift tags or enclosures. Prepare a yard of Christmas fabric with a yard of fusible, and iron it to large sheets of art paper. Involve the children by having them draw on the paper side around shapes (small cookie cutter stars, stockings, and hearts). If they have mastered scissors, let them cut out shapes. With a paper punch, punch a hole at the top of the tag or enclosure, slip a cord through the hole, and knot off. Sell these items individually or as a pack by putting five into a small plastic bag.

Embroidered Cards

Fig. 3.4 *Example of embroidered, double-fold note cards.*

You can purchase cards that are specifically designed with cutouts to showcase your chosen technique (see "Sources of Supplies"), or you can make a card such as described below. Perhaps you have boxes full of half-completed projects. Cut out the good parts, and place them in one of these cards for a special greeting.

Use one of these cards for an occasion when the invitation indicates "No gifts, please." Technically, this isn't a gift, it's a card. Ah, but such a special one! One that says I cared enough to go an extra step, and I stayed within the stated guidelines. Well, maybe I pushed them a bit.

Fig. 3.5 Art Deco card insert

If you are hesitant about designing your own card, use this idea: Find a print fabric such as the one in Figure 3.5 with Art Deco women on it. On this particular fabric, each "picture" averages about 3" x 4" (7.5cm x 10cm). Buy several yards, and embroider cards for everyone who is special to you.

To begin: Take a small scrap of quilt batt and place behind the fabric. Then overstitch a few lines, add a few French knots, several beads as earring or trim, completing it all by hand.

At the time of this writing there are all kinds of wonderful pictorial prints available. You'll find animals and insects, fish and fowl, people and autos—about anything you might want. If you don't have time to add a few embroidery stitches, dot on a bit of glitter or dimensional paint.

Visit a neighborhood printer and ask to buy several sheets of different types of heavy paper, usually called Bristol or cover stock. It comes in smooth and linen finishes and the most delightful array of colors. You can sometimes get envelopes to match. Scale the cards to get two from each sheet. Large cities have paper supply stores that are generally open to the public. The only problem is that you must buy a large quantity, usually at least one hundred sheets. This is great for bazaars, but boring for one person (unless you have five yards of a certain print like the Art Deco one described above).

You will Need:

Heavy paper (art paper, Bristol, or cover stock)
Rotary cutter, ruler, and mat
Olfa circle cutter (see "Sources of Supplies")
Paper glue
Masking tape
Table knife (dull)

1. Decide on the size of your card. Example: If your paper is 8-1/2" x 11" (22cm x 28cm), cut it in half the long way (4-1/4" x 11 [11cm x 28cm]). Measure into three equal areas (approximately 3-2/3" [9.5cm]), and make a light mark at each line. With your ruler and the dull knife, score the two fold lines on the "wrong" side of the paper. Cut a circle out of the center third (Fig. 3.6A).

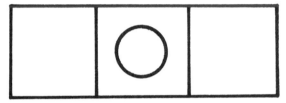

Fig. 3.6A. To make a double-fold card, cut out a circle in the center and score the two fold lines.

2. Fold the right side behind the center (Fig. 3.6B), and the left side back behind the front of the card (Fig. 3.6C). Open out, and slip

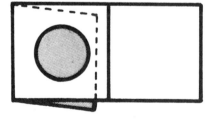

Fig. 3.6B. Fold the right side behind the center.

Fig. 3.6C. Fold the left side back behind the front of the card.

your embroidery behind the opening. Tape or glue it in place.

3. Somewhere along the bottom of the opening, sign your name and mark the date in tiny letters and numerals, using black ink. (A razor point pen such as the Pilot Razor-point permanent ink pen works well for this step.)

Variations:

A. Cut squares, triangles, or ovals—instead of circles—with a craft knife.

> ♥ *When cutting out an area, always place your ruler or guide outside the cutting lines. If your knife slips, it will cut into the area you intend to discard, which is much better than ruining your card.*

B. Using one of the paint pens, especially the gold or silver, draw a line around the opening about 1/16" (1.5mm) to 1/8" (3mm) away from the cut line.

C. Use a straight or decorative stitch on your sewing machine, and stitch around inside the edge of the opening. This procedure attaches the embroidered fabric at the same time you decorate the card.

Production:

Cut up interesting fabrics to highlight in the opening, such as beaded bits from old dresses or embroidery from old linens. Free-machine embroider to highlight aspects of certain prints. We've bought cards at craft shows that are filled with examples of knitting done with interesting yarn on a knitting machine. Perhaps you have a weaver in your group who can do some plain weave with interesting combinations of specialty yarns.

Set up an assembly line: One person cuts the cards, another the openings, and a third glues the embroidery in place.

Envelopes

Fig. 3.7 Make and decorate your own envelopes.

Notepaper and cards are all well and good, but what about the envelopes? A card without an envelope is like a car without a garage, a coat without a closet, or a book without a cover. The easiest envelope to use is one already made, such as the small or large white envelopes we use for business purposes. Another source is all those leftovers you keep in the drawer for the day you'll need them. Surprisingly, that day has come! When you create the notepaper we've described in this chapter, gear the size to fit one of your extra envelopes. Or purchase open stock envelopes in stationery and office supply stores before you make the notepaper.

Don't even think of sending out these envelopes with their blank boring exteriors. Decorate them with stickers from your youngsters' collections, or use rubber stamps.

You don't have any leftover envelopes? It's midnight and all the stores are closed? Not to worry. If you have a sewing machine, read on. Even if you don't have a sewing machine, read on—there is always glue.

Make envelopes from magazine pages. Yes, it sounds a bit zany, but you must have stacks of reading material you'd like to recycle. Many slick magazine pages are a melange of gorgeous color and delightful designs. Envelopes of recipes may be useful to the young adult away at school. Or what toddler wouldn't love colorful cartoon characters? If making envelopes free style is too adventurous for you, use plain heavy art paper and follow the directions below.

You Will Need:

Glossy magazine pages
Sewing machine
Plain address labels 3-1/2" (9cm) wide by
    1-15/16" (5cm) high
Blank mailing labels
Return address labels

1. Cut a piece from the magazine page or art paper twice the size of the folded note, plus 1" (2.5cm) all the way around. When finished writing your note, fold the envelope page in half and slip the note inside. Take it to your sewing machine and stitch around all three open sides close to, but not into the notepaper inside. (There is ample room for stitching.) Trim back to the stitching with scissors, rotary cutter, or paper cutter.

2. Place one of your return address stickers on the upper left-hand side. In the upper right-hand side, place a plain label for the stamp (the postal service takes a dim view if its cancellation can't be seen). Use another larger blank label on the front for the address.

Variations:

A. Open up a standard note card envelope and trace it on heavy art paper or your magazine page. Then fold and glue the new envelope to copy the sample. Watch your junk mail for interesting envelopes that you can use as patterns.

♥ *Make your own "lick'em" glue for the envelopes by boiling flavored gelatin (the old-fashioned real sugar kind) with water in a one to two ratio—one part gelatin to two parts water. Bring to a boil, and stir until all the gelatin has dissolved. Let cool a bit, but apply while it's still warm. Let dry for a day or two. Store extra glue in the refrigerator in a microwave-safe container so you can easily reheat when you need it.*

B. Making envelopes out of old magazines is a good art project for children. Better yet, give the smallest children in your family a pad of plain paper and a new box of crayons. Have them draw pictures or patterns, or write on the paper. Let the children who have mastered scissors cut out the artwork, and fold and glue them into envelopes.

Show children how to score the paper before folding, using their school rulers and a dull knife drawn along the fold line. Slip five or ten envelopes into a plastic sandwich bag to sell at the next bazaar. These envelopes also make great gifts for teachers, aunts, uncles, and grandparents.

C. If you have a sewing machine with an alphabet and numbers, stitch the address to a piece of heavyweight fusible interfacing, and bond it to the front of the envelope.

D. If you have a labels program for your computer, make your own labels. Then keep a good supply of them for your children and family. If you want to hear from children on a regular basis when they're away from home, make up a stack of postcards or envelopes with your address and a stamp for them to take along.

E. Check out the nametag labels at your favorite card store. You may find some that will work on the fronts of envelopes. Jane found "Hi Y'All" tags at a Texas store which work well. Another idea is to glue shaped *Post-it Note Pads* to the envelopes.

F. Save all the perfumed strips from magazine ads. Cut them into one inch pieces, and slip them into the envelope along with the card. Remember the perfumed stationery of the 1940s and 1950s? (But don't send these to your friends with allergies.)

Make-It and Take-It Booth

Fig. 3.8 Make wrapping paper by hand-stamping rolls of plain paper.

When the children were young, one of our favorite Christmas projects was making our own wrapping paper. We have a large collection of rubber stamps, and we used them to stamp images using colored stamp inks on white shelf paper. Sometimes we used broad marking pens to make designs on the paper, and often we combined the two techniques.

At your next bazaar, set up a booth where children can make wrapping paper for a fee. Have a lot of helpers (older children, perhaps ten and above) so that you have about a two or three to one ratio (children to helpers). This also serves as a baby-sitting booth where parents can leave their younger children while they shop the bazaar.

You Will Need:

Nontoxic paints (such as *Createx*)
Sponge stamps
Large roll of 36" (91.4cm) white paper on stand with cutter (you may use old newspapers for sponge printing)
Plastic dropcloths to cover tables and the floor
Styrofoam plates on which to spread the paint
Rubber stamps and stamp pads
Nontoxic broad markers
Low tables such as those used in primary grades
Extra tables or wooden drying racks
Old medium and large T-shirts (try the thrift shops) for the children to wear to protect their clothes
Soap and water for washing hands

There aren't any specific directions. Put all the materials out, slip the T-shirts over the children, and stand back. You could also

---

♥ *You can also print with sliced fruits and vegetables—a project we've done with children as young as nursery school age. They used* **Createx** *to stamp vegetable images on flour sack towels for Mother's Day presents. Or they stamped images on T-shirts.*

---

set up a learn-to-quilt booth for children. Or find volunteers who'll bring sewing machines, squares of muslin, and spring hoops so children can do free-machine embroidery. (From past experience, we promise you'll have a longer line waiting to embroider and quilt than those waiting to play computer games.)

Read on for another idea for a Make-It and Take-It booth.

Filled Plastic Bows

Gifts for men aren't easy to find, so when we found ready-made plastic pouches for bow-making at a craft store, we thought first of filling those bows with something for men and making bow ties. And then we got serious.

Though the bows are supposed to be made into barrettes (and don't discount this use), these have potential as special bows to use instead of ribbon when wrapping gifts. Fill them with items chosen especially for the birthday boy or girl. For example, for a man's gift box, we filled one bow with fishing flies and lures, and pulled the center together by using one repulsive plastic lure with tentacles (Fig. 3.9).

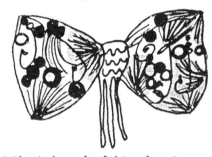

Fig. 3.9 Plastic bow for fishing fanatic

Another bow was filled with sewing items (Fig. 3.10), and a third was made with little

Fig. 3.10 Plastic bow for sewer

girls in mind. The third bow was filled with things girls tend to enjoy: ribbons for their hair, charms, a couple of worry dolls, and buttons of clock faces, pencils, and flowers (which could go on new garments).

The final bow is made for lovers of antique textiles (Fig. 3.11). It's filled with lace, two fine hand-crocheted motifs, small velvet flowers, and French ribbon; and it's decorated with an old pearl button.

Fig. 3.11 *Plastic bow for button lover*

You Will Need:

Plastic bows (see "Sources of Supplies")
Fillings

1. All the bows are filled the same way. Two sides of the bow overlap in back, and that's where you place the "fillings." If you pull out the edge of the underside first, it stays open and is easier to pour things in. Slip the edge back underneath, and fill the other side. Don't glue anything as you want items to slip and slide around inside the bow, or you may want to use all those things later.

2. Pinch the bow together in the middle, and wrap a small fine wire (we use twist'ems) around the center. Then twist the two ends together. If you don't have wire, rubber bands work well, too. Cover the wire or rubber band with an attractive ribbon, glue on a button, or add a worm lure. Put it on top of a package and listen to the compliments.

Variations:

A. Plastic ribbon is available by the yard in craft stores. You can fill it with all these same things and then heat seal it with your iron (directions are available where you buy the plastic ribbon). If you make plastic bows for your bazaar, use the heat-seal type for economy, but use the ready-made bows for speed and simplicity.

B. If children's parties in your area include favors for each of the guests, fill plastic bows with candy, plastic or wooden beads, bubble gum balls, plastic creepy crawlies, a charm or two for the girls, and a tiny car or airplane for the boys. Glue barrette and bow tie clips to the appropriate favors.

C. Check out the miniatures and model train areas of your favorite craft store for particular lilliputian treasures to fill the bows. Find the area in the craft store that has the bags of tongue depressors and popsicle sticks. You'll find a bag of assorted wooden shapes (tiny circles, squares, and ovals) somewhere among them. Cut faces from family photographs (the ones that aren't good enough to mount but you can't bear to throw away), and glue them onto the tiny wooden shapes. Add them to the stuffing in the bows.

D. One further thought: You can offer the plastic pouches and an array of different types of candies, and set up a Make-It and Take-It booth, charging a nominal fee for the bow. Ask an adult on the committee to tie small bows, and use a glue gun to apply them to the center over the wire on the finished product. You can also offer barrette or pin backings, or bow tie clips for the silly ones.

Chapter 4

Knit One
Handknit Gifts

Projects:

- ♥ *The Rag That Started It All*
- ♥ *Knit Potholders*
- ♥ *Coasters*
- ♥ *Baby Blanket*
- ♥ *Scarf*
- ♥ *The Winter of My Warm Shawl*

Fig. 4.1 Knitting can be relaxing.

Several months ago Jane walked into her mother's home and found her Aunt Florence happily knitting. "What are you making?" Jane asked. "Dishrags," came the slightly apologetic reply. Her aunt not only gave her one of the rags, but also the formula she was using. The garter stitch pattern (knit every row) has a nice texture, and there are no purl rows or stitches with which to contend. Aunt Florence gave them away to one and all, and Jane's mother knit a stack for the local church bazaar. Apologies were forgotten as satisfied recipients began requesting additional cloths. While knitting some dishrags for herself, Jane soon realized that many items could be quickly knit using the simple directions.

You begin with four stitches, increasing each row as you knit back and forth, until the stitches on your needle are the number you want for the diagonal of your square. Then begin decreasing stitches until you've created the square. With this square you can make coasters, potholders, slippers, baby blankets, or washrags. If you knit only a triangle, you can make scarves and shawls.

We can make so many things with this formula—depending on the yarn types, needle sizes, number of stitches, and shape—and we found it so easy to master, we began calling it "the Magic Formula."

The Magic Formula

Cast on 4 stitches and knit two rows.
*Knit 2 stitches, yo (yarn over), and knit to the end.**
Repeat from * to ** until the side reaches the desired measurement.

*Knit 1, knit 2 together, yo, knit 2 together.**
Repeat from * to ** until 5 stitches remain.
Knit 1, knit 2 together, knit 2.
Knit one row even.
Cast off loosely.

...at's all there is to it! In the projects that ...w you'll find several variations, and do ...e up some of your own. Use whatever yarns you have on hand and whatever size needles you can find.

> ♥ *Purchase all the yarn needed for any project at one time, checking the dye lot numbers to ensure that they match.*

The Rag That Started It All

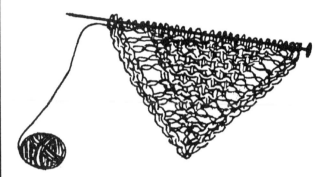

Fig. 4.2 One half of the Magic Formula

Dishrags are usually knit with Lily's variegated *Original Sugar 'n' Cream.* But the solid colors, particularly Cream—the color of kitchen string—is a favorite of ours. For a colorful, schizophrenic look, knit one with the leftover bits of the variegated yarn.

These dishrags are quickly made. If you work outside the home, you can probably knit one in two lunch hours. And if your doctor always keeps you waiting, knit a dishrag to make the time pass quickly. These are a top-seller at our annual Christmas bazaar.

You Will Need:

One 2 oz. (50g) ball *Original Sugar ' n' Cream* by Lily (100% cotton 4-ply worsted weight, enough for two rags)
One pair #10 (6mm) knitting needles

(Before you begin knitting, read the following helpful hint: To avoid weaving in the beginning strand of yarn, knit the first row and the next two stitches of the second row using both ends of the yarn. After knitting these 6 stitches, drop the beginning strand of yarn, and continue with the yarn from the skein.

Do the same thing when you add in another skein of yarn. Knit at least 5 stitches with both ends. When you've completed the item, trim off all these loose ends. Then the only strand to be woven in will be the final one.)

To begin:
Cast on 4 stitches and knit 2 rows.
*Knit 2, yo, and knit to end.**
Repeat from * to ** until you have 40 stitches on the needle.
*Knit 1, knit 2 together, yo, knit 2 together, knit to end.**
Repeat from * to ** until 5 stitches remain.
Knit one row.
Knit 1, knit 2 together, knit 2 (4 stitches remain).
Knit one row.
Cast off the 4 stitches.
Weave in the ends.

There are several pastels in the *Sugar 'n' Cream* line that we use to make facecloths. These make a wonderful "wrapping" for an individual bar of scented soap—another bazaar idea.

Make pastel washcloths for babies, knitting to only 30 stitches before beginning the decreases.

Knit Potholders

Fig. 4.3 Use the same pattern for potholders.

You Will Need:

Two 2 oz. (50g) balls *Original Sugar 'n' Cream* by Lily (100% cotton, 4-ply worsted weight, enough for two potholders)

One pair #10-1/2 (6.5mm) knitting needles

Work with two strands of yarn throughout, and proceed with the formula, knitting until you have 30 stitches. Then begin the decrease rows. When you finish the knitting, chain 12 with an "H" or 8 (5.5mm) crochet hook and both strands to form a loop for hanging. Weave in the ends.

Coasters

Fig. 4.4 *Coasters from the same formula*

You Will Need:

One 1-3/4 oz (50g) skein *Cotton Classic* by Tahki, *Newport Light* by Elite or *Kountry Kabled Kotton* by Lily

One pair #8 (5mm) knitting needles

Wind the yarn into a pull skein. Using the inside and the outside threads, and working with two strands throughout, proceed with the formula—increasing until you have 24 stitches. Then begin the decrease rows. After

> ♥ *If you want to work with both ends of one skein (inside and outside), put the skein in a ziplock bag. Pull both ends out from the top and close the bag, leaving about 1" (2.5cm) open at the edge for the yarn to freely feed.*

you cast off the final four stitches, weave in the ends. One skein of *Cotton Classic* will yield three coasters.

Baby Blanket

Fig. 4.5 *Make baby blankets from the Magic Formula.*

Have you ever checked out one of those USDA Hardiness Zone maps in a seed catalog? Well, if so, you'll know what we're talking about when we say that Jane lives in Zone 9 (Zone 11 being the warmest), and Jackie lives in Zone 5. We began dreaming up baby blankets for each hardiness zone, depending on the yarn and size needles used.

The first baby blanket we made, using the Magic Formula, was made with sport-weight mohair and size 8 (5mm) needles.

After knitting about 10" (25.5cm) it was clear that this blanket would work beautifully in an Alaskan igloo, but would probably cause heat prostration in a Texan baby. The blanket was also as stiff as a porcupine needle. After switching to size 15 (10mm) needles, the blanket grew at a satisfying speed. But when finished, it would better have suited a baby in the tropics: The holes were too big to keep any cold out!

In setting out to develop blankets for each zone, we wanted to be able to produce a blanket in several evenings—not devise a project that required a lifetime commitment.

> ♥ *Study the labels as you consider purchasing yarn. They usually include the following information: fiber content, dye lot, care required, the yardage, weight, recommended needle size and resultant gauge.*

This meant using the larger needles, sizes 11 (8mm), 13 (9mm), or 15 (10mm). We didn't want to use chunky yarn and we didn't want giant holes, so we doubled or tripled the number of strands of yarns. By doing this, you can create your own tweeds as well as combine smooth with fuzzy.

We knit these blankets to be functional, so we're careful to use yarn that can be machine washed and dried. This prerequisite doesn't limit us to acrylics, as there are superwash wools on the market that meet our requirements.

Cotton is a popular knitting choice at the time this book is being written, which means that it is readily available in many colors.

We knitted samples of every weight yarn and combination that we each had on hand by using the Magic Formula and knitting to 15 stitches before casting off. The samples were mounted on cardstock weight paper.

> ♥ *When you give a knit garment to someone, always include one of the labels. As a courtesy, wind a small amount of the yarn onto a piece of card and include this as well. (All expensive items include a length of yarn in case a repair is ever needed.)*

Then we recorded the size needle used, the yarns, and where we had purchased them (if we could remember). We placed the samples in plastic sheet protectors and put them in a notebook. Now we can each go to our notebook when we want to knit something. Be it a blanket or a coaster, we can find the appropriate yarn and needle choice, and knowing the outcome, begin with confidence.

You Will Need:

(Blanket for zones 7 – 10—Summer blanket in all zones)

Two skeins (3 oz. [85g]) of *Red Heart Classic* 100% Orlon (Mexicana)
One pair of #11 (8mm) knitting needles
Tape measure

1. Use the Magic Formula found on page 27, and knit until the side measures 36" (91.5cm).

2. Begin the decrease rows following the formula, and continue until the blanket is finished.

3. Weave in the ends.

To make a winter blanket, use two strands of yarn or a bulky yarn and the #11 (8mm) needles.

Variations:

(Doll Blanket and Washrag)

If you're teaching children to knit, think of how much more fun it would be for them to knit small rags that they could use to bathe dolls, or covers for the dolls' buggies, than to knit the plain scarf we usually teach beginners.

> ♥ *Here's a complete gift idea for a child. Make a tote bag (page 10) with a long narrow pocket on the outside for size 10-1/2 (6.5mm) knitting needles. Buy two skeins of knitting worsted in the child's favorite color. Add a small spiral notebook with the formula written on the first page. Make up several coupons: "This coupon entitles (child's name) to a knitting lesson given by (your name)." The child knits the increase rows with one skein and the decrease rows with the other. Voilà! A doll's blanket!*

Scarf

Fig. 4.6 *Slip a scarf corner through a yarn-over hole on the edge, and pull up to wear.*

Marilyn Kowalski and Jane share the same birthday. Two years ago Marilyn gave Jane a fantastic scarf that she knitted with an eyelash-type yarn. (Lots of fine threads dangle from this yarn.) Marilyn didn't use the dishrag formula, but we thought the formula would work. We used Unger's *Fizz* because it has much the same look as the yarn Marilyn used.

We knit until the yarn was almost gone, saving enough for the cast off row (a length equal to at least six times the width of the row when it is stretched out).

The scarf is smashing, and it took only an hour and a half to knit. The holes (yarn-overs) along the side are ever so handy: Instead of tying the scarf, slip an end through one of the holes about 3" (7.5cm) up the other side of the scarf. (See Figure 4.6.)

You Will Need:

One ball of Unger's *Fizz*
One pair #15 (10mm) knitting needles

You will work only the first part of the formula because the scarf is a triangle, not a square. Work until you reach 50 stitches, and then cast off loosely and weave in the ends.

(If you don't quite reach 50 stitches, don't worry. And if you have a few more, that's okay too. Knit until you have a length of yarn left that is about six times the width of the last row; you'll need this for the cast-off row.)

The Winter of My Warm Shawl

If you live in a Hardiness Zone that doesn't call for heavy woolens, then the following shawl is probably all you need for a light wrap that will offer some protection from the wind.

Even if you live in the cold north and wear down jackets half the year, this shawl can be a gorgeous accent to a plain garment.

> ♥ *If the yarn does not come in pull skeins, wind the yarn into pull balls on a yarn winder. Fold the label and tuck it into the ball at some point.*

Fig. 4.7 *Add tassels of fringe to the shawl.*

You Will Need:

Five skeins (3.5 to 4 oz. each [100g]) crimpy worsted weight yarn
Pair of knitting needles #15 (10mm)
"I" or 9 (6mm) crochet hook

This shawl has a slight variation on the Magic Formula. You will knit only one stitch before the yarn over. This method creates holes right on the edge for the fringe. If you omit the fringe (which uses one and a half balls of yarn), return to the original formula, and knit the side to at least 54" (1.4m) (which might take more than a ball and a half).

Cast on 4 stitches.
Knit two rows.
*Knit one, yo, knit to the end.**
Repeat from * to ** until the side measures 48" (1.2m).
Cast off extremely loosely.

Cut fringe in 20" (51cm) lengths. Take four strands, fold in the center, and slip the folded edge through a hole along the edge. Place the crochet hook inside this loop, reach through and catch the ends, and pull through the loop. Tighten the knot. The longer the fringe, the more elegant the final appearance, and the better the shawl will hang.

> We've taken up knitting by hand again, thanks to this simple Magic Formula. If you want more knit gifts, there are two hats in the children's gift chapter (Chapter 5, "Grandma's Corner")—one knit by hand (page 43) and one by machine (page 44). Now where is that knitting tote I made in Chapter 2?

Grandma's Corner
Gifts for Grandchildren

Projects:

♥ *"Ducks in a Row" Quilt*
♥ *Flannel Receiving Blanket*
♥ *Summer Baby Blanket*
♥ *Grandma's Collar*
♥ *Baby Bonnet*
♥ *Undershirt Dresses*
♥ *Child's 1930s Pixie Hat*
♥ *Machine-Knitted Fair Isle Hat*
♥ *"I Promised You a Flower Garden" Mat*
♥ *Sweatshirt Sizzle*
♥ *Lisa's Card Table Burger Hut*
♥ *Cat Pin*

Fig. 5.1 Gifts from Grandma

Bumper sticker: "If I knew how much fun my grandchildren would be, I'd have had them first."

This chapter is filled with gifts grandmothers wish they'd made for their children—but who had the time? There were car pools and Cub Scouts, school picnics and soccer, flu bugs and doctor checkups, lunches to make and cakes to bake, and on and on. We're grateful to have grandchildren so we can make all the things for them we never got to make when our own children were young. And what better place to start than with a quilt?

"Ducks in a Row" Quilt

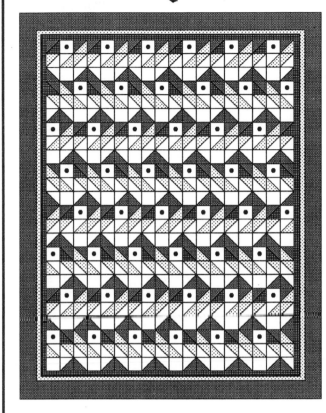

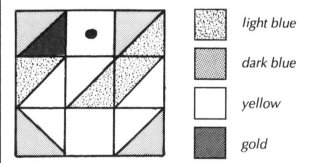

Fig. 5.2 *One section of the duck quilt*

light blue

dark blue

yellow

gold

Given the nurturing quality of quilts, is it any wonder that the first project many women begin making when they find out they're pregnant is a baby quilt? And what do grandmothers begin making as soon as the pregnancy is announced? A quilt, of course.

The quilt that follows is pieced with squares and half-square triangles—a quick job using one of Barbara Johannah's quick-piecing methods (See "Bibliography") and the templates developed by John Flynn (See "Sources of Supplies"). The blocks for the duck quilt can be pieced in less than six hours.

Don't you love quilts made of scraps? The richness of the colors and textures enlivens their surfaces. We also like to use fast-piecing techniques, which demand lots of the same fabric, so we compromised. Flynn's "Half-of-Square Triangles" templates are the perfect answer. Since each use of one of the templates yields 18 pieced squares, you can easily use many different fabrics to obtain all the pieces you'll need.

Flynn's template for the 2" (5cm) pieces, in the quilt that follows, is slightly less than 9" (23cm) square. This makes it perfect for fat quarters or quarter-yard pieces. These templates also answer the main objection to Johannah's method—the required careful and time-consuming measuring in eighths of inches.

The directions that follow will make a quilt that finishes 43" x 55" (109cm x 140cm) when the borders are added. The blocks as given are 6" (15cm) square, but you can make them any size.

If you make quilts around 45" x 60" (1.1 x 1.5m)—they remain useful as the child grows and can be used as an afghan or on a twin bed as an extra layer. If you want a smaller quilt, simply cut down the number of blocks (6" [15cm] square).

If you want to speed up the piecing, use the 3" (7.5cm) template, and the resultant blocks will be 9" [23cm] square. You'll need only twenty blocks instead of forty-eight—a big savings in time.

Use four yellow fabrics for the ducks to get the five colors in the quilt; the polka dot was used on both the right and the wrong sides. Both the right and wrong sides of the blue print were used as well. Yes, you can use both the right and wrong sides of fabrics if you can't find two prints to give you the effect you're after. When you select the fabrics for your quilt, they must be 45" (1.1m) wide; if not, buy an additional 1/4 yd (23cm).

You Will Need:

Six fat quarters of yellow (duck) fabrics
1/2 yd (46cm) 45" (1.1m) gold fabric (beak and 1/2" [1.5cm] border)
1-1/2 yds (1.4m) light blue (water and 1" [2.5cm] border)
1-3/4 yds (1.6m) blue (water and 2" [5cm] outer border)
2 large spools gray sewing thread; invisible thread
2 pkgs wide, double-fold bias tape (5-1/2 yds [5m] needed)
Flynn's Half-of-Square Triangles 2" (5cm) template (If you don't have Flynn's template, look in "Sources of Supplies." Or substitute Barbara Johanna's method—see "Bibliography.")
1-1/2 yds (1.4m) 45" (1.1m) width backing fabric
Quilt batt at least 44" x 56" (1.1m x 1.5m)
Rotary cutter
Pencil
Fabric paint
Potato
1/4" (6mm) seam allowance included throughout

1. Using two 9" (23cm) square pieces of fabric and the 2" (5cm) template, you will have 18 pieced squares. Each block is made of the following squares: three yellow/light blue, two yellow/blue, two yellow, one gold/blue (beak), and one light blue/blue. (See Figure 5.2.)

There are 48 duck blocks in the quilt top. You must piece forty-eight light blue/blue squares or three templates worth (three 9" [23cm] squares of each fabric). This will yield fifty- four squares, six more than you need.

Piece three templates of gold/blue for the beaks (fifty-four squares), and set aside.

Two templates of yellow/light blue (thirty-six squares) and one template of yellow/blue (eighteen squares) will make nine duck blocks. You also need to cut eighteen 2-1/2" (6.5cm) yellow squares for nine blocks.

When using "fat quarters," cut the 9" (23cm) squares for the templates first, and then cut the 2-1/2" (6.5cm) squares from what's left.

Piece all the half-squares. Cut 2-1/2"-wide (6.5cm) strips of yellow. Then cut squares 2-1/2"-wide (6.5cm). Place the pieces into piles comprising one duck block (light blue/blue, gold/blue, three yellow/light blue, two yellow/blue, two yellow squares). Then piece the squares into columns, and the columns into blocks. Piece one duck block facing one way and another facing the opposite until you've pieced forty-two blocks. Press the seams toward the ducks' bills.

> ♥ **When you plan a quilt top, plan your pressing direction as carefully as you do your piecing layout so the seams that will eventually come together are pressed in opposite directions. When you press matching seams in opposite directions, the presser foot on your sewing machine will push these seams together when they are sewn.**

Leave the final six blocks in columns for fill-in around the edges (see page 129 for the partial blocks along the edge). The only rule for laying out the rows of blocks is that the top of one duck's head must come under a blue (water) square—it gives you two possible placements on each row.

2. Lay out the blocks, and choose where you want the different colors (eight rows). Piece one row at a time, placing pins at each block and matching the points. On the wrong side, press the seams between the blocks toward the ducks' bills. Join the rows into the top.

> ♥ **With your vanishing marker, write the number of each row (one through eight) in the upper left corner. Then if the dogs or the children get their hands on them, you'll be able to complete the top without repositioning the rows.**

Press the seams between the rows in one direction. Turn the quilt to the right side, and give the quilt a final pressing.

3. Borders: Cut five 1" x 45" (2.5cm x 1.1m) strips from the gold fabric. Piece the strips

> ♥ **Piece the strips together before cutting them into the lengths needed for each side of the border. This procedure will keep the seams from falling at the same place on both sides of the quilt.**

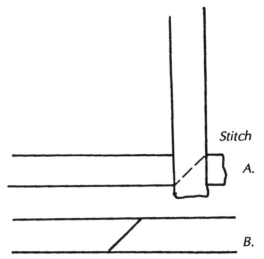

Fig. 5.3 *Piecing the strips for a border with a diagonal seam*
   A. *Place one strip on top of the other and stitch down.*
   B. *Open out.*

together with a diagonal seam (Fig. 5.3A and B). Leaving an extra 1-1/2" (4cm) at each corner, stitch the strips to the top and bottom of the pieced blocks, starting and stopping 1/4" (6mm) in from each edge. Stitch the borders to the sides in the same manner. Miter the corners by bringing the two border strips together and stitching from the corner point out to the edge. Press the seam open. Repeat for the 1" (2.5cm) border (five 1-1/2" x 45" [4cm x 1.1m] strips of light blue) leaving 2" (5cm) at each corner; and for the 2" (5cm) outer border (six 2-1/2" x 45" [6.5cm x 1.1m] blue), leaving 3" (7.5cm). Miter as before. Press the quilt top.

4. Press the backing, and lay wrong side up on a flat surface. Smooth the quilt batt in place over the backing, and put the pieced top right side up over the batt. With safety pins, join the sandwich every three or four inches. Place the monofilament thread on your sewing machine, and set the machine for darning. Using a darning foot or a darning spring, quilt the top.

5. Round the corners by using your rotary cutter and mat and a mug or small plate as a template. Bind the outer edge with the wide double-fold bias tape. Follow the directions on the package if you wish. We prefer to open out one side, stitch it on the front all around on the sewing machine, turn to the back and handstitch into place.

6. Machine or hand embroider the child's name ("Collin's Quilt"), your name, and the year somewhere on the front or back of the quilt.

Flannel Receiving Blanket

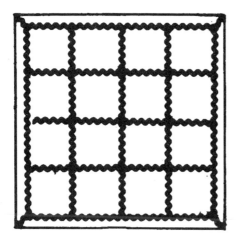

Fig. 5.4 *Flannel receiving blanket*

This baby blanket is a most welcome gift. Instead of the skimpy receiving blankets we know and dislike, this one is a generous size, warm, soft, and washable.

You Will Need:

Two 1-1/4 yds (1.1m) of coordinating 45"-wide (1.1m) flannel fabric (one plain and one printed)
One 4-3/4 yds (4.3m) packet of satin blanket binding to match one of the colors in the print
Machine embroidery thread to match binding
T-square, rotary cutter, and mat
Sewing machine
Walking foot (optional)
Vanishing marker
Yardstick

1. Flannel shrinks, so before you make this receiving blanket, wash both pieces of fabric and dry in the dryer. Next, iron them (wrong sides together), starting at the top and pressing all the way to the bottom. This holds the fabrics together while you cut. Use a T-square, rotary cutter, and mat to even up the top and bottom edges. Fold the square in half, and press in a crease. Fold again and press, dividing the blanket into four parts. Open up the fabric. Turn it 90 degrees, fold in half, press, then fold in half, and press again to divide the blanket into eight sections.

2. With a vanishing marker and yardstick, draw in lines at the folds. This is a small project, so use only quilter's pins to hold it together while you stitch. If you have a walking foot for your machine, use it. If not, then use an embroidery foot. Choose a decorative stitch for the quilting lines. Remember that the lines will intersect, and you may not want the jumble that can occur if the stitch is not chosen wisely. A favorite is the feather stitch or the serpentine (sewn-out zigzag) stitch. Whatever you use, choose a symmetrical stitch. Stitch down on each line you've drawn across the blanket, then turn the blanket 90 degrees, and stitch down the other rows. When the embroidery is finished, check to see if the blanket edges are still even, using a T-square. You can make your own T-square by using two rulers—one perpendicular to the other—to make a square corner. Don't worry that the blanket is no longer 45" (1.1m) square (it won't be after washing and drying), but it must have square corners.

3. To hold the two flannel pieces together at the edges, straight stitch all around the outside, placing the outside edge of the presser foot at the edge of the blanket.

4. Start at one corner and slip the edge of the blanket down into the fold of the purchased satin blanket binding, and pin in place. Miter the corners as shown (Fig. 5.5). Baste

Fig. 5.5 *Miter the corners.*

by hand for exactness, paying careful attention to the corners. Then machine stitch at the edge of the binding, with the same decorative stitch used to hold the blanket together. Remove the basting thread and press.

Variations:

Use striped flannel and hold the striped fabric to the lining by stitching on appropriate stripes—you won't have to draw in stitching lines. Checks and plaids are also good choices for the same reason.

Summer Baby Blanket

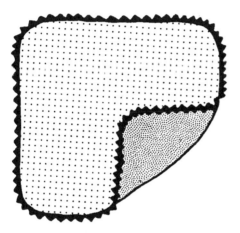

Fig. 5.6 Summer baby blanket

Receiving blankets don't always have to be made in two layers of flannel. Use a single layer and hand roll the hem, holding it in place with a blanket stitch or single crochet in #8 pearl cotton. Modern grandmas can serge the edges.

Or you may choose a nonshedding fabric such as cotton or a cotton/poly blend to back the flannel top. Winter babies' blankets? Back them with the finest white pinwale corduroy and trim the blankets with a narrow, heavy, crochet-type lace. Summer blankets can be backed with seersucker or plissé and trimmed with narrow gathered cotton eyelet.

This summer blanket is made with flannel on one side and plissé on the other. It has a masculine look with its bright colors and rick-rack trim.

You Will Need:

1-1/3 yds (1.2m) of 45" (1.1m) cotton flannel
1-1/3 yds (1.2m) of 45" (1.1m) plissé or seersucker
5 yards (4.6m) of rick-rack
Sewing machine
Thread to match one of the above
Pencil
Coffee cup

1. Wash the flannel in hot water and dry in your dryer. Also wash and dry the plissé. Press the flannel.

2. Measure the width of both fabrics. Cut a square from the one with the narrower width. Cut a matching square in the other fabric. Use the coffee cup to round the corners (Fig. 5.7).

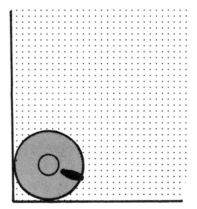

Fig. 5.7 Use a coffee cup as a pattern to round corners.

3. Matching the selvages, place the plissé on top of the flannel, right sides together. This will ensure that the grain runs in the same direction in both the flannel and the other fabric. Stitch around in a 3/8" (1cm) seam, leaving 5" (12.5cm) open for turning along one side. Clip into the seam allowance at the rounded corners.

♥ *To clip wedges on outside curves, pinch the fabric together and snip on a slant about every inch. Or, use pinking shears.*

4. Turn to the right side and press, turning under the fabric at the opening. Stitch 1/16" (1mm) inside the edge all the way around, which will close the opening.

5. Pin the rick-rack (or desired trim) around the perimeter so half of it extends off the edge. Stitch the rick-rack down through the middle, overlapping the beginning and ending about 1/2" (1.5cm).

Variations:

A. Omit the trim and stitch one of the decorative stitches around the edge.

B. Place the wrong sides of the fabrics together and bind them with purchased or self-made bias tape, OR, serge them together using decorative threads in the lower loopers.

C. Trim with a beaded trim and thread ribbon through the beading for a fancier finish on plain fabrics.

> ♥ *Construct a matching shield for the shoulder out of an 8" x 22" (20.5cm x 56cm) piece of flannel and fabric. When in use, remember to put the flannel side up and the fabric side next to your garment.*

Grandma's Collar

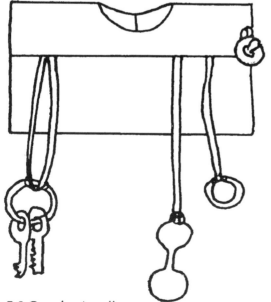

Fig. 5.8 Grandma's collar

Babies aren't choosy about the sex or age of the person on whom they drool—any shoulder will do. The other day we met a grandmother carrying her six-month-old grandson and wearing a collar much like the one that follows. She said that the collar had come from a baby's specialty shop outside the area (and we were sure it was outside our pocketbook).

Mostly, we liked the idea of a gift for grandmothers—that's what our contemporaries are becoming these days. Mothers can wear these too, but grandmothers will appreciate them more.

The feature we like best about this collar—and it isn't the protection it affords our best clothes—is that toys and pacifiers don't fall on the ground.

If you've been sewing for a few years, you probably have the start of what will become an extensive pattern collection. Look through this collection, and chances are you have a pattern for a collar like the one shown. If not, follow the directions for creating the pattern (step 1 below).

Pattern companies periodically produce patterns for different collars; do add one to your collection at the next opportunity.

The collar is lined for two reasons: It's quicker and it adds one more layer of protection. A fine wale corduroy lining keeps the collar from slipping around and adds a little extra weight. Flannel or cotton velveteen also works. We thought about using a pre-quilted fabric for the collar, but we didn't want to wear the extra bulk.

A busy multicolored print is used for the collar so spit-up won't show and so the collar will go with as many outfits as possible.

You Will Need:

1/3 yd (30.5cm) outer fabric
1/3 yd (30.5cm) lining
Fat quarter or scrap for yoke
Lace or rick-rack trim (optional)
Sew-on snap size 1
2 yds 1/8" (3mm) ribbon
Several small toys (e.g., rattles, teething ring)
Pacifier

1. If you don't have a square collar pattern: Take any bodice pattern, and trace the front and back about 8" (20.5cm) down from the shoulder seam. Tape the front and back together to eliminate the shoulder seam. The front fold of the collar should be placed on the lengthwise grain. Make a mark 3" (7.5cm) down from the neck at the center front. Draw this line straight out to the edge. Repeat at the center back. Trace this yoke area onto tracing paper as shown in Figure 5.9.

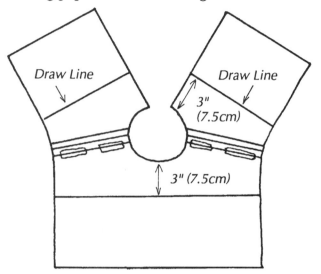

Fig. 5.9 Trace yoke area.

2. Cut out the collar, lining, and yoke. Turn under 1/2" (1.5cm) along the straight edges of the yoke. Place into position on the top collar. Stitch 1/8" (3mm) from the edge at the neck. Cut the ribbon into three 20" (51cm) to 24" (61cm) lengths, and fold in half. Slip under the yoke on the front 3-1/2" (9cm) from each edge, plus 1-1/2" (4cm) from the left edge. Topstitch the yoke into place at the front and back, securing the ribbons at the same time. Place the lining on top of the collar with right sides together, and stitch all the way around, leaving a 4" (4cm) opening for turning below one side of the back yoke. Turn to the front and press. Topstitch 1/16" (1.5mm) away from the edge all the way around, closing the opening.

Fig. 5.10 Sew snap to back of collar.

3. Sew the snap to the back as shown in Figure 5.10. Attach the toys by taking the loop of ribbon through the toy and slipping the toy back through the ribbon loop.

Baby Bonnet

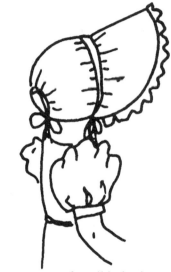

Fig. 5.11 One-size-fits-all baby bonnet

After we tell you what we like about this bonnet, you'll be convinced to make them whenever a baby gift is called for—whether it's one at a time for a special baby or by the tens for a bazaar. The bonnets are flat construction, fold flat when finished, are large enough to keep sun out of any baby's eyes, and yet can be made smaller as easily as cutting the length or width to your specifications. You can get six bonnets out of 2 yds (1.8m) of fabric.

You Will Need:

- 1 yd (.9m) of outside fabric (we used embroidered cotton)
- 1 yd (.9m) of lining (we chose peach to show through the open places in the embroidery)
- 24" (61cm) of 1" (2.5cm) ruffled eyelet for the brim
- 1-3/4 yds (1.6m) of 1/4" (6mm) or 3/8" (1cm) ribbon
- 1/4" (6mm) seam allowance included throughout

1. Make a pattern by drawing a rectangle 21" x 11" (53.5cm x 28cm) (Fig. 5.12). To trim off

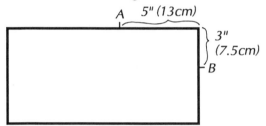

Fig. 5.12 *Pattern starts with rectangle.*

the corners, first place a mark 3" (7.5cm) from one corner on the short side. Make another mark 5" (12.5cm) from the same corner along the long edge. Fold the pattern in half and draw a gentle curve between the two marks (Fig. 5.13). Using your pattern,

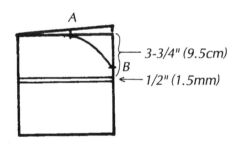

Fig. 5.13 *Fold in center, then cut curved corners from A to B. Draw in casing lines.*

stack the outside and lining fabrics. Then cut out. Mark the front casing lines on the embroidered cotton with a vanishing marker; the first line is 3-3/4" (9.5cm) from the top edge, and the second line is 3/8" (1cm) away (1/4" [6mm] ribbon) or 1/2" (1.5cm) away (3/8" [1cm] ribbon) as shown on Figure 5.13.

2. Fold over one cut edge of the ruffled eyelet twice and pin at the curved edge of the right side of the embroidered fabric, placing the gathered edge of the eyelet along

the edge of the bonnet fabric. Check to be sure the top surface of the ruffle faces the top side of the embroidery (the side folds of the ruffle are underneath facing the top side of the lining) (Fig. 5.14). Cut off the ruffle if too long, but leave enough to fold twice, as you did at the start. You'll slipstitch these ends later.

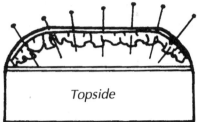

Fig. 5.14 *Pin ruffle to top edge of brim.*

Place the lining fabric on top (right sides together), and begin stitching in the center of the back edge. Stitch up one side (leaving the space between the casing lines open), across the brim (capturing the ruffle between the layers), down the other side (leaving the casing line open), and across the bottom (leaving an opening for turning) (Fig 5.15).

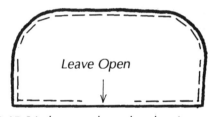

Fig. 5.15 *Stitch around at edge, leaving openings for casing and turning.*

Turn the bonnet to the right side, and press. Straight stitch on top of the bonnet next to the ruffle to hold the fabric in place. Pin near the casing lines, and stitch on the marks you've drawn (Fig. 5.16).

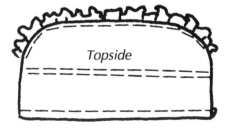

Fig. 5.16 *Turn right side out, topstitch, then stitch in casing lines.*

Turn under 3/8" (1cm) for 1/4" [6mm] ribbon or 1/2" (1.5cm) for 3/8" [1cm] ribbon at the back of the bonnet, turning the raw edges of the opening to the inside. Stitch 1/16" (1mm) from the folded-under edge to form the casing.

3. Finishing: Cut the ribbon into two pieces: 27" (69cm) and 40" (1m). Thread the 27" (69cm) piece through the back casing and the 40" (1m) piece through the front casing. At the ends, tie overhand knots and dab the threads with *Stop Fraying*. Pull up on the ribbon in back and tie into a bow to form the bonnet. When the bonnet is on the baby, the front ribbon ends are pulled up and tied in a bow under the baby's chin.

Variations:

A. Sew lines of decorative machine stitching across the brim.

B. Carve a small heart or some other appropriate shape out of a potato, and print the hearts across the brim with textile paint. Use the sponge shapes available at craft stores to print designs on the brim.

Undershirt Dresses

Fig. 5.17 *Embroidered undershirt dress*

Take a baby's undershirt, trim a little fabric off here, add a little fabric there, and incorporate a bit of lace and decorative stitching. Presto! Chango! Abracadabra! A dress! These little dresses make wonderful gifts, but they are even better to make for

sale at your bazaar or the hospital auxiliary gift shop. Why? Most of the work is already done for you. You purchase the baby undershirts (no cutting out or sewing together). They're inexpensive if purchased at your local discount stores—about $1.25 each if purchased in a package of three, slightly higher if they're in colors. The little shirts are also available everywhere—even your local grocery store.

Use knit scraps for the skirts. If you need to purchase knit, you'll also find T-shirt or single knit at any fabric store. And if you can't find it, use men's undershirts (new, if these dresses will be made for sale).

Tiny embroidered flowers can be used on some of these. Check your treasure box to see what you have on hand to add a little something extra. Remember, it's the little extra touches that make the sales.

While this may seem like the most abject heresy, don't use stabilizer when stitching

> ♥ *Buy some tiny decorated socks and offer them with the dress as a set. You'll be able to charge much more for the set than the price of the socks plus the price of the shirt and fabric.*

knits because the slightly uneven quality of the stitching looks more like hand stitching. But our suggestion to you is that you try it each way and see which you prefer.

You Will Need:

Newborn-size pullover lap-shoulder undershirt
Single-knit scrap at least 4" x 28" (10cm x 71.1cm) in same color as the undershirt
Water-soluble stabilizer (optional)
Vanishing marker
Scissors
6" (15cm) of 1/8" (3mm) double-faced satin ribbon (you can purchase tiny bows in packages at most craft stores)
6" (15cm) of narrow lace or crocheted trim
Sewing machine
Cording and transparent embroidery feet
#70/10 universal sewing machine needle
Rayon machine embroidery thread such as *Natesh* or *Sulky* Thread to match the undershirt

Cordonnet or heavy thread for gathering knit

1. Cut the knit piece for the skirt 4" x 28" (10cm x 71.1cm). Thread the top and bobbin of your machine with the rayon thread and do all of your decorative stitching. To stitch around the neck, turn the shirt wrong side out and fold the lapped area out of the way when you're stitching. Do this rather than use the free arm if your machine has one, so you can start stitching right at the sleeve seam. Either anchor the threads by taking a few straight stitches in place or pull the threads to the back. Tie and clip. One line of stitching is enough on the back if you're trying to save time.

Catch the lace in with the stitching on the front bottom row by choosing a stitch that

> ♥ *Magic trick number one: On knits use decorative stitches with a reverse action and the knits won't stretch out of shape (e.g., feather stitches, the stretch stitches [utility or decorative], and many of the pictorials). Always test your choices before you actually stitch on the shirt—perhaps on the knit you're using for the skirt or the pieces you cut from the shirt. If you want to use other stitches, such as the close satin stitches, only use them at the waistline seam or the one directly over the neckband. (These two places have several layers of fabric, so they are naturally stabilized.)*

has a straight line at the bottom. You could, of course, zigzag (stitch width 3, length 1-1/2) this in place with thread to match the

> ♥ *Magic trick number two: When stitching without stabilizer on soft knits, don't pull or push the fabric in the least little bit. Most machines feed so evenly that you can hold these knits as gently as you would the wings of a butterfly—just enough to keep the stitching in line.*

shirt before you stitch the decorative line, if you feel it's necessary. Place the line of stitching along the sleeve 1" (2.5cm) from the

> ♥ *A justification to use if you own two or more sewing machines: "Two machines save me so much time when I'm making these little dresses that I can make twice as many in half the time. I thread one machine with rayon thread, and set it up for the embroidery. Then I thread the second with the sewing thread that matches the undershirt."*

edge. Stitch line on the skirt however you wish, vertically or horizontally as shown in Figure 5.17.

2. Replace the rayon thread with the sewing cotton. Cut 1/2" (1.5cm) off each sleeve edge and 2" (5cm) off the bottom edge. Sew the center back skirt seam with the elastic overlock stitch. Stitch shell hems at the bottom of the skirt and at each sleeve edge by turning the knit under 1/2" (1.5cm) and placing the fold to the left under the presser foot. Using the blind hem stitch (5 to 7mm wide), stitch so the straight stitches are parallel to the hem, and the left swing of the needle sews over the edge creating the shell.

3. Put the cording foot on your machine, and gather the skirt by zigzagging over the heavy thread 5/8" (1.5cm) from the edge. Pull up the gathers to fit the bottom of the skirt. Return the transparent embroidery foot to the machine and stitch the skirt in place by stitching with a slight zigzag (stitch width 1, stitch length 1-1/2) right beside the heavy cord. Turn the seam toward the shirt.

4. Return the rayon embroidery thread to the machine and stitch one or two lines of decorative stitches directly above the seam line, stitching through all the layers. Add any embellishment such as the ribbon.

Variations:

A. Buy the sleeveless shirts, make ruffles of the fabric cut from the bottom of the shirt, and stitch them in the armholes. Finish the ruffle edge with the shell hem or with lace.

B. Use a white shirt and a colored knit for the skirt. Stitch the decorative stitching on the shirt in the color of the knit, and embroider the skirt with white thread.

C. Stitch decorative stitches with white thread over colored narrow ribbon.

D. Use a soft cotton batiste or dimity for the skirt, and make a bonnet to match.

Production:

Work on ten or more dresses at one time. Cut out all the skirts. Do all of the decorative stitching on the skirt and the shirt except where the skirt is attached. Next thread your machine with thread that matches the shirt, and sew all the skirt seams. Then stitch all of the shell hems. Gather the skirts and stitch to the shirts. Return the embroidery thread to the machine (or use a second machine). Stitch the decorative stitching around the waist. If you don't have large blocks of time available, you can do one step on the ten garments at a time, and before you know it they're all finished.

Child's 1930s Pixie Hat

Fig. 5.18 Pixie hat

Just about every baby that has touched Jane's mother's life has been the recipient of one of these pixie hats. They're quick and easy to knit, and the finishing is simple. One of the best features is that the tie acts as a muffler, keeping out the cold wind and staying tied because it's knit. The hats are "climate rated." Work with one strand in the warmer regions and two strands in the colder zones. You'll need twice as much yarn, but the child's head will be twice as warm.

The hat is constructed of a rectangle that is equal to two squares. A child's hat is made of an 8" x 16" (20.5cm x 40.5cm) rectangle; a baby's hat of one 7" x 14" (18cm x 35.5cm). A 5" x 10" (12.5cm x 25.5cm) rectangle will make a nice hat for a 16"-18" (40.5-46cm) doll. Make the tie 10 stitches wide and 28" (71.1cm) long (between the points) for a baby, and 6 stitches wide and 18" (46cm) long for a doll.

You Will Need:

One 3oz. (85g) ball of Red Heart *Maypole* or a comparable 4-ply knitting worsted-weight yarn
One pair #9 (5.5mm) knitting needles
Yarn needle
Gauge: 4 stitches equal 1" (2.5cm) (measured over stockinette)

♥ *Use your heavy clear plastic ruler (e.g., Omnigrid)* *to measure your gauge by placing it over your swatch and counting the number of stitches between the 1" (2.5cm) and 2" (5cm) markings.*

---

1. Hat Directions:

Cast on 30 stitches.
*Knit one row.
Purl 23, knit 7.**
Repeat from * to ** until piece measures 16" (40.5cm).
Cast off.

♥ *Inc = increase   Dec = decrease*

---

2. Tie Directions:

Cast on two stitches.
Knit all rows (garter stitch).
Increase one stitch at each end until there are 12 stitches on the needle.
Knit even until straight area measures 30" (76cm).
Decrease one stitch each end until 2 stitches remain.
Cast off.

3. Finishing:

Fold the hat in half across the middle of the rectangle. Sew the back seam. Pin the center of the tie to the seam at the neck edge. Measure 4-1/2" (11.5cm) from this pin on each side of the tie. Pin the tie to the front edge of the hat at this mark. Sew these 9" (23cm) of the tie to the hat with a backstitch and matching thread, gathering the hat to make it fit the tie (Fig. 5.19).

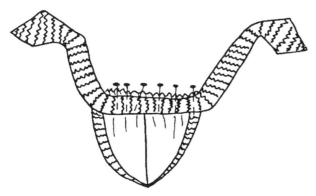

Fig. 5.19 Pin tie to bonnet.

Variations:

A. For the body of the hat (the two-square rectangle) you could knit in any pattern and yarn you choose (even crochet if you'd rather).

Simply knit a swatch to obtain the gauge, and multiply times width (8" [20.5cm]) to find the number of stitches. For example: If you are knitting with a fine yarn and the gauge is 8 stitches equal 1" (2.5cm), you will need 8 x 8, or 64, stitches.

The pattern is: *Knit one row, turn, purl 56, knit 8.** Repeat from * to ** until piece measures 16" (40.6cm) long. Cast off.

B. Cut an 8" x 16" (20.5cm x 40.5cm) rectangle of wool or cotton fleece. Fold in half, and sew the back seam. Blanket stitch or bind the edge that surrounds the face. Stitch a purchased long scarf to the neck edge, or knit a tie that complements the fabric and stitch it in place as above.

Machine-Knitted Fair Isle Hat

Fig. 5.20 Fair Isle hat

You'll find charts on page 130. This one was knit on a twelve-year-old Knitking (Brother) Compuknit with a ribbing attachment. The hats are so fast to knit, you'll see to it that everyone's ears are warm—whether they want them to be or not.

You Will Need:

2 skeins Unger's *Roly Sport* (enough for two caps with reverse colors; e.g., white with blue and blue with white)
Knitting machine
Ribber (optional)
Lace carriage (optional)
Jumbo pompom maker
Gauge: 7 stitches and 10 rows equal 1" (2.5cm)

1. Always knit at least a 3" x 3" (7.5cm x 7.5cm) sample swatch, and let it rest overnight. Steam lightly, and count to check the gauge. Adjust your tension to obtain the proper gauge. Set up the Fair Isle pattern (punch a card or mark off the design for the Compuknit).

2. Cast on 133 stitches in a 1 x 1 rib. Knit for 4" (10cm) (40 rows). Transfer all the stitches to the main bed of your machine.

♥ *Make the hat to fit a baby or toddler by reducing the number of stitches to 100, the rows of ribbing to 30, and the rows of pattern to 40. Finish as described.*

3. Knit ten rows with the main color. Add the second color, and work in the Fair Isle design for 45 rows (55 rows from ribbing; 95 rows from start). Transfer every other stitch to the stitch next to it. Tighten the tension at least three numbers—more if possible without bending the needles. Knit fifteen rows. Cut the yarn, leaving a long end.

4. Thread the long end into a large yarn needle. Take the stitches off one by one with the needle onto the yarn. Lightly steam the hat. When it is dry, pull the stitches as tight as possible to shape the top of the cap. Sew back and forth across the top to secure. ***Do not cut off the long yarn end.***

5. Place the right sides together, and sew the center back seam on your serger or by hand, beginning at the top of the ribbing (Fig. 5.21). Do not sew the ribbing in the same

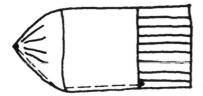

Fig. 5.21 Sew hat together inside: Stitch from top edge of ribbing to top of hat.

seam. When you've finished with the back seam, turn the hat to the right side. Placing the wrong sides of the ribbing together, sew the ribbing seam (Fig. 5.22). Turn half the ribbing up to form a cuff, which can be turned down to protect the ears in freezing weather.

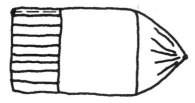

Fig. 5.22 Turn hat right side out, and stitch up ribbing.

6. Make a large pompom with the accent color, and sew it to the top of the hat with that long piece of yarn you left dangling in step 4.

Variations:

Make the hat all one color, stripes of a lot of different colors, or a plain color with one or two different colored stripes. One word of warning: Don't knit in the child's name, as it allows strangers to approach the child and convince him or her that they know the child.

"I Promised You a Flower Garden" Mat

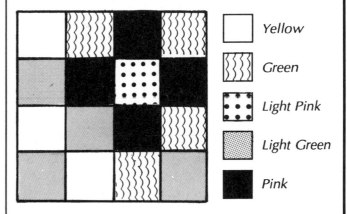

Fig. 5.23 One section of the flower garden quilt

What child could resist a nap on this delightful flower garden? Make this one for your grandchildren's nursery school rest periods (see page 131 and Color Plate 8).

Twenty-one 6" (15cm) square flower blocks are pieced from four 45" (1.1m) bands of fabric strips (16 strips) to make a mat 19-1/2" x 46-1/2" (50cm x 1.2m). Placed in a square, that's enough strips to make a crib quilt with twenty blocks: four blocks (24" [61cm]) by five blocks (30" [76cm]) before adding the border. Eight bands would yield forty-two blocks, a personal sized quilt 36" x 42" (.9m x 1.1m) before the borders (six blocks by seven blocks).

We wanted grandchildren to feel as though they're lying down in a meadow of wildflowers (we've never done that, but someday. . .). To accomplish the look, we used small floral prints, except for the lightest green, which looks like a sponge print.

Cut enough 1-1/2" (4cm) squares out of your fabric choices to make two blocks. Draw a 6" (15cm) square divided into sixteen 1-1/2" (4cm) squares on two pieces of paper. Dab a spot of glue on the back of your fabric squares and place them in position as shown. Trim the square on one piece of paper so you can lay them side by side. Study the squares to be sure the flowers come forward and catch your eye first. If there's a war going on between the colors within the block, change the fabrics. The top is made of twenty-four blocks and one column of segment *a*. Seven of these blocks, the ones down the center, are vertical mirror images of the primary block A. (If you placed a mirror at the bottom on the block and looked at the reflection, you would see block B.)

All the blocks are pieced from the same bands; the segments are turned upside down and pieced as shown in Figure 5.24 for block B.

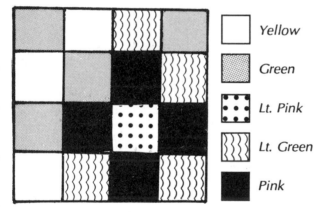

☐	*Yellow*
▨	*Green*
⊡	*Lt. Pink*
〰	*Lt. Green*
■	*Pink*

Fig. 5.24 *Mirror image of the section*

If you pieced all the blocks the same, and turned them upside down, you would have a different variation formed by rotating the block.

You Will Need:

2" x 45" (5cm x 1.1m) strips of the following fabrics:
- 9 green (18" [46cm])
- 8 pink (16" [40.5cm])
- 8 light green (16" [40.5cm])
- 2 light pink (4" [10cm])
- 7 yellow (14" [35.5cm])

24" x 60" (61cm x 1.5m) backing (can be pieced)

24" x 50" (61cm x 1.3m) quilt batt
2" (5cm) of 1/2" (1.5cm) Velcro
3/4 yd (69cm) of 1/2" (1.5cm) grosgrain ribbon
Pearl gray sewing thread
Monofilament thread
Safety pins (1" to 1-1/2" [2.5cm to 4cm]) for pin basting
Sewing machine
Rotary cutter, ruler, and mat
1/4" (6mm) seam allowance included throughout

1. Cut the strips with your rotary cutter. Sew the strips of fabric into eight bands, two each of *a*, *b*, *c*, and *d* (see page 131).

Set the remaining two strips aside (one green and one yellow). Press the seams on *a* and *c* toward the bottom and the seams on *b* and *d* toward the top.

2. Cut the bands into 2" (5cm) segments. Count out and stack the segments for the sixteen A blocks. Make separate stacks for the eight B blocks, and reserve the extras for another project.

Stitch the segments for the A blocks first by stitching all segment *a*s to segment *b*s and *c*s to *d*s.

Finish the blocks by joining the *b*s and *c*s.

Repeat for the eight B blocks, turning the segments upside down before stitching *a*s to *b*s, etc.

Press all the blocks, with the seams between the segments in opposite directions on every other block. This way the seams will butt into each other as you sew the blocks into columns. (It took longer to write this than it did to stitch it!)

3. Sew the blocks into columns: two columns of eight block A and one column of eight block B. Stitch the columns together.

Segment *a* is designed with the alternating colors (yellow and green), so when it's repeated on the right side of the top, it would appear almost like a border.

Stitch the additional strips into a two-strip band, and cut it in half. Put one half under the other and stitch them together. Cut it in half again, and stitch. Keep doing this until the band measures a little more than 4" (10cm) wide.

Return to the cutting board and cut two 2" (5cm) wide segments (really l-o-n-g segments). Place one under the other, and stitch together into a column. Add this column to the right side of the top.

> ♥ *The technique of making a band, then cutting it in half, stitching it together, etc., is a super way to create a pieced inner border (an inch or less) for a quilt. The strips can be various widths, and there can be as many of them as you wish. The more strips in the band and the wider they are, the greater the length that will be produced.*

4. Press the top. Make a sandwich of the top, batt, and backing, and pin the layers together with safety pins. Quilt the mat on your sewing machine. Thread the top of your sewing machine with monofilament thread, and the bobbin with thread to match your backing fabric. When the quilting is com-

> ♥ *Set your machine for darning, and use your darning foot. Roll up the mat and begin quilting at the end so that the roll is under the arm of your machine. The quilting lines meander around the top.*

Roll up quilt and let it feed off to left of your sewing machine.

plete, round the corners and bind the mat with the wide double-fold bias tape.

5. Finishing: Turn under 2" (5cm) at each end of the grosgrain ribbon, turning one toward the front and one toward the back. Stitch one side of the *Velcro* to each end, and stitch the ribbon to the bottom of the mat. Now the recipient can roll up and tie your gift. Make a label with your sewing machine alphabet or with a *Pigma* pen, including the child's name, your name, and date.

Variations:

A. Increase the size of the squares (2" to 3" [5cm to 7.5cm]) for a full-sized quilt.

B. Out of another fabric (bonded to *Wonder-Under*), cut 6" to 8" (15cm to 20.5cm) high letters for the child's name. Bond the letters to the front and machine appliqué (satin stitch) into place.

Sweatshirt Sizzle

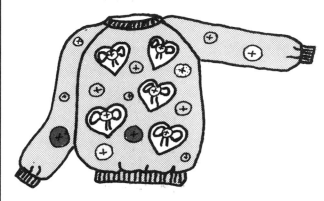

Fig. 5.25 Sweatshirt with appliqués and buttons

These filled plastic-heart appliqués embellish an otherwise mundane piece of clothing and are guaranteed to get attention whenever your grandchild wears it.

You Will Need:

Child's sweatshirt
Washable lightweight, clear plastic (available at hardware and discount stores if your local fabric store doesn't have it)
Decorative buttons
Nylon decorative cord
Bits of ribbon, rick-rack, sequins, glitz
Teflon presser foot
Vanishing marker

1. Wash and dry the sweatshirt *twice.* Heart templates are available in quilt and craft shops. Or, make your own by folding a piece of paper, cutting out half a heart shape and unfolding. Cut out different heart sizes from scrap paper, and arrange them on the sweatshirt to decide where you should place the plastic appliqués. Once you've decided, use a vanishing marker or chalk pencil to draw around them on the sweatshirt so placement isn't a question later. Cut out hearts from clear plastic.

2. For the filler in the hearts, cut up narrow ribbons, rick-rack, thread, metallic sequins, stars, and strips of lamé. Remember, this is going into the washing machine (delicate cycle), so everything must be washable (the plastic precludes it going into the dryer).

Use glacé and punchinello (sequin waste), too. (Both are available in sheets and ribbons at craft stores.) Place washable ribbons, rick-rack, and the large pieces of glitz inside one of the heart outlines on the sweatshirt. Cover with a plastic heart. Use a straight stitch (not too short, as you don't want too many holes in the plastic) and a *Teflon* presser foot to stitch from the top side of the heart, down around the point, and up the other side—leaving enough top area open so you can sprinkle in all the small metallics and ribbon bits you want inside the appliqué. Use a hemostat or a screw driver to place the ingredients where you want them. Remember that all but the large pieces will move—which is part of the fun of this appliqué. Put the sweatshirt back under the presser foot, and continue to sew around the heart to close it.

3. Use an acrylic or nylon decorative cord to cover the edge of the heart, leaving two ends at the top long enough to tie into a bow. Zigzag over the cord to couch it down (Fig. 5.26). (We used a stitch width 3 to cover the

Fig. 5.26 *Couch down cord around the appliqué.*

cord and a 1.5mm length.) Tie the ends of the cord into a bow, and attach a colorful button on top of the bow to hold it in place. Dab glue stick underneath the buttons, press into place, and sew the buttons on by machine if you can—the job will go faster than if completed by hand, and you have many buttons to apply (Fig. 5.27).

Fig. 5.27 *Attach button on top of bow.*

Continue applying all the plastic hearts the same way. Place the sweatshirt on a table in front of you and fill in empty areas on the shirt with more colorful buttons of different sizes. Once arranged, mark each spot with a marker (color and size noted), then take off the buttons and proceed to sew them on by machine. Never decorate just the fronts of sweatshirts, but sew buttons on the sleeves as well as a few on the back.

Variations:

A. Fill and stitch two plastic hearts together. Then spread *Sticky Stuff* (available from Clotilde—see "Sources of Supplies") or Aleene's *Tack-It* on the back, which allows you to place the appliqué on the shirt when you wear it and remove it for washing. Ask for this type of adhesive in craft and fabric shops, too—they do work!

B. Buy plastic ribbon (the type you fill and heat seal) at the craft store, and fill it with decorative elements. Seal the edges, and use as you did the removable heart. What possibilities!

Lisa's Card Table Burger Hut

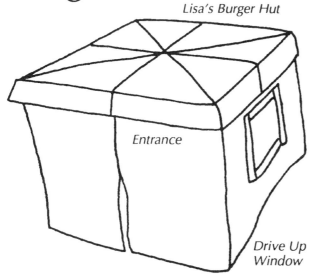

Lisa's Burger Hut

Entrance

Drive Up Window

Fig. 5.28 *Card table fast-food restaurant*

Did you ever build caves and forts with blankets, tablecloths, sheets, and bath towels when you were a child? We did, and so did our children. Our kids would have blankets and quilts strung all over their rooms, draped from bed to dresser, desk over chair—wherever a suitable surface was found, and sometimes a not so suitable one.

Maybe you always thought of making your children one of those fabric houses that card tables can wear, but you never did. Today we have grandchildren, and today Jane made her granddaughter her own card table play-house.

To make your own fast food restaurant like Lisa's Burger Hut, set up your card table and carefully measure it.

The top of Jane's table is 30-3/4" (77cm). You may want to cut the top the size of the table, plus a 1/4" (6mm) seam allowance. But if you want to piece a stripe as shown on Color Plate 2, and then bring the fabric down around the top for an "awning," divide the measurement in half (15-3/8" [38cm]), and construct the triangular pattern (Fig. 5.29)—adding 6" (15cm) for the "awning."

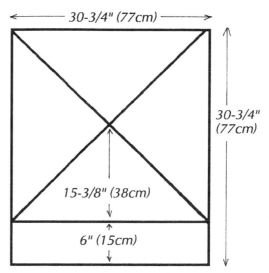

Fig. 5.29 *Construct top by sewing four triangles together, then adding an "awning."*

Jane's table measured 26" (66cm) from the top to the floor, so she needed 26" (66cm), plus 1/4" (6mm) seam allowance and 2-1/4" (6cm) for the hem or 28-1/2" x 31-1/4" (73cm x 79.4cm).

There's a "door" on one side, which meant she needed two pieces of fabric 28-1/2" (72.4cm) by 18" (46cm).

With those basic pattern pieces, you're free to turn your own "building" into any business establishment. The directions that follow cover most of the possibilities, from lettering to landscaping. Each side was worked separately for ease in handling and stitching. Work with a heavy sport cotton/ polyester blend, for its weight, wearability, and washability. Also, use the clear vinyl found at local do-it-yourself centers. The awning (striped cotton) and decorations were chosen strictly for their visual effect.

> ♥ **Check area discount upholstery and drapery stores for inexpensive heavy fabrics.**

You Will Need:

1 yd (.9m) 45" (1.1m) heavy sport cotton/ polyester blend fabric for the top

2-1/2 yds (2.1m) 45" (1.1m) striped cotton fabric for awning (use scraps for window trim)

3-1/2 yds (3.2m) 45" (1.1m) solid color fabric (see above) for the sides, or 3-1/3 yds (3m) 60" (1.5m) solid color fabric for top and sides

1/3 yd (30.5cm) *Clear-Vu* double polished vinyl

Sewing thread to match

Pencil

Happy Chalk transfer (see page 7 in Chapter 2)

Masking tape

Stencil brush

1" (2.5cm) alphabet stencil

Fabric or acrylic paint

Use 1/4" (6mm) seams, then zigzag edges together to strengthen

1. Cut a 31-1/4" (79.4cm) square for the top. Cut three 28-1/2" x 31-1/4" (72.4cm x 79.4cm) sides. Cut two 28-1/2" x 18" (72.4cm x 46cm) pieces for the fourth side.

2. Back: On the wrong side, draw the window opening 7-1/2" x 9- 1/2" (19cm x 24cm) in the center of the back 8" (20.5cm) down from the top. Cut four window "trim" pieces from striped fabric: two 1-3/4" x 10-1/2" (4.5cm x 27cm) and two 1-3/4" x 11" (4.5cm x 28cm). Place the two 10-1/2" (27cm) pieces on the top and bottom window lines, with the right side of trim to the wrong side of back (Fig. 5.30). Stitch in a 1/4" (6mm) seam

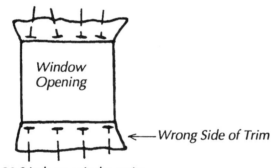

Fig. 5.30 *Stitch on window trim.*

starting and stopping 1/4" (6mm) beyond the line. Stitch the side trim in place the same way, starting and stopping at the point of the previous stitching (the pieces will extend beyond the stitching to the end of the top and bottom trim). Do not start stitching at this point. Cut out the window on the drawn line, clipping to the stitching at the corners.

Turn the trim to the right side, turn under 1/4" (6mm) along all sides, and stitch down. Cut a piece of clear vinyl 12" x 10-1/2" (30.5cm x 27cm), and with masking tape, tape in place inside above the top trim

stitching line. Stitch it in place with a long stitch and a piece of tissue paper on top, which usually comes with vinyl. If you don't have paper, stitch from the right side with the vinyl against the throat place.

3. Sides and Front: Place windows in side and front just as you did in step 2. For front entrance, turn under 1/4" (6mm) on one 28-1/2" (72.4cm) side on the two smaller pieces; turn under an additional 2" (5cm) hem and stitch in place. Overlap pieces with hems 1/2" (1.5mm) at center top so front measures 31-1/4" (79.4cm) across. Stitch down 3" (7.5cm) with a close satin stitch to secure overlap.

4. Follow directions included with the *Happy Chalk* transfer, applying the transfer to the right of the back window. Cut a pocket 10" x 5-1/2" (25.5cm x 14cm) from the scraps. Press under on both 5-1/2" (14cm) ends. Fold in half with right sides together, and stitch the side seams in a 1/4" (6mm) seam allowance. Turn to right side and press. Stitch pocket on three sides under the window. Stencil appropriate words with the alphabet stencil, paint, and brush. Stencil

---
♥ *Dip your brush in the paint, wipe it on a paper towel, and then begin the stenciling.*

---

ideas similar to "Lisa's Burgers" and "Drive-in Window" on one side, "Entrance" beside the side with the opening, "Specials" over the transfer, and "Chalk" under the pocket. Let dry thoroughly.

5. Stitch the four sides to the top in a 1/4" (6mm) seam, leaving 1/4" (6mm) open at beginning and end of each side. Stitch the side seams. Press under 1/4" (6mm) all around the bottom, and turn up and stitch a 1-1/2" (4cm) hem.

6. Awning (optional): Cut four triangles as previously described, matching the stripes. Make a mark at the table top measurement on each corner. Stitch from the mark to the center on each piece. Turn under and press 1/4" (6mm) on bottom and sides. Straight stitch into place. Secure the awning to the top by stitching in-the-ditch along the top seams.

Variations:

A. Work each side as a different building to create a card table town.

B. Add a print of large floral motifs along the bottom for landscaping. Bond to *Wonder-Under*, cut out around the flowers, and then bond to the sides. Outline the flowers with glitter dimensional paint.

Cat Pin

Fig. 5.31 Cat pin

Jane was checking out new arrivals at a favorite craft store several weeks ago when she spotted a package of "Cat Whiskers." She bought two packages (twelve pieces, each 12" [30.5cm] long), black and crystal. She had an idea for a cat pin floating around in her head for awhile, and the whiskers were the catalyst she needed. They're super quick to stitch, and if you can't find the whiskers, use stiffened carpet thread.

Make the pins of silk or lamé for an elegant look, or a tiny floral print or check for a country look. Make them flatter by using pieces of quilt batt rather than loose stuffing.

You Will Need:

Scrap of fabric 2" x 6" (5cm x 15cm)
#3 pearl cotton for tail
Gold cord for collar
Small black bead
Cat's whiskers
Thread to match fabric
Tiny jingle bell
Stop Fraying
Pin back

1. Body: Cut a rectangle of fabric 2" x 6" (5cm x 15cm). Turn under 1/4" (6mm) on both 2" (5cm) ends and press. Match 2" (5cm) ends right sides together and stitch 1/4" (6mm) side seams. Turn. Stuff. Make a twisted cord tail about 4" (10cm) long with #3 pearl cotton, ribbon thread, *Candlelight,* or anything comparable that complements the fabric. Close the opening by hand, slipping in the tail at one side.

2. Ears: Working with doubled thread, run small gathering stitches in the center of the cat's head, beginning 3/8" (1cm) down on the back and continuing up, over, and 3/8" (1cm) down onto the front. Pull on the thread to gather. Then loop the thread around the top over the gathering stitches and poke the needle from the starting place through the cat to the back. Again pull tight and end off the thread with several tiny backstitches. Take the needle into the body at this point and bring out about 1/2" (1.5cm) away. Clip the thread. This makes ear shapes on the cat's head.

3. Collar: Cut a 9" (23cm) piece of gold cord. Thread a tiny brass jingle bell on the cord, then wrap the cord twice around the neck. Pulling tight, tie a square knot at the back, being sure the bell is at the front. Clip the threads and put a drop of *Stop Fraying* on the knot.

4. Face: Sew or glue a small black bead on the face for a nose. Cut the whiskers into six

♥ *Add googley eyes if you want or substitute a tiny pompom for the bead nose. Use any ribbon, cross-locked beads, or small trim for the collar.*

1" (2.5cm) pieces. Insert the ends into the cat, three on either side of the nose. Put a drop of *Stop Fraying* where the whiskers enter the fabric.

5. Finishing: Glue or sew the pin back to the back of the cat.

> ♥ *If you don't have any pin backs, sew a safety pin to the back.*

Variations:

A. Fold the fabric in half, right sides together. Make a pencil mark 1/4" (6mm) in from the edge at the bottom and 1/2" (1.5cm) in at the top. With a ruler, join these two dots with a pencil line. Sew the seams on the drawn lines. Proceed as above.

B. Make the cat of unbleached muslin and paint the face, including the whiskers, after the cat is stuffed. Paint designs on the body or sew on charms.

> Don't stop at this chapter if you're looking for gifts for children. There are baby blankets to knit in Chapter 4, page 29. And ornaments in Chapter 8, page 110, can be enlarged as suggested in variation E (page 112) and made into a stuffed animal or doll.

Chapter 6

A Woman's Touch
Gifts for Women

Projects:

- ♥ *Buttons and Button Covers*
- ♥ *Needlepoint Earrings*
- ♥ *Crocheted Cords*
- ♥ *Flat Braid Bracelet*
- ♥ *Quick Glitz Earrings*
- ♥ *Angel Doll Pins*
- ♥ *Memories and Remembrance Framed Collage*
- ♥ *Heart Pincushion*
- ♥ *Hat Pincushion*
- ♥ *Needlepoint Needlecase*
- ♥ *Needlework Frame Weights*
- ♥ *Sewing or Jewelry Bag*
- ♥ *Humbug Make-Up Bag*
- ♥ *Heirloom Apron*
- ♥ *Exercise Mat*

Any lady on your list will be lucky to receive one of the gifts within this chapter. You'll find gifts to give as well as gifts to make for yourself. Women's gifts range in size from buttons to exercise mats. Whether you crochet, needlepoint, embroider, sew, or enjoy assembling collages, there is something here for you.

Fig. 6.1 *Polymer clay buttons and button covers*

Buttons and Button Covers

Warning: Working with *Sculpey, Fimo,* or *Cernit* is habit forming! If you've never tried these polymer clays but have always wanted to experiment with them, what's stopping you? They are easy to use, and the results are so professional that you'll never stop at buttons, but go on to creating beads and small pins. Also, if you need small sculptured hands, heads, or feet for doll making, this medium may be the answer.

You'll find the clays at craft shops and art supply stores in arrays of colors, including neons and metallics. Adding special glitter is also a possibility.

There are differences in the three clays. *Cernit* gives a porcelain-like finish. *Fimo* takes longer to manipulate into a soft workable clay. *Sculpey III* works up quickly into a malleable clay and is readily available in craft stores—reasons why we use it. All three clays stay soft until baked.

You Will Need:

A large supply of clay in many colors
Wallpaper razor blade
Button covers
Household Goop (available at hardware stores)
Finishing glaze (specially made for use with clay)

1. Buttons: To make buttons, work the bar or bars of clay into soft moldable blobs. If you have a pasta machine, run the clay through the machine several times. (Jackie bought a machine she uses only for *Sculpey*, even though the clay is nontoxic. The rollers on the pasta maker clean up easily with alcohol.)

Once you have workable pieces of clay, roll them out into cylinders the diameter you want for your buttons (Fig. 6.2). Use a wall-

Fig. 6.2 Make disks by slicing rolls of clay.

paper razor blade to slice them into disks. But don't limit yourself to disks. Use small cookie or canape cutters to cut shapes after you've rolled out a slab of clay (Fig. 6.3).

Fig. 6.3 Use cookie cutters for button shapes.

Again, the pasta maker is perfect. You can roll out even slabs as thick or thin as you wish. If you don't have a pasta machine, use a rolling pin.

After the buttons are shaped, use a darning needle or ice pick to poke holes in the buttons. We use a store-bought button, lay it over the clay button, and poke through the holes and into the clay. Then all our button holes are the same distance apart.

Don't make buttons of one color only. Try this idea: Roll out cigarette-sized clay pieces in many colors. Twist two or more colors together to marbleize (Fig. 6.4). Or, combine

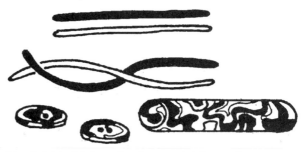

Fig. 6.4 Marbleize clay by combining colors.

several of these long rolls and cover them with a thin slab of clay. Roll on a flat surface to combine the colored tubes into one roll. Slice with the wallpaper razor blade. Each button will look different, but related.

Another idea is to roll out two slabs of clay of different colors. (We used black and white.) Layer one on top of the other, and roll a rolling pin over them to make them stick together. Then roll up the slab from the long side, creating a spiral. (Remember pinwheel cookies?) Slice buttons from the roll. To make them more colorful, we added rolls of yellow, green, red, and blue as we rolled the pinwheel. When sliced, the buttons had an interesting colorful design that looked a lot more complicated than it was to make (Fig. 6.5).

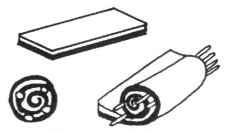

Fig. 6.5 Slip in skinny rolls of colored clay while rolling slab pinwheels.

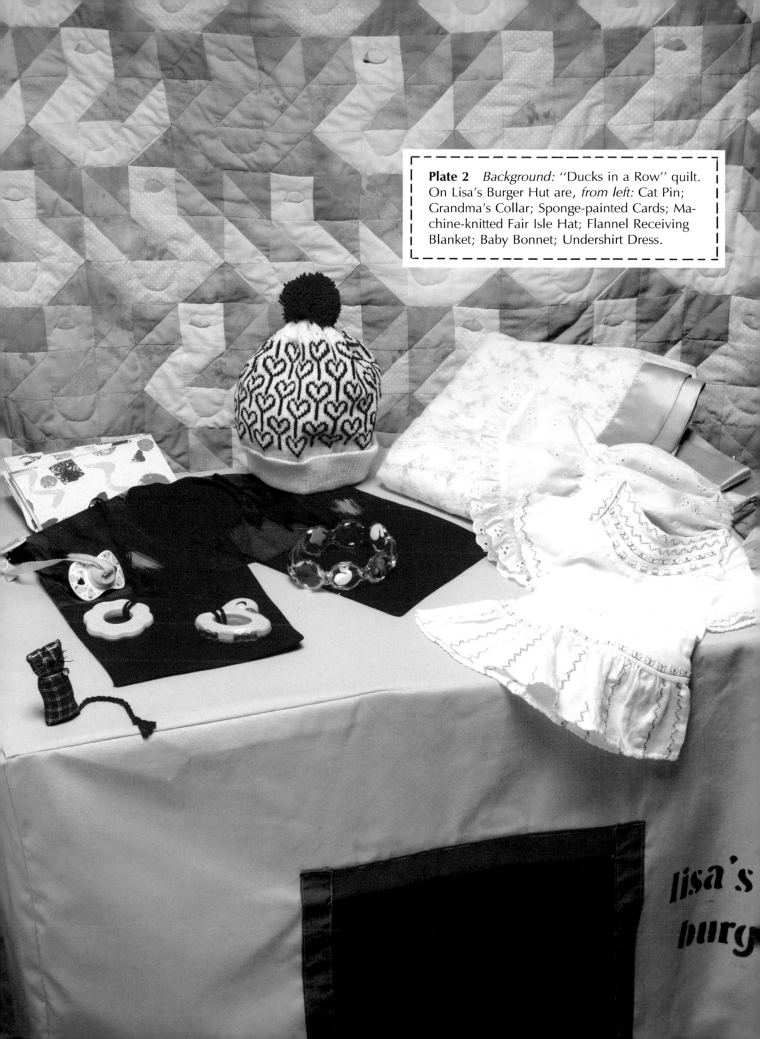

Plate 2 *Background:* ''Ducks in a Row'' quilt. On Lisa's Burger Hut are, *from left:* Cat Pin; Grandma's Collar; Sponge-painted Cards; Machine-knitted Fair Isle Hat; Flannel Receiving Blanket; Baby Bonnet; Undershirt Dress.

Plate 3 The Exercise Mat is on the Fur Lap Robe. *From top to bottom on the mat:* Hooded Bath Towel; Scout Wreath; Cheerleader Wreath; Sporty Hang Towel; People Wrapper; Card Holders; Ultrasuede Pocket Tissue Holder.

Plate 4 *Clockwise from noon:* Memories and Remembrance Collage; Victorian Christmas Stockings; Cathedral Window Ornament variation; Christmas Tree Skirt. *Lower left and center:* Five Hand-made Postcards, with Fabric-covered Card immediately below the collage.

Plate 5 *From top left corner:* Baby Blanket; Scarf; "The Rag That Started It All"; Warm Shawl; Knitted Potholder.

Plate 6 *Clockwise from top left:* Grocery Sack; "Knit One" Tote; Fanny Pack; Grocery Sack; Metamorphosis Bag.

Plate 7 "Phone Home" Afghan.

Plate 8 *Left to right:* Embroidered Art Deco Card; Frame Weight; Filled Plastic Bows; Humbug Make-up Bag; "I Promised You a Flower Garden" quilt; Sculpey Buttons; Hat Pincushion; Bird Doll Pin.

Plate 9 Angel Doll Pins.

Plate 10 *Top:* Advent Calendar. *From left, row 1:* Glitzy Boot Ornament; Seminole Patchwork Ornaments; Glitzy Double-fold Card; Cathedral Window Ornament. *From left, row 2:* Lamé Stars; Christmas Memory Collage; Mr. and Mrs. Santa; Crocheted Wreath Pins. *From left, row 3:* Battenberg Star; Lace and Wire Ornament; Fabric-covered Tags; Needlepoint Ornaments; Lamé Star.

Don't throw away any scraps. Combine them, and slice or cut out to size to make different, less perfect designs—which tend to be more interesting anyway.

2. Button Covers: One of the easiest gifts to make, yet one of the most original, is a set of button covers. The findings are readily available at craft shops. Two types of covers are available—the hinged type and the type that slide over the button.

Make clay buttons as above, but don't poke holes in them. You can also use clumps of clay embedded with beads, stones, jewels, or glitter. A friend knitted a sweater scattered with yachting flags. For her buttons she used *Sculpey* flags to match.

3. Finishing: Once the buttons are made, they must be baked. To do this, place the buttons on a cookie sheet and bake them at 275–300 degrees for ten or twelve minutes—depending on the thickness of the clay. When the clay cools, paint the buttons with the special matte or glossy glaze for *Sculpey* (available where you bought the clay). This glaze enhances the colors and protects at the same time.

> ♥ *Use an inexpensive clear nail polish, which comes complete with brush (no messy cleanup) and is easy to apply.*

Use *Household Goop* to attach buttons to button covers. *Goop* is an extremely thick adhesive that holds the buttons securely on the covers—no sliding while drying. Also, if you want to take the covers off later, it is quite easy to pry them off if you've used *Goop*.

Button covers are wonderful cuff links for long-sleeved shirts. If you make cuff links for a man, create a tie tack to match. (Tie tack findings are available at your local craft shop.)

Variations:

A. Use small silk flowers, turquoise stones, Indian head pennies, or buffalo nickels. Heavy cardboard or wood can also be covered with fabric or pieces of maps showing favorite towns. Protect with clear acrylic spray. Cut out favorite comic strip characters, or become Picasso, and paint the wood with gesso. Add a background color if you wish, dots and squiggles, streaks of lightning, smears, lines, crosses, and circles. Cleanup is easy if you use acrylic paint.

B. Glue beads, washers, screws, and such to the painted wood. Paint the glued objects, and spray a coat of clear acrylic over them for protection.

Needlepoint Earrings

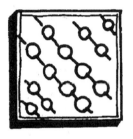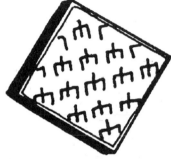

Fig. 6.6 Use pearl cotton on fine mesh when making needlepoint earrings.

We suggest you keep small frames with stretched canvas in them in a tote bag beside your favorite chair. Whenever you sit down for a few minutes, you can stitch on the earrings that follow.

We work on 18-mesh tan canvas or whatever colors we've found in remnant pieces at our favorite shops. Don't rush out and buy some canvas; use whatever you have on hand. Our preferred thread for the earrings is stranded floss, which comes in over 360 colors and is available everywhere. It's inexpensive, easy to use, and looks like silk. There are metallic ribbons and threads of all sorts to use in combination with the floss for a sparkly look. Use single strands of

Watercolours (gorgeous variegated thread in muted colors available at needlework shops). We use leftovers from other projects in place of floss. Anything goes. Apply *Needlework Finisher* to the finished earrings to protect and stiffen the stitches. *Ultrasuede* and iridescent dimensional or glitter paint can be applied for a quick professional finish.

You Will Need:

4" (10cm) square piece 18-mesh canvas
4" (10cm) frame (optional)
1 skein stranded floss
1 tube 1/16" (1.5mm) metallic ribbon
    thread
#24 tapestry needle
 Needlework Finisher (see "Sources of
    Supplies")
Small paintbrush for finisher
Iridescent dimensional or glitter paint (see
    "Sources of Supplies")
Ultrasuede or felt scraps
Earring findings (Figs. 6.7–10)
Household Goop
#2 pencil
Waxed paper

1. Stretch the canvas on the frame. Count down and in five or six threads from the inside of the frame. With your pencil, outline a square seventeen threads by seventeen threads. Count across four threads and mark an identical second square. Mark squares for the second pair of earrings, leaving six threads between the two pairs. Work one of the charts on page 132, using four to six strands of floss. (You may work these on any even-weave or cross-stitch fabric. If you want to work on fourteen-mesh fabric or canvas with threads appropriate to the count, you will have larger earrings.)

2. Stitch both pairs (four squares). Cut a 2-1/2" x 2-3/4" (6.5cm x 7cm) square of *Ultrasuede* or two pieces 2-1/2" by 1-1/4" (6.5cm x 3cm). Remove the canvas from the frame. Turn over, and thoroughly paint the back of the stitched blocks with the finisher. Paint the wrong side of the *Ultrasuede*, being sure to paint the edges as well. You need a completely bonded back, so the edges will not separate after trimming. Press the backing on the stitching. Place the earrings between two pieces of waxed paper and place under several heavy books. Let dry overnight.

3. When thoroughly dry, trim around the square, leaving one unworked thread. Use any dimensional or glitter paint that comes in a "writer" bottle. Carefully squeeze a line

> ♥ *When painting the line of glitter glue around the edge, place the index finger of your nonpainting hand in the center of the earring to hold it in place. Test the paint to be sure that it is flowing properly. Holding the paint between your thumb and index finger, rest and stabilize your hand on your little finger. Place the drawing tip at the top of one side, squeeze the bottle, and draw the line down the side without moving your little finger. Repeat for each side.*

of paint along the unworked thread. Let dry overnight.

4. Using Goop, glue the earring findings (Figs. 6.7–10) to the back of the stitched

Fig. 6.7 Posts   *Fig. 6.8 French ear hook*

Fig. 6.9 Kidney wire   *Fig. 6.10 Clip*

squares. Let dry for several hours. If you want the square to dangle from a french ear hook finding, take a large crewel needle and push it through the backing about two threads in at any corner. Place a 9mm jump ring through the hole, and attach the ring to the finding. Repeat for the second earring.

Variation:

Glue magnets on the backs instead of earring findings, and you'll have the most elegant refrigerator in town.

Crocheted Cords

Fig. 6.11 Crocheted cord

We've made notebooks with directions and samples of every kind of cord we could find in all our different books—twisted, braided, crocheted, knit, sewn, and knotted.

♥ *Make twisted cord on the sewing machine by either looping or tying your doubled cord (at least five-and-one-half times the desired finished length) on a bobbin. Place the bobbin on the winding pin, and set your machine for winding. Put your index finger in the loop of the cord at the other end of the cord, stretching the cord to keep tension on it. Run the machine until the cord threatens the blood supply in your finger. Stop the machine, find the middle of the cord, and take it in your other hand. Bring your finger to the bobbin and let the cord twist on itself. Grasp it tightly right above the bobbin, cut the cord from the bobbin, and immediately tie an overhand knot to secure the twists.*

With all those possibilities we still didn't have the kinds of cord we wanted for the purses in this book as well as some jewelry we'd been making. Jane picked up a crochet hook and yarn, and discovered a whole series of new cords—some flat, some twisted, and some round, but all fast to do. We've made some suggestions on how they can be used. Do try them in different threads and with different size hooks. We make them from fine crochet cotton and a size 10 (3.25mm) hook all the way to rattail cord with a "J" (6.5mm) hook and everything in between.

♥ *We've used the standard crochet abbreviations: ch=chain, sc= single crochet, dc=double crochet, yo=yarn over.*

---

1. Lover's Knot (Solomon's Knot) chain (Fig. 6.12):

Fig. 6.12 Lover's Knot chain

*Ch 1, pulling up loop to desired length, yo and pull loop through, sc in back loop to lock the chain.**
Repeat from * to ** for desired length.

Make a cord of Lover's Knot, keeping loops even length from 1/2" (1.5cm) to whatever length desired. The length of the loop will depend on the weight of the thread used (the finer the thread, the shorter the loop).

This is excellent for purse handles when done with rattail cord and hooks from "H" (5.5mm) to "J" (6.5mm), or chains for necklaces when worked with gold or silver metallic cord and a "D" (3.25mm) hook.

2. Leaf chain (Fig. 6.13):

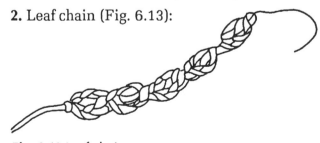

Fig. 6.13 Leaf chain

The cord that follows looks like a string of leaves and is especially effective when worked in #10 crochet cotton with a size 5 hook.

*Ch 4, yo, and insert hook in top thread of third chain from hook, yo and pull up a loop, yo and draw through 2 loops, yo, and insert hook in same space, yo and pull up a loop, yo and draw through 2 loops, yo and draw through 3 loops.**
Repeat from * to ** for desired length.

Variations:

A. Ch 3.

B. Ch 5.

C. Add one yo: Insert hook in same space, yo and pull up a loop, yo and draw through 4 loops.

D. *Ch 3, yo, insert hook in top of third chain from hook, and draw up loop, yo, insert hook in same chain and draw up loop, yo and draw through 5 loops.** Repeat from * to ** for length desired.

3. Mediumweight chain (Fig. 6.14):

Fig. 6.14 *Mediumweight chain*

*Ch 2, sc in top of second chain from hook.**
Repeat from * to ** for desired length.

Variation:

*Ch 3, sc in top of second chain from hook.**
Repeat from * to ** for desired length.

   Crochet this with floss and a zero-sized hook for the chain on the next pendant you make.

4. Knotted chain (Fig. 6.15):

Fig. 6.15 *Knotted chain*

Ch 2, sc in second chain from hook, ch 1. Turn in clockwise direction away from you.
*Sc in sc, ch 1, turn away from you.**
Repeat from * to ** for desired length.

Turn this chain as you work it. It isn't one of the twisted chains.

Try this with #3 pearl cotton and an "E" (3.5mm) hook.

5. Spiral cord chain (Fig. 6.16):

Fig. 6.16 *Spiral cord chain shown flat*

Ch 3, sc in third chain from hook, ch 2. Turn counterclockwise or toward you.
*Sc in previous sc, ch 2, turn toward you.**
Repeat from * to ** for desired length.

This cord will spiral and twist more, depending on the size of the yarn and the hook.

Record all your experiments so you can repeat them when you want to use this cord.

6. Narrow flat cord chain (Fig. 6.17):

Fig. 6.17 *Narrow flat cord chain*

Ch 2, sc in second chain from hook. Pull loop a shade long.
Turn clockwise (away from you).
*Sc in sc just completed. Turn away.**
Repeat from * to ** for desired length.

   Following is a flat braid that has a slight built-in elasticity to use as a bracelet.

Flat Braid Bracelet

Fig. 6.18 Flat braid

You Will Need:

Unger's *Pima Cotton*
Aluminum crochet hook size "E" (3.5mm)
#18 tapestry needle

1. Use the cotton and "E" (3.5mm) hook. Ch 3, insert hook in top of second chain, yo and draw up loop, insert hook in top of third chain, yo and draw up loop (3 loops on hook), yo and draw through all 3 loops.

Turn work away from you (clockwise). *Insert hook in stitch just made, yo and draw up loop, insert hook in loop along side, yo and draw up loop, yo and draw through all loops on hook. Turn work away from you.**
Do not pull stitches tight.
Work this cord in a relaxed manner with stitches a bit longer than usual. Repeat from * to ** for 8" (20.5mm).

2. End with ch 1, and pull the thread through to finish off. Bring the ends together, noting how they fit.

Thread one of the ends in a tapestry needle, and sew the two ends together. Weave the ending threads in as inconspicuously as possible (Fig. 6.19). Clip the ends and put a few drops of *Stop Fraying* on them.

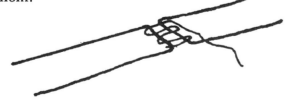

Fig. 6.19 Finish bracelet invisibly.

3. One inch of finished braid takes about 24" (61cm) of *Pima Cotton* when worked with an "E" (3.5mm) hook. Thus, one ball would yield about 130" (3.3m) of braid.

There is a built-in elasticity in this braid so it slips easily over the hand. Crochet the bracelet to any length desired (smaller for children, larger for men). The braid is also effective when worked in *Watercolour*.

Quick Glitz Earrings

Fig. 6.20 Make instant earrings: Glitz up purchased appliqués with paint.

Here's a super quick idea when you need some special earrings, which happen to be great sellers at bazaars. Have an earring afternoon with several friends, and you'll make enough to stock your booth at the fair.

You Will Need:

Matching pair of embroidered appliqués (available at fabric stores and by mail)
Glitter paint in colors to match appliqué
Small paintbrush
Earring backs (clip-on or posts for pierced ears)
Household Goop
Waxed paper

1. Place the appliqués (embroidered side up) on the waxed paper. Paint glitter over the different areas. Let dry.

2. Using *Goop*, glue the glittered appliqués to the earring findings.

Variation:

Buy sequined appliqués and skip the glitter paint. Simply glue to findings. Don't make a matched pair, but use appliqués that are related in color or theme.

Angel Doll Pins

Fig. 6.21 *Angel with twig arms and feet*

When we decided to use geometric shapes in the book, Jackie changed her generic doll pin pattern (in *How to Make Soft Jewelry*, Chilton, 1991) to an elongated triangle. Once decorated with feathers and beads, she realized she'd made a pin that resembled an opera singer/singing teacher/dramatic coach who lived in her town when she was a child. Always festooned with furs, feathers, and jewels, she used to let Jackie and friends look through trunks of old costumes and wear the clothing. Mrs. Northrup is one of Jackie's favorite childhood memories, and these dolls are her favorite contribution to the book.

The triangle pattern is modified a bit, to enable you to sew on the button face (by adding a half-circle of fabric in the center back). In order to add twig feet, we cut off the bottom point of the triangle and folded the raw edge up inside.

You Will Need:

Small bits of white or unbleached muslin, lace fabric (pieces at least 3-1/2" [9cm] square)
Fiberfill
Tacky glue
White or glitter-covered twigs
Beads, feathers, pearl charms or fetishes, pearl buttons
Sewing machine
Hemostat or point turner

1. Begin by making a pattern. Use the one pictured in Figure 6.22 or enlarge it to fit

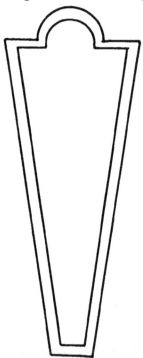

Fig. 6.22 *Basic pattern for all angels—enlarge or reduce size.*

your needs. We've made the angels in all sizes—small to use on swags of evergreens or glued to wreaths, and large to adorn the top of a Christmas tree.

2. Use lace fabric for the front of the dolls, but back it with a plain white or off-white muslin. Cut two pieces of the lining so you can back the doll with muslin, too.

Draw the pattern on the wrong side of a piece of solid fabric. Place a layer of lace underneath and another piece of plain fabric under that for a lace sandwich (Fig. 6.23). **Do not cut out.** Stitch around the entire shape except for the straight bottom. Once stitched, cut out the angel body, clip in at the tab corners, and clip off corners at shoulders. Go back and zigzag around each doll (still leaving the bottom open).

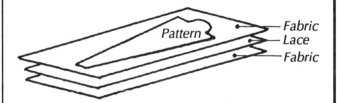

Fig. 6.23 *Layer fabric, lace, and fabric again to make an angel.*

3. Turn the angels right side out. You can do this by reaching up inside to the tab with a hemostat, grasping the fabric, and pulling down (if the opening at the bottom is large enough for the bulk of the fabric). If this method is too difficult, slit open the back of the doll and turn (the slit won't show later because the pin back is sewn there). We prefer to cut up the back, because when the slit is sewn together later, the doll becomes rounder in front (like Mrs. Northrup), and has a more interesting shape.

4. Stuff the angel lightly with fiberfill or batting and turn the bottom edge up inside the doll. If you slit up the back, now is the time to stitch it shut.

5. The fun begins! Choose a button for the face. We like real pearl buttons, flat, and with two holes. After stitching it in place, we add beads as if they were eyes (in the button holes), but string them on one thread from hole to hole. Between the eye-beads we add something appropriate for a nose—a small heart, a tiny, long crystal, or pearl drop bead (the hole should be at one end and allow the bead to drop).

Once the face is in place, the personality evolves. Stitch white glittered twigs to each shoulder for arms. (Branches are available at flower shops, or make your own by spray painting branches from your own trees. Glue or spray glitter, or leave them plain white.) Look for that part of the branch with a curve (elbow) to it. At the end we want a few small branches off the main one to look like hands.

Sometimes we sew the hands to the sides or in front of the doll to protect them from breakage later. Both arms are different and probably different lengths—that's part of the charm of this doll. If you can't find branches, or live in an area with no trees, then use this idea: String long bugle beads and seed beads together to create arms (Fig. 6.24). Add

Fig. 6.24 *Angel with beaded arms and feet*

charms and more beads where the hands belong. Do the same for the feet: A bugle bead and a few seed beads are sufficient for each foot. Go back to the branches you've painted, and find two pieces that look like high heels or chicken feet (Fig. 6.25).

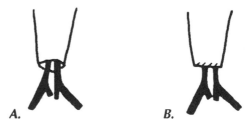

Fig. 6.25
   A. Break off twigs and place inside bottom opening for feet.
   B. Stitch opening closed.

Cut off those parts, leaving about an inch for the leg. Squirt a bit of thick tacky glue inside the doll, and push the legs up inside, heels together. Determine how much leg you want to show, and then stitch by hand across the bottom of the doll.

Go back and decorate the head of the doll. Use thick tacky glue. Start by placing a large glob of it between the button and the tab. Then down between and into the glue goes feathers, strings of beads (string them on wire or buy them that way), tiny paper flowers, ribbons, rick-rack, ribbon, lace, tassels, and yarn. You probably won't use all of that on one doll, but those are all excellent choices.

Decorate the body by stringing a potpourri of beads, trinkets, and sequins and hanging them from the shoulders in swags. You can also hang them at the sides of the head to reach halfway down the doll for ridiculous earrings, or at the ends of the twig arms.

Do stitch beads on the lace dress as well. Cut lace motifs from other fabrics and add those, too. Bead over them to hold them in place.

6. The last step makes your doll an angel, and we have several ideas for wings: (1) Use plain white feathers available at craft stores. (2) Use flower petals (bridal department do-it-yourself in the same craft store) made from covered wire—sometimes beaded—with transparent fabric stretched between. (3) Use white silk flower leaves. (4) Use whatever you find in the bridal area that were meant to go into bridal headpieces or bouquets, but are appropriate as "wings."

One of our favorite sets of wings are two hunks of clam shells found while on vacation. They'd been in the lake a long time and were easy to cut into shape, though sometimes we left them in the shape they were. We also found birch bark curled all over the ground and cut wings from the whitest parts.

Variations:

A. Tree-top Angel (see Color Plate 9). Another idea for wings, and one I used for the tree-top angel, is to find a piece of lace and a piece of floral wire covered in white. Set the sewing machine on a wide zigzag and a stitch length about 1.5mm. Stitch the wire to the lace in a wing shape (Fig. 6.26). Clip

Fig. 6.26 Couch wires inside lace to stiffen wings.

back on the lace to even it up, if needed. The lace on this angel was a terrific find; it's scalloped as you see it in the photo.

At the back of the tree-top doll, sew two strips of *Velcro* across the back, one several inches from the other. To attach the doll to the tree top, open the strips, place the angel against the top of the tree, and close the *Velcro* back on itself (Fig. 6.27).

Fig. 6.27 Stitch two Velcro *strips to the back of angel, and attach to Christmas tree.*

B. Bird Pins (see Color Plate 8). The bird doll pins were born after the angels, because of the shreds of an Indian rug we can't throw out. We made the birds the same way as the angels, but used plain twigs for arms and legs and antler buttons or gorgeous handmade wooden buttons bought at a gallery store for faces. (Look in fabric stores—you'll find beautiful commercial wooden buttons.) On the faces of the birds we strung beads and turquoise chips for beaks.

To decorate the birds, we used tiny pearl birds from an old Indian necklace, pottery-looking beads, and a lot of turquoise. White sequins with brown, turquoise, and orange beads in the centers were also used. The wings are clam shells or birch bark, and the birds are decorated with feathers, strips of suede, rick-rack, ribbon, and other appropriate "bird" things. Wear the smaller pins or use them on a tote bag or purse. Make a large one for the wall, and attach a wire loop for hanging.

These dolls are hazardous to your health because you stop doing everything else—including eating—when you begin making them. One doll leads to another and another and another.

(Move over Jenny Craig. We've invented a new method of losing weight!)

Memories and Remembrance Framed Collage

Fig. 6.28 Assemble a memory collage of special collectibles.

Wilfred J. Funk once published a list of the ten most beautiful words in the English language. The sound, not the meaning of the word, was the criteria. Understandably the most beautiful words contained long vowels and the soft sounds of consonants *m* and *r*.

Memory is an example of a beautiful word, and *remembrance* comes close. Not only the sounds, but the meanings as well make these two words beautiful. We're not referring to remembering a broken tooth or that needle in your foot (we're trying to forget those), but remembering past beauty and beautiful people, family, and treasures tucked in drawers and run across only occasionally.

Instead of hiding your momentos, get them out and place them on a table. This is the first step to making this special collage.

Memory collages are personal gifts you should make for loved ones as well as yourself. The following collage is a remembrance of two grandmothers.

You Will Need:

Frame (we used 13" [33cm] square) with glareless glass
Plywood or canvasboard to fit your frame
Stapler (if using plywood)
Tacky glue
Kraft paper
Serrated picture hanger
Memorabilia and related items (read through before beginning)

Even if your grandmothers never gave you a pieced quilt top, the colors of the background quilt scrap may remind you of them, so use it. Place the fabric piece in front of you. Then put the frame (minus glass) on top of it so you can work within the frame's boundaries.

Now begin arranging your collection. If your grandmothers did needlework, add a collection of tatting, Teneriffe, beadwork, a card of buttons, a package of needles, and a strip of lace—whatever they've left you or whatever reminds you of them. Perhaps you're lucky enough to have a wedding announcement or invitation. Copy the original, reducing the size if necessary, and perhaps, aging your copy by tearing or burning the edges with a match for that older worn look. Include flowers—pictures from magazines, silk, pressed petals—they loved, had worn, or had pressed in old books.

Once you've arranged your remembrances, take off the frame. Then cover the plywood with *Pellon* fleece.

Now, you ask, how can you take the memorabilia off the backing, attach the backing to the plywood, and then get the items back in the same arrangement? Do one of three things: Try to memorize the arrangement, sketch the arrangement before taking it off the backing, or take a *Polaroid* picture of it.

Stretch the quilt piece backing over the plywood and staple the fabric to the board.

Use a smudge (only a light one) of glue stick on everything to hold the collage together until the glass is put over it and it's framed.

When you're satisfied with the arrangement, cover it with glareless glass and the frame. Flip it over and secure the wood backing with long nails.

Finally, spread tacky glue around the back of the frame and place it on a piece of brown kraft paper. Use a razor blade to slice off the paper all around the frame. A serrated hanger completes the project.

Variations:

A. Make these collages for children, collecting their favorite comic strip characters, games, candy wrappers, bottle caps, report cards with super grades as well as drawings they've sketched and awards they've won.

B. For the teens in your life, find pictures of their idols, words of songs they love, favorite colors, pressed flowers, invitations, and graduation memorabilia. Yes, this project is the same as arranging a bulletin board, but it's permanent. If they like the gift now, in a few years they'll treasure it.

Heart Pincushions

Fig. 6.29 Embroider and bead hearts for gifts.

Make velveteen hearts all year long while waiting for children at lessons, for the doctor at the office, or in front of the TV. Pile them into a basket at Christmas, and give them to unexpected guests. Or, place them on dressers in your home so favorite pins are on view.

Embellish the hearts with beads, lace, embroidery, buttons, old jewelry, or whatever is at hand.

You Will Need:

Velveteen fabric for the hearts
Old jewelry
Old buttons
Old beads
Lace
Ribbons
Beading needle
Embroidery thread
Stuffing

1. Heart: Take a 6" (15cm) square of paper, and using most of it, cut a heart pattern like you did in grammar school. (You remember: Fold the paper in half, and cut an angel's wing.) Cut two hearts out of a project you no longer want (these were made from a log cabin pieced fabric). Place right sides together, and stitch around in a generous 1/8" (3mm) seam, leaving an opening for turning. Turn, stuff firmly, and close the opening.

2. Embellishment: Yes, it would be easier to embroider and bead if the hearts were not sewn together, but use a beading needle. Stitching through the fat heart with this extremely long needle to attach lace or sew on buttons isn't hard at all.

To rule out having to bead heavily on one of them, first bead another piece of fabric and stretch it over lightweight cardboard to make an appliqué. Then glue it in place on the heart to hold it while you add more beads to the edge to make it look like you

Fig. 6.30 *Attach an appliqué of beads to a heart.*

did all the work on the heart itself (Fig. 6.30). Also, add brass leaves and beads (purchased as part of an old necklace) to hide the appliqué edge completely. You can fudge with embroidery as well by decorating ribbons or appliqués and then attaching. Decorating with old buttons is even easier (Fig. 6.31). Opaque white and pearl buttons

Fig. 6.31 *Sew an assortment of buttons to a heart.*

with red, pearl, and white beads are sewn down and layered on the heart. Beaded lace motifs are also stitched to the heart. Buttons over them help hold them in place as well as decorate the heart (Fig. 6.32).

Fig. 6.32 *Decorate with lace, beads, and buttons.*

What about the underside of the heart, which is now dotted with stitches? Cover it with lace, attaching it at the seam around the perimeter of the heart. Pearls strung with wire are stitched down to cover the edge (Fig. 6.33). At the upper curve, bend the wire

Fig. 6.33 *Add wire strung with beads around the seam line.*

into a double bow, and sew more beads over the stitches used to tack it down. Cording is another choice for covering the seam. Gold cording with the red heart looks gorgeous. The cord is wrapped and couched from the point, around the heart, and back to the starting point (the couching thread is hidden in the twist of the cord). Add ribbons, a bow of a dozen loops of gold cord, and more beads (Fig. 6.34).

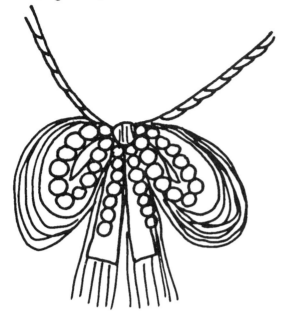

Fig. 6.34 *Form a bow with ribbons, cord, and strings of beads.*

Now you tell us, are these decorative pincushions? Victorian ornaments? Goodies for a designer basket? Embellishment for a pine wreath? Favors for a special dinner? If someone questions their use, quote this ever-useful phrase, "Beauty is its own excuse for being."

Hat Pincushion

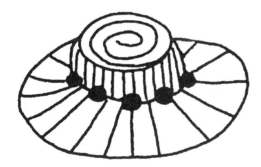

Fig. 6.35 *Hat pincushion from a 1920s pattern*

Jane's Aunt Ella, who's been supplying bazaars with handmade items for more years than either one of us will ever tell, shared this hat pincushion with us. In Victorian times, pincushions like these were used on a lady's dressing table as a temporary parking place for m'lady's brooch. These days, we use the hats for pincushions.

We often buy leftovers (bits of unusual yarns) from weaving shops, and use these for the accent area on the brim. These hats are crocheted with two strands of a fine rayon chenille, which creates a rich velvety surface.

You Will Need:

2 oz. (50g) rayon chenille (see "Sources of Supplies")
1/4 oz. (12.5g) for contrast (can use left-overs)
Size "H" or "I" (5.5mm or 6mm) crochet hook
#18 tapestry needle for finishing

1. Crown:
   a. Chain 83 stitches.
   Double crochet (dc) in fourth chain from hook.
   2 dc in same chain.
   1 dc in next 77 chains.
   6 dc in end chain.
   1 dc in other side of starting chain (77 dc) to beginning of round.
   3 dc in starting chain.
   Slip stitch to third chain at top of round.
   b. Ch 1 (do not turn), and 2 sc in same place as last sc.
   2 sc in next 3 dc.
   1 sc in next 77 dc.
   2 sc in next 6 dc.
   Change to contrast yarn. Sc in next 38 stitches.

2. Brim:
   a. Working in the back loop of each sc around, 1 sc (first stitch of the brim) and 1 hdc (half double crochet) in the next sc, 2 dc in next 37 sc, 1 hdc and 1 sc in next stitch, ch 1, turn. 1 sc in each of next 77 stitches.
   b. Attach main yarn. Ch 1, turn.
   1 sc in next 79 stitches.
   Slip stitch into next stitch of crown.
   End off.

3. Finishing:
   a. Roll the band into a hat shape by beginning at the curved end away from the brim area. Sew the rounds together on the bottom. Using two strands of the accent yarn, chain a 15" (38cm) length.

b. Starting at one end, make an overhand knot (not pulled tight) about 1" (2.5cm) from one end. Continue making overhand knots every inch until you reach the other end. Tack this band around the hat where the brim meets the top.

Variations:

A. Decorate the hat with ribbon and silk flowers.

B. Use one strand of chenille and another fiber in a similar weight and color for the crown and brim. Work a row of single crochet around the brim in a glitzy yarn for the accent.

The Needlepoint Needlecase

Fig. 6.36 Needlepoint needlecases make special gifts for sewing friends.

Jane's friend, Phyllis Tucker, has a collection of antique needlepoint and beaded bags. When Phyllis decided to reproduce one of the antique bags for a friend of hers, she asked Jane to chart the design. She used the computer program "Stitch Grapher" (see "Sources of Supplies") and her IBM to produce the charts. Jane felt that Phyllis's unselfishness deserved a gift of its own, so she isolated one of the flowers, a rosebud, and stitched a needlecase for her. The colors used are the same as the ones on the antique bag.

The charts for the needlecase are found on pages 134, 135, and 139.

You Will Need:

6" x 9" (15cm x 23cm) 18-count interlock canvas
3 skeins #310 DMC stranded floss
1 skein each DMC stranded floss #934, 732, 734, 739, 3773, 309, 815
4" x 6" (10cm x 15cm) black taffeta
6" x 5" (15cm x 12.5cm) linen
#24 tapestry needle
Velcro dot (black)
Pencil
Black sewing thread

1. With the pencil, mark off a rectangle of 56 threads x 90 threads about 1-1/2" (4cm) from the left edge of the canvas. Count forty-four threads from the left edge, and draw a pencil line. Skip two threads, and draw another line. Skip fourteen threads, and mark a rectangle 56 threads by 18.

2. Front: Work the rose, background, and tab in diagonal tent (basketweave). If you want to add a monogram, do so in the upper left corner. Jane worked hers in the deep rose #309. The scroll border is worked in a three-thread cross-stitch with the top leg tied down (the magic stitch). Work one row of tent stitch all around the border.

3. Back: Count in and down four threads from the upper left corner of the marked line. Draw an inner rectangle 36 by 48 threads (same as above). Work this inner area in diagonal tent with #310. Work the scroll border and the tent stitch outline as before. There will be two unworked threads at the center.

4. Tab: Work the tab (1" [2.5cm] x 2" [5cm]) in diagonal tent with #310.

5. Long-legged cross-stitch: Cut out the case and the tab, leaving seven empty threads all the way around. (If you haven't done long-legged cross-stitch as a binding, work the tab first for practice.) On the tab, fold the excess threads to the back, leaving two threads on the turn. Fold the tab in half. Work the cross-stitch along both sides, working through all four exposed threads (two on each side of the tab). Fold the excess threads of the needlecase to the back, leaving the two exposed for the long-legged cross-stitch. Fold the case along the two unworked lines and work the long-legged cross-stitch as before. Now work it around the edge of the case.

6. Finishing: Using small backstitches, stitch the tab in place. Fold the edges of the taffeta to the underside, and press so the piece measures 3-3/8" x 5-1/4" (9cm x 13.5cm). Slip stitch the lining to the case all the way around. Cut the linen into two pieces, each measuring 2-1/2" x 6" (6.5cm x 15cm). Work one line of stitching (either by hand or machine) 1/4" (6mm) away from the edge all the way around, and withdraw the linen threads to this line. Fold in half, and place in the center of the case. Backstitch into place. Stitch the *Velcro* dots on the tab and on the back.

Variation:

If you're a cross-stitcher, work the design on a 6" x 9" (15cm x 23cm) piece of ecru or cream Aida 18. You'll need one skein each of DMC stranded floss #934, 732, 734, 739, 3773, 309, 815, and a #26 tapestry needle.

1. With a sewing thread, mark a rectangle 56 threads by 90 threads. Using four strands of #309 and the #24 needle, work the first step of the scroll border (cross-stitches over three threads). Work the second step (tie-downs) with four strands of #739. The color of thread used in step 2 must match the color of the Aida for the border to appear as it does in the original. A different border appears if you use a nonmatching color for the tie-downs.

2. Using two strands of floss, work the rose and monogram (if desired) in cross-stitch.

3. Cut out the case with 1/2" (1.5cm) Aida extending beyond the border. Cut the tab piece 3-1/2" x 1-1/2" (9cm x 4cm). Fold the tab piece and stitch the sides. Turn. Stitch the tab to the front 1/4" (6mm) away from the stitching. Cut the lining from the cotton fabric the same size as the case. Place the lining and case with right sides together, and stitch all the way around in a 1/4" (6mm) seam, leaving a 2" (5cm) opening for turning at the center of the bottom. Turn to the right side and slip stitch to close the opening. Stitch the *Velcro* in place on the tab and at the back. Prepare and stitch in the linen "flaps" as described in the Needlepoint Needlecase above.

Needlework Frame Weights

Fig. 6.37 Embroidered glove frame weight

Using a glove as a hand to hold a needlework frame on the table while you're stitching is a super idea. You're recycling old gloves, perhaps one left from a pair—and that's a laudable pursuit in itself. We're not at all sure, however, that you should put one of these "hands" in a gift box for presentation unless you first call the paramedics.

The idea for this frame weight came from our embroiderers' guilds (Fig. 6.38). We all

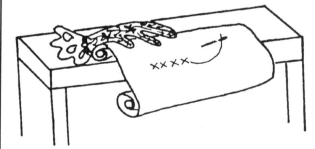

Fig. 6.38 Weight your needlework frame with a glove.

decorated gloves, then filled them with sand, shot, or whatever we had on hand or could beg, borrow, or buy to weight the glove when the embroidery was complete.

Buy gloves at thrift stores. Long formal types are fun and afford ample room for decoration. If you're in a hurry, decorate a child's glove.

You Will Need:

Child's glove
Several colors of *Designer Dye*
Embroidery thread or pearl cotton #8 or #5
#8 or #10 shot, fine grade blaster's sand, aquarium gravel, or rice

1. The weight pictured is a child's size 5 glove. It is made of knit fabric so it stretched. We transformed it completely because the rice used for weighting showed through. (It was also slightly spooky when pristine white—like that old Peter Lorre movie).

To decorate the glove, first hold it under the faucet and let water soak it completely. Then wring out the water and flatten the glove on a stack of newspapers. Use *Designer Dye*, which is available at craft shops, and dot the surface with yellows and greens. When the dye is dry, begin to decorate. First draw on the design with a vanishing marker. Each fingertip has a flower of lazy daisy stitches, a center French knot, and a feather-stitched stem with French knot buds traveling back on top of each finger. After the flowers are in place, go back and fill in the rest of the glove with more stems and buds of French knots.

2. When satisfied with your design, fill the glove with rice. Then place a ruffle of cotton embroidered fabric inside the wrist edge and pin it in place. Attach the ruffle and close the opening at the same time by sewing across it several times on the sewing machine. Then, to hide the stitching, knot a piece of yellow grosgrain ribbon in three places, dab glue stick on it, and place it over the stitching and around to the back of the glove. Go back and stitch down the ribbon invisibly by hand, catching only a tiny bit of the edge with each stitch.

Variation:

If you like the idea of a frame weight but you're a little uneasy with one that looks like a hand, use your heart pattern from page 64. Make the frame weight of *Ultrasuede* scraps that you stitch to a muslin foundation, and stuff with shot or aquarium gravel.

Sewing or Jewelry Bag

Fig. 6.39 Sewing bag

There's a pattern for a bun warmer some-where in our files. It lays flat until a series of ties are tied, at which point a lot of little pockets are drawn up and formed. That bun warmer led to designing a sewing kit that had little bun-warmer pockets (as best we remembered them).

The sewing bag is made with circles: A smaller circle is stitched inside the larger. Three intersecting lines of stitches divide the smaller circle into six pockets and attach the smaller circle to the larger outside circle.

You Will Need:

Two pieces fabric 14" (35.5cm) square for outer bag
Four pieces contrasting fabric 9" (23cm) square for inner bag
Fourteen 1/8" (3mm) eyelets
1-1/2 yds (1.4m) 1/8" (3mm) ribbon or rattail cord
Two pony beads
Posterboard for pattern
Hole punch or awl
Strawberry emery
Tape measure
Ruler
Eyelet pliers
Vanishing marker
Compass

1. Pattern: Make a circle pattern with a 7" (18cm) radius (14" [35.5cm] diameter).

Make a smaller circle pattern with a 4-1/4" (11cm) radius (8-1/2" [22cm] diameter). Mark a circle with a 1-3/4" (4.5cm) radius (3-1/2" [9cm] diameter) in the center of the smaller circle. With a compass, divide the perimeter of the smaller circle into six equal areas. With your ruler, construct lines dividing the small circle into wedges. Cut out the small center circle of your pattern. Cut a tiny notch at each line on both the outer and inner edges of the pattern (Fig. 6.40).

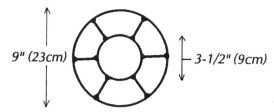

Fig. 6.40 *Circle pattern for pockets*

Make a mark 1/2" (1cm) in from the edge of the large circle. Measure 3-3/8" (9cm) and make another mark.

Continue around the circle until you return to the starting mark. You will also need two holes 1/2" (1.5cm) apart at the center front of the larger circle. To accomplish this, make a mark 1/4" (6mm) on either side of one mark. Punch holes 1/2" (1.5cm) away from the edge at each mark (14 holes) (Fig. 6.41).

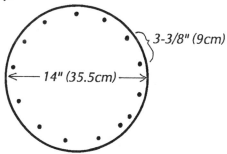

Fig. 6.41 *Mark grommets inside edge of large circle.*

2. Outer Bag: Place the right sides of the outer fabric together. One side will be the lining. Cut out the large circles. Stitch all around the edge in a generous 1/8" (3mm) seam allowance. Cut a slit in the center of the lining circle, and turn through this opening. Press around the edge.

3. Inner Bag: Stack two fabrics for one part of the inner bag with right sides together and cut out, using the small circle pattern. Do the same for the other two fabrics. Stitch around one set of circles in a generous 1/8" (3mm) seam. Cut a slit in the center of one circle and turn through this opening. Press. Repeat for the second set. You do not need to close these slits; later you will simply place the circles so the slits are sandwiched between the two. Decide which circle you want to be the inner "petals," and place your small circle pattern on top. Draw around the small center circle with your vanishing marker. Make a mark at each notch. With the marker and your ruler, draw the stitching lines between the notches. Stack the two small circles and stitch on these lines (Fig. 6.42).

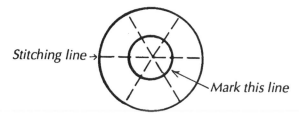

Fig. 6.42 *Mark center circle. Stitch circles together on dotted lines.*

4. Joining Bags: Cut a piece of ribbon 22" (56cm) long and fold in half. Place the two stitched small circles in the center of the outer bag. Pin in place, slipping the cut ends of the folded ribbon under these circles so they will be caught in the stitching.

Slip the 60" (1.5m) end of the tape measure under the circles as you did with the ribbon loop. Stitch around the small marked center circle (Fig. 6.43). Mark the center of each wedge on both the petals and the inner bag.

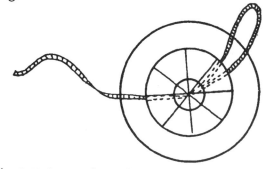

Fig. 6.43 *Sewing bag: Slip tape measure and ribbon loop for scissors under center marked circle. Stitch around circle to attach.*

5. Finishing: Mark the position of each eyelet, and apply eyelets with the pliers on the outside of the outer bag. Thread a hand

> ♥ *You'll get a neater, firmer lock when you first punch the holes using an awl and then apply the eyelets, rather than doing it all in one step. Don't use the pliers for this step alone, as the hole is larger than necessary.*

needle, double the thread, and knot it. Take a small backstitch at the marked center of one of the inner circle wedges. Then take a small stitch in the corresponding marked center of each "petal" wedge, pulling them tightly together to form the center "flower." If you are adding the strawberry emery, catch the loop with your needle and thread now. Whip over this loop at the center several times. Take three backstitches at the

> ♥ *If you don't add an emery, add a bead or several beads at the center.*

center through all the layers. Run the needle between the layers about an inch away, and clip the thread. Weave the ribbon in and out the eyelets, beginning and ending at the two eyelets that are 1/2" (1.5cm) apart.

Thread a pony bead on each end and make enough overhead knots to hold the bead on the ribbon. If you are going to include scissors, loop them over the folded thread.

> ♥ *Make this a family project by having your children use aspic or cookie cutters to make beads for the ends out of Sculpey, Fimo, or Cernit. Punch the holes with a yarn darner or small knitting needle.*

Variations:

Make these in velveteen and silk as jewelry bags. Omit the ribbon loop. Cut the ribbon into two pieces and attach one on either side of the inner circles about 2" (5cm)

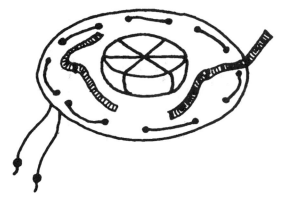

Fig. 6.44 Jewelry bag: Attach ribbons on large circle to hold necklaces in place.

from the bottom stitching (Fig. 6.44). Necklaces are placed around the inner circle and tied in place with the ribbon ties to keep them from getting tangled.

Humbug Make-Up Bag

Fig. 6.45 Humbug shapes

This exciting print fabric of lipsticks, eye shadows, blush, and all kinds of make-up items, begs to be made into a make-up bag—not any ordinary cosmetic case, but one with a twist. This bag is a humbug shape (a hard-boiled British sweet, usually having a striped pattern) with a 7" (18cm) nylon zipper across one long side. Although humbug shapes are unusual when finished, they begin with a simple rectangle. Their simplicity makes them great choices for demonstration purposes—a sure way to get the crowds to your bazaar booth.

You Will Need:

6" x 18" (15cm x 46cm) rectangle of
   double-sided pre-quilted fabric
7" (18cm) zipper
Scissors
Sewing machine
Zipper foot

1. Mark the rectangle by folding it in half
6" x 9" [15cm x 23cm]), and notching the
fold (Fig. 6.46). Then fold again (6" x 4-1/2"

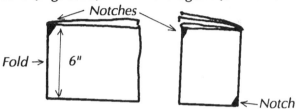

Fig. 6.46 Fold rectangle in half and notch.

[15cm x 11.5cm]), and make tiny notches on
the other side of the rectangle at both folds
(Fig. 6.47). Open the fabric flat.

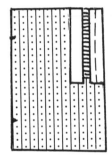

Fig. 6.47 Refold and notch opposite edges.

2. Put a zipper foot on your machine, and set
the machine to needle left. Place the zipper
tape at the long edge of the fabric, right sides
together. Stitch close to the zipper teeth to
the end of the zipper tape (Fig. 6.48). Fold

*Fig. 6.48 Apply zipper to long edge, right sides
together.*

the fabric back at the center notch, and line
up the fabric and zipper edges. Continue
stitching the zipper to the other half of the
fabric edge (Fig. 6.49).

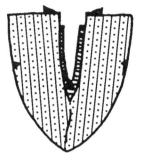

*Fig. 6.49 Fold fabric back at the notch, and stitch
down the other side of zipper.*

Leave the zipper open for the next steps.
Remove the zipper foot and attach the general purpose/zigzag foot. Stitch down the
side from under the zipper to the other edge
(Fig. 6.50). Neaten up the edge with scissors.
Change to a zigzag stitch, and zigzag the raw
edges together.

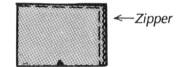

Fig. 6.50 Stitch down short side.

3. Now open the humbug and refold on the
two notches at the other side (the seam
you've sewn on the short side will be in the
middle and perpendicular to the stitching
line). Straight stitch across (Fig. 6.51).

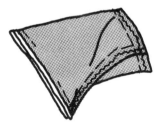

*Fig. 6.51 Refold edge at notches and stitch across.
Stitch under zipper 1" (2.5cm) at each side.*

Go back to the zipper edge. Arrange the
fabric edges so the top "zipper" edges meet
exactly. Then stitch straight across from the
edge, barely under and past the zipper's
metal stopper (you can mark this first before
you stitch if you can't feel the stopper
through the fabric). Stitch in approximately

1" [2.5cm] at each side, as in Figure 6.51, to neaten the corners.

4. Clip corners and cut edges to neaten. Then zigzag the raw edges together at the bottom and the zipper tape to the fabric edges on each side. Finally, turn the make-up bag to the right side. Poke out the corners and admire your quickie creation.

Variations:

A. Plain quilted fabric begs to be embellished when used on the outside. Use a quilted muslin, and decorate it by stitching on top of the quilting with a built-in machine feather stitch and variegated machine embroidery thread to punch up an otherwise ordinary fabric.

Another idea: Following the quilting lines, couch down #5 or #3 pearl cotton by zigzagging over it with monofilament or a thread that matches the pearl cotton. Choose a single large motif on your machine and place one in the center of each square.

B. Line the bags with plastic purchased in a fabric store. (Plastic is sold for tablecloths and comes in several weights.) You'll need a *Teflon* presser foot for your sewing machine.

C. Make humbugs in all different sizes for different uses: coin purses, toy bags, and jewelry. Sew a cord or fabric loop in a corner on the zipper side for hanging on to later (especially for a coin purse). Search fabric shops for appropriate material for particular uses.

D. If your fabric isn't quilted, bond fusible fleece to the outside fabric, place on top of the lining fabric, and quilt using decorative stitches or straight stitching with metallic or multicolored rayon thread.

Heirloom Apron

We've probably given more aprons as gifts through the years than anything else. We made floor-length aprons when hostess skirts were long and pants suits were not passé, short and sassy ones when skirts were the same, and butcher aprons when the sexes dressed alike. We've made them plain and we've made them fancy, and through the years we've made a lot of them.

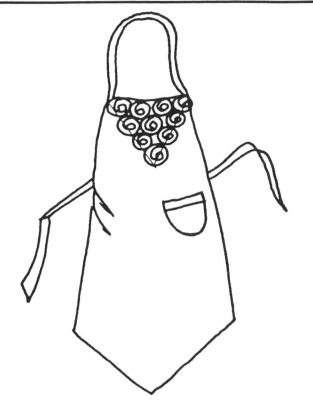

Fig. 6.52 Stitch an heirloom apron.

A few days ago we discovered this apron in an old Singer sewing book from the 1920s. What really interested us was the triangular area at the top. Jane used a 36" (91.5cm) square cutwork luncheon cloth embroidered by her mother to form the bibs on aprons for herself and her three daughters, avoiding the age-old "Who gets the cloth?" question.

You Will Need

(makes four aprons):

    4 yds (3.5m) of 45" (1.1m) cotton-linen
        blend (the one we found was 56" [1.5m]
        wide) for the apron body
    Thread to match
    32" (81.5cm) square embroidered lun-
        cheon cloth or fat quarters for contrast-
        ing bibs (10" to 14" [25.5cm to 35.5cm]
        square napkins with a pretty embroi-
        dered corner may be substituted) (Look
        for tablecloths and napkins in thrift
        stores.)
    Spray Starch or *Fabric Finish*

1. Cut the apron body fabric into one-yard pieces. Cut a 36" (.9m) square from each yard (after straightening the ends, our square ended up 34" before hemming). Cut three 2-1/2" to 3" (6.5cm to 7.5cm) wide strips (ties) from the remaining fabric in each yard.

2. Spray the cloth with starch and iron. Measure the corner design on your luncheon cloth (16" [40.5cm] on the one we used). Make a mark 1/2" (1.5cm) less than the corner measurement on each side of the apron square (15-1/2" [39.5cm]). To hem the apron, make a clip 1" (2.5cm) deep at these two points (Fig. 6.53). Press under 1/4"

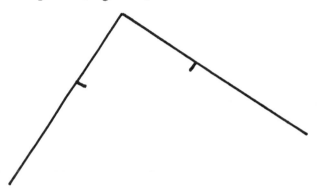

Fig. 6.53 Clip in 1" (2.5cm) at each side.

(6mm) all the way around the apron (but not between the clips) (Fig. 6.54). At the clips,

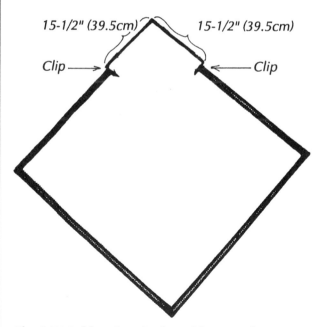

Fig. 6.54 Fold under 1/4" (6mm) hem, and press from clip to clip as shown.

fold the hem on the diagonal, then turn the hem under 3/4" (2cm) and press (Fig. 6.55).

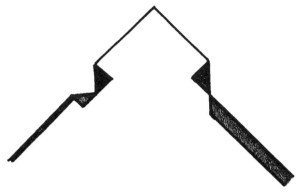

Fig. 6.55 At the clips, fold hem on the diagonal and press. Turn hem 3/4" (2cm) more and press.

Miter the three corners by folding and stitching as shown in Figure 6.56. Stitch the hem

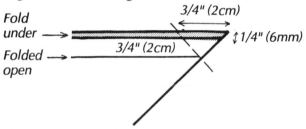

Fig. 6.56 To miter the corners: Fold out the 3/4" (2cm) hem, pinch corners together, and stitch on line shown.

in place with a straight stitch. On the remaining corner, turn and miter the hem as you did before, but turn it toward the front.

3. Fold over the corner you intend to cut off the cloth, and press (16" [40.5cm]). Cut on the pressed diagonal line (Fig. 6.57). Repeat

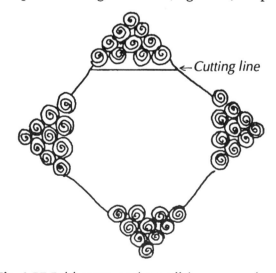

Fig. 6.57 Fold, press, and cut off the corner of an embroidered tablecloth.

for the other three corners. Press 1/2"
(1.5cm) under on each of the diagonal edges.
Place one bib corner on the under side of
one apron corner (the one with the hem
turned to the front). Pin in place and stitch
along the diagonal. Stitch close to the embroidery along the outer edge to hold in
place, then stitch around all the embroidery,
following the design (Fig. 6.58). The more
stitching you do to hold the bib in place, the
easier it will be to iron this area.

Fig. 6.58 Stitch embroidered corner in place on apron.

4. Fold two ties in half, right sides together,
and join together with a generous 1/8"
(3mm) seam allowance, stitching one end to
a point. Turn and stitch in place 10"
(25.5cm) above each side corner by placing
the wrong side of the cut edge 1/4" (6mm)
over the hem stitching on the underside of
the apron (Fig. 6.59). Stitch in place. Then

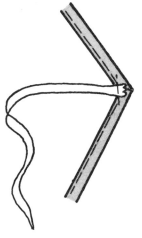

Fig. 6.59 Attach a tie in corner at back edge of the apron.

bring the tie over the stitching to the outside.
Stitch along the outer edge, burying the raw
edges of the tie (Fig. 6.60).

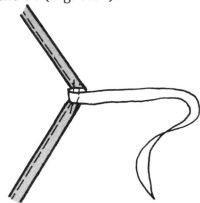

Fig. 6.60 Fold tie to side, and stitch in place on hem and on fold.

Stitch the third tie by folding in half, right
sides together, with both ends open and
turn. Cut 25" (63.5cm) long, and finish both
ends with a close machine satin stitch. Lay
the apron flat, bib side up. Make a mark 5"
(12.5cm) either side of the center bib. Place
the outer side of the neck strap on the mark,
extending 1/2" (1.5cm) onto the apron body.
Stitch strap in place on the line of stitching.
Try on to check the neck strap length before
stitching the other side of the strap, then
stitch in place. Stitch slightly above the satin
stitching on both sides to anchor the strap.

5. If you have napkins to match, you can use
one for a pocket if desired. Jane felt the
napkin drew attention away from the bib,
and since she had extra fabric (thanks to the
extra width), she made a 5" x 6" (12.5cm x
15cm) pocket out of the apron fabric and
stitched it in place with the top edge of the
pocket on the same line as the corner and
20" (51cm) in from this point (Fig. 6.61). You
can stitch it on either the right or left side.

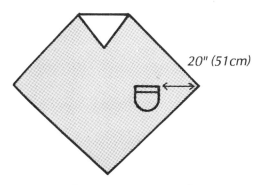

20" (51cm)

Fig. 6.61 Sew pocket to apron across from corner.

Variations:

A. If you don't have any old linens to use for the bib area, work machine or handmade cutwork in the area. If you make the apron out of a complete square, the fabric should be the same on both sides.

B. Make the bib area out of an even-weave ground fabric on which you have cross stitched a border or worked hardanger or other hand cutwork embroidery.

C. Cut the bib and ties out of print fabric. Turn under 1/2" (1.5cm) on the diagonal edge. Place the right side of the print to the wrong side of the apron and stitch on the two sides. Turn and press. Topstitch the print to the main fabric along the diagonal edge.

D. You may make the apron out of an entire embroidered luncheon cloth, but you will need to cut the bib area off, turn it over, and stitch it back or the bib area will be on the wrong side.

Exercise Mat

Fig. 6.62 Exercise mat of batting-filled tunnels

The dimensions for this mat are the same as a store-bought mat (24" x 72" [61cm x 1.8m]), but mat size is arbitrary, and you may not need an exercise mat this long. However, like any quilted fabric, the exercise mat shrinks in size once it is stuffed with batting. The more batting, the shorter it becomes. Although we began with the size stated, our mat ended up shorter than 72" (1.8m) because it was so plump.

This project is tailor-made for recycling fabric scraps. The mat can be constructed from different widths or the same widths of fabric. If you have only scraps of fabrics, those can be sewn into strips as wide as you need and work as well as whole cloth.

Remember to always prewash fabrics to prevent surprises later. Dry and press the

fabric. Then cut strips using a rotary cutter, mat, and 6" x 24" (15cm x 61cm) ruler. These strips of corduroy are 5" x 24" (13cm x 61cm). We chose corduroy because it washes well, wears well, and we had a lot of it from past sewing projects. Our corduroy strips are different colors and different wales.

You Will Need:

18 strips of fabric 5" x 24" (12.5cm x 61cm)
2 yds (1.8m) fabric for backing and binding
Bonded batt 72" x 90" (1.8m x 2.3m), plus scraps for binding
Rotary cutter, mat, and 6" x 24" (15cm x 61cm) ruler
Monofilament thread or thread that matches backing

1. Cut the backing the size of the mat—24" x 72" (61cm x 1.8m). Cut bindings from the same fabric on the straight of grain. You'll need two 26" (66cm) strips and two 72" (1.8cm) strips, each 6" (15cm) wide.

2. Unroll the roll of bonded batting, but don't unfold it. Cut into eighteen strips, each 5" x 24" (12.5cm x 61cm) wide. Cut 1" (2.5cm) wide strips of batting to stuff the bindings as well. Use any scraps of batting you have—they are single layers.

3. Wind the monofilament thread on a bobbin, or use a polyester thread the perfect match of your backing fabric. Use a color that matches any strip on top, as it won't show no matter what strips are sewn.

4. Mark stitching lines on the wrong side of the corduroy backing piece. Guide lines are drawn 4" (10cm) apart across the backing down the entire length (use a colored pencil or marker that won't soak through to the front).

♥ *Start at the left-hand side of the backing, which means the bulk of the fabric is between the needle and the machine at this time. Roll up the backing, unrolling as you proceed. The batting bulk feeds off to the left of the needle as you stitch strips in place, and you never have to wrestle an unwieldy exercise mat.*

5. Sew on the marked side. Wrong sides together, line up the long edge of the first strip with the edge of the backing and sew. Use a straight stitch slightly shorter than normal and a seam allowance the width of the presser foot.

6. Slip a strip of batting between the backing and the strip you attached. To do this, fold the batting the long way and push it to the left of the first guide line. Then pin the remaining raw edge of the strip to the backing, aligning it with the guide line. Again, use the presser foot as a seam-allowance guide, letting it ride on top and a hair off the right edge of the strip as you stitch the first strip in place (Fig. 6.63).

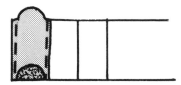

Fig. 6.63 Stitch strip to backing at edge, slip in batting, and stitch down other side at mark.

Place another strip of corduroy, right sides together, on top of the previous strip. Pin the raw edges together. This time place the edge of the presser foot exactly at the edge of the strip (to hide the first row of stitching) as you sew the second strip in place (Fig. 6.64). Add another folded strip of batting as you did the first. Flip the strip over the batting up to the next guide line, pin, and sew down the edge. Continue across the mat.

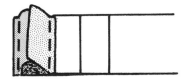

Fig. 6.64 With right sides together, stitch down second strip on top of first.

When all the strips are in place, sew the last strip to the right edge of the backing. Then pull on the bottom fabric a bit (to prevent pleats) as you stitch down each side with 1" (2.5cm) seam allowances. Even the edges neatly.

7. To attach the binding, first fold the binding strips in half the long way, wrong sides together. Stitch at the raw edges to hold them in place (Fig. 6.65).

Fig. 6.65 With wrong sides together, stitch at the edge to hold binding strip together.

Bind the two long sides first. With raw edges together, place one of the bindings on top of the mat. Stitch 1" (2.5cm) from the raw edge (Fig. 6.66). Slip one of the long,

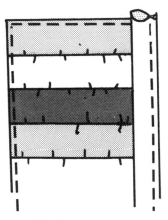

Fig. 6.66 Stitch down strip on top and side of mat.

1"-wide (2.5cm) batting scraps in on top of the edge before you fold the binding around to the back side. After folding the binding around the edge, hand tack the fold to the stitching line. Or, pull the edge slightly past the stitching line (trim the raw edge if you must) and stitch-in-the-ditch (between

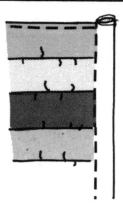

Fig. 6.67 *Fold strip over to back, and stitch-in-the-ditch to hold in place.*

binding and mat) from the top (Fig. 6.67). Stitch the opposite side in the same way.

Stitch the top and bottom edges. To do this, first fold in the extra binding at each corner and proceed as with the side bindings. When stitching is complete, hand stitch the corners closed.

Start your push-ups!

Variations:

A. Make the mat longer by adding more strips, or wider by increasing the length of each strip (24" [61cm] above).

B. Make a nap mat for the nursery school or kindergarten student in your life. The finished size is 20" x 44" (51cm x 112cm), so you will need 12 strips 5" x 20" (12.5cm x 51cm), and binding strips that are 44" (112cm) and 22" (56cm) long. Add a 12" (30.5cm) loop of elastic at the back so the mat can be rolled up and tied securely.

C. Use striped fabric and extra-loft batting or thin foam rubber available at fabric stores (they'll cut any size for you). Use the stripes as guides to sew the batting or foam to a backing by stitching one stripe, stuffing, stitching the next stripe, and so on.

D. Use striped fabric and batting to make speedy crib quilts, lap robes, and baby-changing pads. Make baby quilts 45" (1.1m) (the width of most cotton fabrics) x 2 yds (1.8m)—extremely generous for a baby. The quilts can be used on the floor to play and crawl on, and later as a cover in which to cuddle. Jackie's eight-year-old granddaughters still use their quilts when they sleep in the back seat on long car trips. Use the large width double-fold bias tape as a binding. Make changing pads smaller, and bind them with narrow bias double-fold tape.

If you haven't found exactly what you want to make and give a special lady in your life in this chapter, check out "The Christmas Exchange" (Chapter 8) or try totes and purses (Chapter 2). In Chapter 7 (page 91), you'll find a super purse-sized sewing kit. And if you're wondering what to make for us—we'll take one of everything!

M is for Male
Gifts for Men

Projects:

- ♥ *Fur Lap Robe*
- ♥ *"Phone Home" Afghan*
- ♥ *People Wrapper Blanket*
- ♥ *Sporty Hang Towels*
- ♥ *Card Holders*
- ♥ *The Parallelogram Manicure Kit*
- ♥ *Hooded Bath Towel*

We'd rather shop for a three-toed sloth than for a man! We've bought more ties that were never worn (even made a few back in the 1960s), more shirts that only hung in closets, more games that were never played, and more silly gifts that only we found funny. We've had some successes along the way, and we can promise that the following have been gift-tested—happily given and received—and will bring joy to the man in your life.

Fur Lap Robe

***Fig. 7.1** Cuddle up in a furry lap robe.*

These furry lap robes are so cosy, that every one in the family will want one. A friend has one in fake sable with a designer-labeled lining for chilly nights in front of the TV. We've made them in pastel fur with soft flannel lining for babies, and sent them to college in dark blue fur with a denim lining. So many combinations! This is an ideal bazaar idea. It sews up in a flash, and there is one to appeal to everyone.

Buy fabric and lining according to the size of the person for whom you're making it. Store-bought lap robes are usually too skimpy, so use this rule of thumb: Make the lap robe at least the height of the person who'll receive it, plus enough snuggle room. If it's meant for a crib, then make it to cover the length of the crib. If you plan to make these to cover only laps, legs, and feet, then govern the length and width accordingly. (We've also made these predicated on the remnant of fur we bought, no matter what the size—as long as it looks big enough.)

Remnants, sold by the pound in some stores or wrapped in paper sleeves in others, should be the first place you look when buying fur for this lap robe. Never buy off the bolt unless you want an exact type of fur because you can save so much money choosing ready-cut pieces. And look for fur that has a short nap as opposed to fake wolf, fox, or coyote. Long-napped furs shift too much in construction, and more time is needed to sew and then ease the long strands of fur from the seam when you finish. Of course, you can trim back the fur at the seam allowances before you begin, but this also eats up your time.

Usually, you'll piece the lining fabric because fur comes in much wider widths than regular fabric. To save time in sewing the lap robe, choose a plaid fabric for the lining. Then, when cutting it to size and sewing it to the fur, you have stitching lines already built in. The fabric chosen for the lap robe pictured (Color Plate 3) is lined with a soft brushed-nap polyester that looks like a heavy flannel. It's plaid; the fur is a curly, short nap; and with its simple construction, we can make the lap robe in an afternoon and still have time to spare.

You Will Need:

Fake fur
Lining
T-square ruler
Rotary cutter and mat

1. Wash and dry both the lining and the fur. Use a T-square to even up the fur (no one ever cuts these straight at the fabric store). Cut the plaid to even that up also. Piece the lining, if necessary. If using a plaid, stitch a seam to fall down the center of the robe. If you use a plain fabric, you may want to cut one of the lining pieces in half, then piece it so there is a seam on either side of the middle section. (You can even try color blocking by piecing different fabrics together for an attractive lining.)

2. Pin the fur and lining, right sides together. Start stitching approximately 18" (46cm) from the corner on a short side. First anchor your thread by stitching up and back a few stitches; then straight stitch (toward the corner) around the edge, nudging as much fur inside as you can before you begin stitching. (Clip the fur off in the seam allowance first if it is too bulky.) Stitch to the corner, turn, and continue around the lap robe and up to the side you started on. Turn that corner, and stitch in on the fourth side. Leave an opening long enough to enable you to easily turn the lap robe right side out, which depends on how bulky the fur is (Fig. 7.2). Anchor your thread by stitching up and

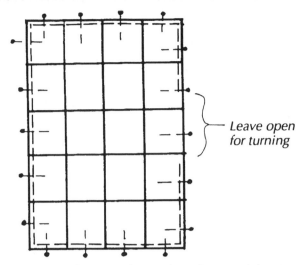

Fig. 7.2 *Pin lining to fur, and stitch around, leaving an opening for turning.*

back at the end. When you stitch, use the machine's presser foot as a guide by placing it directly over the edge of the lining and fur. Or, use a line in the plaid fabric as a stitching guide. Clip the corners to eliminate bulk, and zigzag the edges flat. Turn the lap robe right side out, and push out the corners with a blunt instrument (no scissors allowed). Handsew the opening shut. With a pin or needle, ease out any fur that may be caught in the seam.

3. **Finishing:** Take it to the ironing board, and press from the lining side to flatten the edges.

Variations:

A. Jan Saunders of Dublin, Ohio, gave us another quick blanket idea: She bought a wool Navy blanket at an Army-Navy store, bound it with gold felt (school colors), and appliquéd a large felt crest with a fraternity monogram to the blanket. The blanket is big enough for two at a football game.

B. Make a small (24" [61cm]) square fur throw for baby's first photograph.

"Phone Home" Afghan

Fig. 7.3 Pieced phone motifs

When is a quilt not a quilt but an afghan? When it contains only two layers. Add a batt and "Phone Home" can become a quilt.

Autograph quilts are an established part of the tradition of quilting whether they were made by church members for a favorite minister, or by the female members and close friends of a bride's family. Make "Phone Home" for a graduation present and have family and friends sign their names and phone numbers with *Pigma* pens. When they become famous athletes or authors, cinema stars or rock singers, the quilt will develop a value beyond the sentimental one.

The charts for the afghan are found on pages 137 and 138, and it is shown in Color Plate 7.

This as an enjoyable project to piece. Cut the rectangles and triangles out of twenty different solid-colored fabrics, and set them around the sewing machine like a painter's palette. Begin to piece, deciding on the colors as you go along. The only rules are: (1) the dark colors go in one direction, and the light colors in the opposite; (2) no two phones in any row or column can be the same color; and (3) the mid-value colors are lights or darks, depending on what colors are around them. Divide the drawing of the top into blocks of seven rectangles x five rectangles, working across and down. (You can plan out where you want each color to go—boring as that would be in our opinion.)

Pin the afghan on the wall in front of you to keep the phones in their proper colors as you piece the blocks. (And, yes, sometimes you may have to rip out a patch or two.) We used only fabrics we had on hand. If you don't have a stash of fabrics, and to reduce shopping time, buy medleys of fabrics (quarter-yards of eight to ten dark blues, light blues, grass greens, etc.) in quilt shops or by mail order.

You Will Need:

1/4 yd (23cm) of at least twenty different solid-colored fabrics
2 large spools of medium gray sewing thread
2 yds (1.8m) of 100% polyester felt (ours was 54" [1.4m] wide)
Rotary cutter, ruler, and mat
Sewing machine
Monofilament thread
Thread to match the felt
1/4" (6mm) seam allowance included throughout

♥ *If we suspect a fabric may not be colorfast, we wash it alone with a scrap of white fabric. If the scrap isn't pristine white at the end of the cycle, we don't use the fabric.*

1. Machine wash and dry all the fabrics, especially the felt. We used felt because it looks more masculine and adds body, since there's no batting in this afghan. Felt is also less slippery than cotton and it comes in a wider width than most cotton fabrics.

2. Fold the fabric so you have four layers. Then from each fabric, cut out two rectangles 2-7/8" x 4" (7.5cm x 10cm) with your ruler and rotary cutter. (Fabric yields eight rectangles.) Cut the rectangles in half on the diagonal (producing sixteen triangles) as shown in Figure 7.4, and clip 1/4" (6mm) off the points (Fig. 7.5). With the fabric still

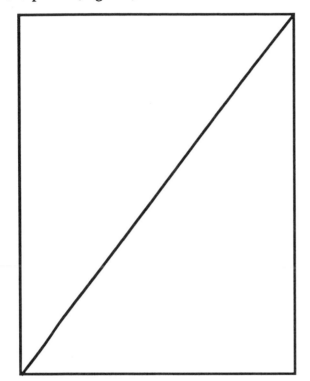

Fig. 7.4 *Cut the rectangles into triangles.*

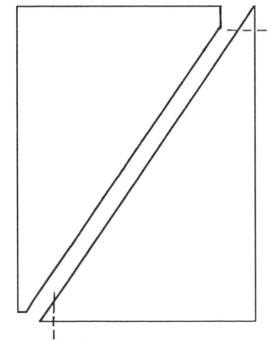

Fig. 7.5 *Clip bulk from triangle corners.*

stacked, cut an additional six rectangles 2-1/2" x 3-1/2" (6.5cm x 9cm). (Fabric yields twenty-four rectangles.) You will have enough rectangles to make eight "phones" of each fabric.

> ♥ *You will definitely have leftovers from this meal. Save them to use in a small wall hanging.*

3. Copy the diagram for the quilt shown on page 137, and color the phones to show where each color goes. Piece each block of seven by five rectangles, working row by row as shown on page 138, first stitching all the triangles in the first row into rectangles. Press the seams in one direction. Work the second row and press the seams in the opposite direction. Then join the two rows. Work this way so if you goof, you have only one row to rip.

4. Cut your piece of felt 46" x 70" (1.1m x 1.8m), and spread on a long table or the floor. Lay the pieced fabric on top of the felt, right side up. Pin the two layers together with safety pins. Set your sewing machine for darning and attach the darning foot. Thread the monofilament on top and the thread that matches the felt on the bobbin. Quilt the two layers together with your sewing machine. Use tight spirals that look like a telephone cord, beginning at the bottom on one of the phones (Fig. 7.6). Stitch enough to hold the layers together, but don't stitch cords on every phone.

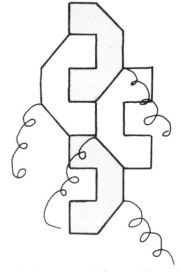

Fig. 7.6 *Telephone cords free-quilting designs*

5. Round the corners by drawing around a kitchen glass or cup. Bind all around with double-fold bias tape. Put your name and the year on either the front or back of the afghan.

Variations:

A. Limit yourself to three or four colors for a different look.

B. Do all the shapes facing one way in many bright colors, and the reverse shapes in one tinted or grayed color.

C. Turn page 81 by 90° and look at the shape. We see squatty, little huts, and the reverse shapes look like U's.

D. Make a quilt by substituting batt and a backing for the felt.

People Wrapper Blanket

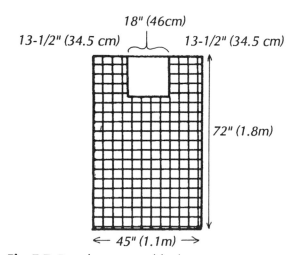

Fig. 7.7 People wrapper blanket

This wool blanket is large enough to keep you warm in the football stands, and small enough to fold into the attached pillow slip, making a pad to sit on when not functioning as a blanket. There's no extra bag to fall into the peanut shells and spilled drinks under-foot—an unqualified plus.

The best idea is to use plaid fabric for the blanket. Then cutting square corners, and

measuring and sewing straight lines is a breeze. The pillow case is a generous 18" (46cm) square. A plain fabric (one of the colors in the plaid) was used for the pillow case so you can see it better in the photo. But use a matching plaid, if you prefer.

You may want to finish the edge with a serger and a thick thread in the upper looper (and cover the edge with close stitches), but we used a sewing machine.

You Will Need:

45" x 72" (1.1m x 1.8m) plaid wool fabric
18" x 18" (46cm x 46cm) plain wool fabric
#5 pearl cotton
Tear-away stabilizer or adding machine tape
Sewing machine
Cording presser foot
Rotary cutter and mat
Machine-embroidery thread
Aleene's *Stop Fraying*

1. First, trim your fabric (use a T-square if you don't use plaid). Then place #5 pearl cotton in a cording foot or on the top edge of the blanket under an open embroidery foot. Slip a piece of tear-away stabilizer (or use adding machine tape) under the edge you are stitching to keep it from rippling.

Set your machine on stitch width 4mm and a stitch length slightly longer than a satin stitch. Sew over the pearl cotton as shown in Figure 7.8. Use either rayon or cotton machine embroidery thread on the

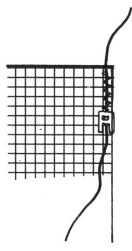

Fig. 7.8 Stitch over pearl cotton for a raised edge.

top and bobbin. Begin sewing down one long side on top of the blanket edge, stitch the other long side, then stitch across one short side. Edge stitch around the three sides of the pillow-case square as you did the blanket.

2. Put the pearl cotton away. Set your machine to stitch slightly wider and much closer (satin stitch). Again, stitch both long sides and the short side of the blanket, and the three sides of the square.

3. Fold the pillow-case square in half, and mark the center of the unfinished edge. Do the same with the blanket. Place the square over the blanket, matching the marks, with the *wrong* side of the square to the *right* side of the blanket. Pin together at the top and around the square.

Set the machine on straight stitching, and stitch the unfinished edges of the square and the blanket 1/8" (3mm) from the edge to hold the two together (Fig. 7.9). Stitch down the

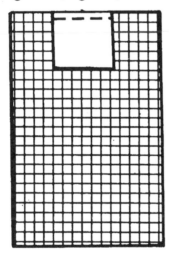

Fig. 7.9 Straight stitch across top to hold pillow case to wrapper.

sides of the square, stitching in-the-ditch (the "line" between satin stitches and fabric). Anchor your thread with a few backstitches at each end. **Do not stitch across the bottom of the square.** Leave the bottom end of the square open. Go back and stitch again, this time at the outer edge of the satin stitches (Fig. 7.10).

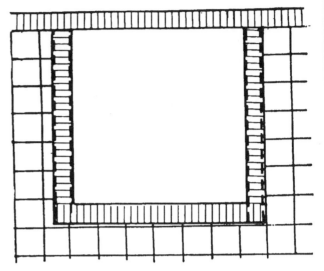

Fig. 7.10 Topstitch at both sides of satin stitches on the pillow case to keep it in place.

4. Finishing: Finish the top edge with the same method you used on the other three sides. Clip all the threads at the corners when completed, and dab *Stop Fraying* at each corner to keep the stitching in place.

5. To insert the blanket into the case, first fold back the blanket the long way at each side of the pillow case (Fig. 7.11). Enclose

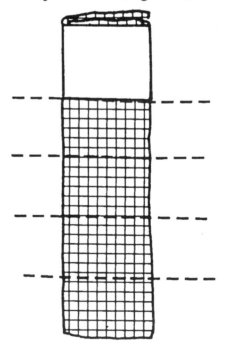

Fig. 7.11 Fold back sides of blanket the long way.

the top part of the blanket with the pillow case by turning the case over to the back (Fig. 7.12). Now fold up the end of the blanket about 1/3 of the distance to the top (Fig. 7.13). Fold again, and slip into the square (Fig. 7.14).

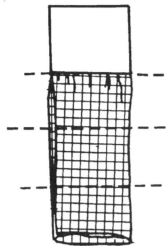

Fig. 7.12 *Turn pillow case over the back of the blanket.*

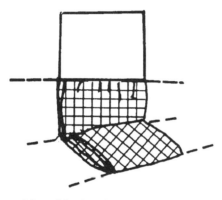

Fig. 7.13 *Fold up blanket from bottom and on other dotted lines.*

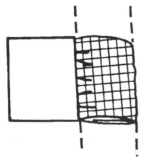

Fig. 7.14 *Slip folded blanket into pillow case.*

Variation:

Make a loop of fabric or cord, and stitch this between one corner of the pillow and the blanket for ease in carrying it to the ball game.

Sporty Hang Towels

Fig. 7.15 *Sporty hang towels*

The day we found fingertip towels with an even-weave area for cross-stitching on sale at our craft store for 88 cents was the day we thought about using our decorative machine stitches in the cross-stitch area. We didn't buy one or two towels; we bought ten.

The fingertip towels, however, seemed a bit dainty for masculine hands, so we took ourselves back to the craft store for another look. What to our wondering eyes should appear, but hang towels—half hand towels gathered into snap tabs. You might think they're made to slip around the handle on your oven, but we saw them attached to handles of golf bags, tennis racquet covers, sport bags of all kinds.

Machine stitching on the even-weave fabric is not done to imitate cross-stitch. If you have a sewing machine with decorative stitches and an alphabet, put the two together to create special towels related to the man in your life's favorite sport.

These gifts can literally be made in minutes because all you have to do is stitch. The towels are pre-finished.

You Will Need:

Charles Craft Hang towels
One small pkg of 14-count Aida fabric
Natesh or *Sulky* rayon machine-embroidery thread
Sewing machine with decorative stitches
Aleene's *Stop Fraying*
Vanishing marker
Water-soluble stabilizer (optional)
#90 (#14) machine needle

1. Thread the top and bobbin of your sewing machine with the rayon embroidery thread. Set your machine for full-width decorative stitching. Use the even-weave fabric to make a stitched record of the different stitches available on your machine. If the widest width stitch is splitting one of the threads, instead of laying between two threads, slowly turn your width down until the stitch fits exactly between however many threads it will cover. (The number of threads covered depends on your sewing machine.) If you're not satisfied with the stitching, place a piece of water-soluble stabilizer behind the fabric. For a stronger line: Wind an extra bobbin with your thread and place it on the second spool holder. Thread the machine with both threads, holding them together and threading them through the needle together. (Large-eyed needles [top stitching needles] are available from your sewing machine store if you have trouble threading a regular needle.) When you're satisfied with

> ♥ *Become familiar with all the stitches on your machine. Remember that utility stitches can also be used decoratively. Do lots and lots of samples with different threads, combinations, and rhythms (open, closed; spiky, smooth; narrow, wide; etc.).*

the stitching, write the machine settings on the fabric with a permanent pen, and put away the fabric for future reference.

2. If you think you might have trouble staying on the lines, take the vanishing marker and mark the line before you start stitching.

Anchor the threads at the beginning and end of each line by stitching several stitches in place. (To do this, set stitch width and length at 0.) Clip the thread, and dab a drop of *Stop Fraying* at each end.

3. If you have an alphabet, write the names of favorite sports figures, famous golf courses, makes of cars and so on. Some machines have several sports designs: bicycle, golf green with flag, a ball. If possible, program designs of your choice into your machine. If you have a fish stitch, do a line of fish and then a line of fish names. You can write, "I love you, honey" or "Bill Bailey, Won't You Please Come Home" over and over. Or you may stitch in the names of jazz musicians if he's into this music, or Country and Western songs and stars if that's where his interests lie.

> ♥ *If you have access to a copy machine, copy each towel as you stitch it and keep these pages with your practice cloth.*

Variations:

There is almost nothing you can think of that isn't available pre-made with an area of even-weave waiting for you to stitch. Check the "Sources of Supplies" for mail-order shops. Any crafts or needlework store has the more common items, such as all sizes of towels, washcloths, baby bibs, placemats, napkins, bread cloths, and plaid and checked fabrics. Ads in the back of cross-stitch magazines have such items as tote bags, eyeglass cases, T-shirts, canvas baseball caps, and greeting cards. Also, you can fill all sorts of plexiglas items such as key rings, soap dishes, frames, coasters, etc.

Card Holders

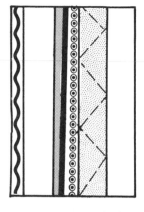

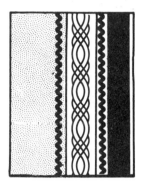

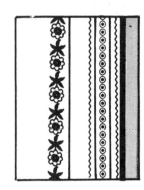

Fig. 7.16 Decorated Ultrasuede *card holders*

When a son is granted his first credit card, make him his own special card case. *Ultrasuede* scraps are available locally or by mail order (see "Sources of Supplies"). The size of the scraps doesn't matter because you can piece several together, if necessary. You'll also need wallet inserts, which are readily available at stationery stores, card shops, and drug stores, and come in several sizes from small to large. Certainly, the card holder is a unisex gift. Everybody has cards of some kind or another—driver's licenses, insurance cards, membership cards, check cashing cards, student cards, and social security cards. We added the even-weave stitched area on several of the holders for contrast and for a simple division of space (Fig. 7.16), decorating the holder differently each time.

Measure the plastic holder. You will need to add at least 1/2" (1.5cm) to the width to accommodate the thickness of the cards. Purchase your insert first, or use the mea-

surements given and hope you can find ones in the stated size—around 3" x 4" (7.5cm x 10cm). The finished size (opened) of the smaller holders is 6-1/2" x 4-1/2" (16.5cm x 11.5cm); the larger finishes at 8" x 6" (20.5cm x 15cm).

Ultrasuede holders are pricey in the better stores and they're also not lined or interfaced. Card holders are easy to mail and the right size to serve as a stocking stuffer.

You Will Need:

Scraps of *Ultrasuede* and even-weave fabrics
#80/12 sewing machine needle
Natesh or *Sulky* rayon machine-embroidery thread to match the even-weave and *Ultrasuede*
Vanishing marker
Rotary cutter, mat, and ruler
Wonder-Under
Teflon presser foot or lubricant such as *Tri-Flow* or *Needle-Ease* for the needle and presser foot
Sewing machine with decorative stitches

1. Cut a piece of even-weave fabric 2" x 5" (5cm x 12.5cm) (Fig. 7.17). Mark a 1" (2.5cm)

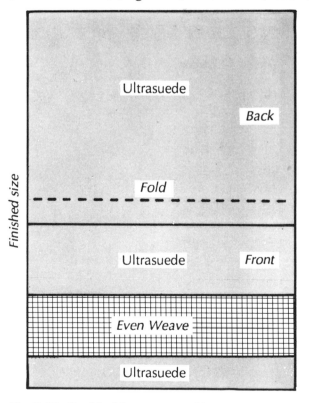

Fig. 7.17 Card holder pattern with even-weave insert

wide area lengthwise down the center with the vanishing marker. Stitch decorative stitches inside this area. Cut *Ultrasuede* scraps slightly larger in all directions than the areas on the pattern to allow for some overlap. You may use narrow strips of *Wonder-Under* to bond these pieces together before you stitch if you want. Also, cut out the inside flaps at this time: 3" x 5" (7.5cm x 12.5cm).

2. Place the small pieces on either side of the even-weave area first, putting the edge right on the marked line. Stitch these together using the triple stretch stitch and topstitching a scant 1/8" (3mm) from the edge. Use thread that either matches the decorative stitching or the even-weave fabric. If you have small strips of *Ultrasuede*, you can apply them with the triple stretch stitch or a decorative stitch as shown on one of the holders. Do any stitching you want on the *Ultrasuede*, drawing the lines with the vanishing marker.

3. When you've finished all the decorative stitching, mark the stitching line around the entire cover (6-1/4" x 4-1/4" [16cm x 11cm]) with the vanishing marker. Put the two inside flaps behind the cover at each end, and begin stitching at the center of the top on the marked line with the triple stretch stitch (0 width), catching in the flaps as you stitch (Fig. 7.18). Continue topstitching around, overlapping your beginning stitches by 1/8" (3mm). (You may use a plain straight stitch if you prefer.) Clip the threads.

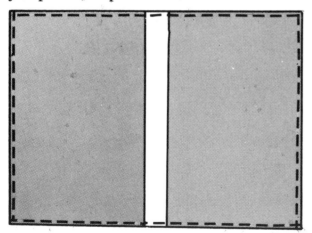

Fig. 7.18 Flaps are added to inside of holder.

4. Trim to within 1/8" (3mm) of the topstitching with the scissors by holding the scissors at a 45° angle to the edge. Be sure you have the finished side uppermost. When you trim in this manner, the underneath (flap) is automatically trimmed a scant smaller. Thread your machine with a color to match the even-weave fabric, and sew a close satin stitch at the top and bottom of this area.

> ♥ *Always trim seams in this manner, and they will be automatically graded (one smaller than the other to eliminate bulk).*

Variations:

A. You can make these out of any fabric. Divide the area any way you want, or make them from one piece of *Ultrasuede* with stitching, if your scraps are large enough. You can also piece the flaps if you can't find large enough scraps.

B. Put in a separate small pocket on one of the flaps (to hold your driver's license) before you stitch it to the front. This pocket is handier than having your license inside one of the plastic slips. Make a holder with the largest size holder (3-1/2" x 7" [9cm x 18cm]), and make a pocket on one side for your checkbook.

C. Make a checkbook holder using the measurements from the one the bank gave you.

> ♥ *Use little bits of leftover* Ultrasuede *for barrettes, scarf clips, and pins. You can get the findings (the pin-backs and barrettes) at any crafts store or check the "Sources of Supplies." Bond two pieces of* Ultrasuede *together, using* Wonder-Under *for the base. Bond on some decorations and stitch on top of these. Then use your trusty hot glue gun to attach these to the findings.*
>
> *Talk about getting something for almost nothing—and they're great stocking stuffers. Wouldn't a basket of these items be great at your table at the next crafts fair? You could charge 50 cents for them, and then there would be something children could buy.*

D. A pocket tissue holder for briefcases (Fig. 7.19) is another holder to make, if any of

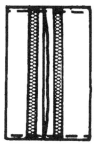

Fig. 7.19 *Tissue holder*

your *Ultrasuede* scraps are at least 5-1/2" x 8" (14cm x 20.5cm). They're also great sellers at bazaars. Bond 1/2" (1.5cm) under on both 5-1/2" (14cm) sides. Then bond and stitch 1/2" (1.5cm) strips of a contrasting *Ultrasuede* on either side 3/8" (1cm) away from the bonded hem. With wrong sides together, turn the two edges until they meet in the middle (Figs. 7.20 and 7.21).

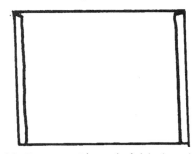

Fig. 7.20 *Pattern with ends folded under*

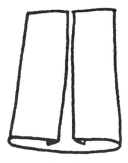

Fig. 7.21 *Pull folded ends around until they meet in the middle.*

Stitch the sides in a 1/4" (6mm) seam, and trim the *Ultrasuede* right next to the stitching. You can make scores of these in an evening. If your scraps aren't big enough, piece them by overlapping before cutting out the 5-1/2" x 8" (14cm x 20.5cm) piece, but keep the pieces as large as possible.

Production:

Cut patterns from poster board if you're producing a lot to speed up your sewing time. You can piece and stitch the outer covers, and then cut to size. If you don't mind making two exactly the same and your scraps allow, you could double the length (4-1/2" [11.5cm]) to 9" (23cm), do the decorating, cut to size, and complete each separately.

The Parallelogram Manicure Kit

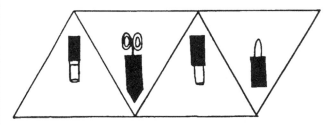

Fig. 7.22 *Open manicure kit*

This kit is made with four equilateral triangles (three 60° angles and sides the same length) (Fig. 7.23). You can construct any

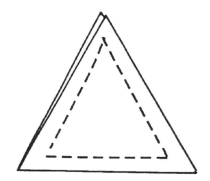

Fig. 7.23 *Closed kit*

size equilateral triangle with this pattern. Draw a straight line on tracing paper, and make a mark at both ends of the line. (A 5" [12.5cm] line was used for this project.) Place the marked straight line over one side of the equilateral triangle (Fig. 7.24) with a

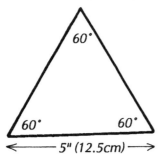

Fig. 7.24 *Equilateral triangle for kit pattern*

corner of the triangle directly under the mark at the beginning of the line you've drawn. From that point, draw a line 5" (12.5cm) long, following the side of the equilateral triangle seen underneath the tracing paper. Slide the equilateral triangle (under the tracing paper) to the other end of the first 5" (12.5cm) line you drew so the corner of the triangle is under the other mark. Draw a line from that mark, following the side of the triangle underneath. The triangle you've drawn is your pattern: an equilateral triangle with 5" (12.5cm) line.

Four equilateral triangles placed side by side will create a parallelogram (Fig. 7.22). In order to fold up the case when finished, leave 1/4" (6mm) between each traced triangle as shown in Figure 7.25. Add 1/4" (6mm) seam allowance all around the parallelogram as well.

Fig. 7.25 *Pattern for kit with stitching space between triangles*

You Will Need:

Piece of felt or interfacing 6" x 15" (15cm x 38cm)
Piece of fabric for lining 6" x 20" (15cm x 51cm)
Ultrasuede scraps
Piece of needlepunched batt 6" x 18" (15cm x 46cm)
Fingernail and toenail clippers, scissors, tweezers
Vanishing marker
Wonder-Under (optional)
Velcro dots (one)

1. Construct the pattern as described above. With your vanishing marker, draw the parallelogram on the piece of felt. Place *Ultrasuede* scraps on the felt, extending slightly beyond the drawn lines. Using as large scraps as possible, overlap and stitch down. (You may bond *Wonder-Under* to the back of the *Ultrasuede,* and subsequently, bond to the felt.) Place the felt side of the pieced *Ultrasuede* on top of the batt.

2. Use the pattern to cut out the lining. Cut patterns for small rectangular and triangular pockets (four) to hold the utensils you've purchased. Use the utensils themselves as patterns, making the pockets large enough to hold them, but not so large that they fall out. Cut out these patterns from *Ultrasuede* scraps. Place the pockets on the lining piece and stitch in place (Fig. 7.26).

Fig. 7.26 *Stitching on kit showing placement for* Velcro *dots or snaps*

3. Place the lining over your pieced *Ultrasuede,* right sides together. Stitch all around in a 1/4" (6mm) seam, leaving a 5" (12.5cm) opening along one long edge for turning. Turn to the right side. Turn the seam at the opening to the inside, and press. Stitch a scant 1/8" (3mm) from the edge all around, closing the opening at the same time. Stitch on the lines between the triangles, starting and stopping at the outer stitching line (Fig. 7.26).

4. Bond the *Velcro* dots to the appropriate points as shown in Figure 7.26. Fold in the triangle without the *Velcro*. Fold it again. Then fold the remaining single triangle over the previous folds and press the *Velcro* to hold the kit closed.

Variation

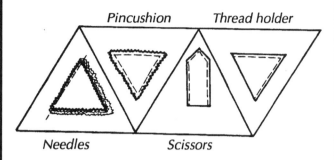

Fig. 7.27 Needlework kit showing sections for needles, pincushion, scissors holder, and slot for buttons and thread

The parallelogram makes a wonderful sewing kit (Fig. 7.27), and can be made of cloth or *Ultrasuede*. The cloth directions follow:

You Will Need:
Two pieces of fabric 6" x 15" (15cm x 38cm) for outside and lining
Small scraps of fabric for pincushion and pocket
Small scrap of flannel for needles
3" (7.5cm) piece of 1/2" (1.5cm) grosgrain ribbon for scissors holder
Pinking shears

1. Construct the pattern as described above. Place the lining and outer fabric right sides together, and cut out the parallelogram. Also cut one out of batt. Place the two fabrics on top of the batt, and stitch around in a 1/4" (6mm) seam. Leave a 5" (12.5cm) opening for turning along one long side. Turn to the right side, turn the seam at the opening to the inside, and pin. Stitch a scant 1/8" (3mm) in all around the edge, closing the opening at the same time. Stitch on the lines between the triangles, starting and stopping at the outer stitching line (Fig. 7.26).

2. Cut out two 3-1/2" (9cm) equilateral triangles from the batt, and stitch together with a 4mm width zigzag stitch. With the pinking shears, cut out a triangle slightly larger than the batting. Place the batting and fabric in the center of the second triangle as shown in Figure 7.27.

3. With the pinking shears, cut out three 3" (8cm) triangles from the flannel. Stack them, and stitch along one side in the first triangle on the left as shown in Figure 7.27. Add some needles.

4. Add a scissors holder as seen in the manicure kit (Fig. 7.22).

5. Fold a scrap, and place one side of the 3" (7.5cm) triangle pattern along the fold. Draw in the other two lines. Cut out, allowing a 1/4" (6mm) seam line along the two edges. Fold back, and press 1/4" (6mm) along one edge. Stitch the other side, and turn to the right side. Position as shown in Figure 7.27, and stitch in place.

Sew the two parts of the snap to the appropriate points as shown in Figure 7.26.

Cut a piece of index card that will fit into the triangular pocket. Wind some lengths of thread around it, and glue on several shirt buttons to create a masculine traveling sewing and mending kit.

Production:
Put lining and outer fabrics with right sides together, and cut into 5" (12.5) strips across the width. Each strip will yield three parallelograms—with enough left over for the pockets and pincushions, if you alternate the fabrics as outer and linings.

Hooded Bath Towel

A hooded bath towel can be made quickly, and adding a zippered pocket for keys or coins, will take only a few minutes longer. These popular towels are ideal for bazaars and sell out quickly.

If sewing for a bazaar, buy inexpensive towels at a discount store, and skip the pocket. The towels may not be heavy plush,

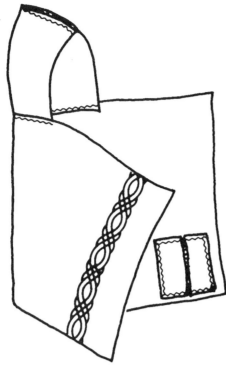

Fig. 7.28 Make a hooded bath towel from washcloth, hand towel, and bath towel.

but they are more than adequate. When the towel is worn, it hangs from a hood, leaving hands free to carry snorkels, shoes, shells, and other beach necessities. The hood also keeps children and adults warm after swimming.

Writing directions for this gift would be simpler if all bath towels were one size—but they aren't. However, this project doesn't need a pattern and it's not based on exact measurements. What matters is finding towels of adequate size for your use (at a bazaar you may want several sizes), then folding, marking, and stitching them.

For small children, buy the smaller bath towels; adults love the size of a large bath sheet. If you find sets of matching towels, you're in luck, as your ensemble will look smashing. (Also, don't ignore irregulars or seconds.) But don't despair if you can't find towels that match. Buy multicolored or printed bath sheets at a discount store, and team them with washcloths and hand towels that sport colors found in the bath sheet. When making the towels for preteens, we only used smaller bath towels and hand towels. We cut off both ends of the hand towel to make the pocket (Fig. 7.29).

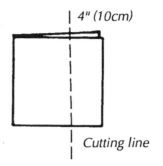

4" (10cm)

Cutting line

Fig. 7.29 Make a pocket and hood from a hand towel.

We like adding pockets to the towels because they're useful for swimming lesson cards, watches, sun glasses, small change, and a myriad of other items you want at the beach or pool, but not in the water.

You Will Need:

Bath towel or bath sheet
Hand towel
Washcloth for hidden pocket (optional)
12" (31.8cm) zipper for hidden pocket
    (optional)
Sewing machine

1. First fold the long sides of the bath sheet to find the top center of the sheet, and then mark it with a pin. Match the short ends of the hand towel, and stitch it together (1" [2.5cm] seam allowance) along one side edge. Clip the seam at the fold almost to the stitching line. Open the seam, and zigzag through all the layers at each edge to hold them in place (these stitches are hidden in the terry cloth and practically invisible).

♥ Buy all the towels and washcloths at the same time to be sure you can match them. When you want to save money for the bazaar, cut a hand towel in half to make two child-sized hoods.

2. Match the pin at the center of the bath sheet and either the center fold of the hood or the seam line of the hood. This puts the seam either on the top of the head or at the back. You decide, based on the design of the hand towel and what looks more attractive.

To hold the hand towel in place, place the hood's selvage edge under that of the sheet, pin in place, and stitch at the edge of the bath sheet. Go back again, and zigzag stitch at the other edge of the selvage.

3. Pocket (optional): If making a pocket, you'll need a 12" (31cm) nylon zipper to match the towel color. (Cut it to size if too long when constructing the pocket.) To make the pocket: Fold the washcloth in half, and cut down the fold. Place a zipper on top of one cut edge, right sides together (Fig. 7.30) and stitch it in place along the right side of the teeth. Fold the zipper back, and zigzag along the edge to hold it in place (Fig. 7.31). Do the same to the other side (Figs. 7.32 and 7.33).

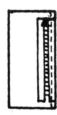

Fig. 7.30 *With right sides together, sew down zipper at cut edge of toweling.*

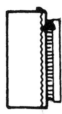

Fig. 7.31 *Fold back and zigzag topstitch.*

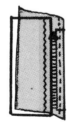

Fig. 7.32 *Attach the other side of the zipper as you did the first.*

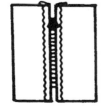

Fig. 7.33 *Fold back and zigzag topstitch to finish.*

If you must cut off the zipper to fit the washcloth (12" [30.5cm] zippers fit the washcloths we used), stitch across the teeth at the length you want, and cut off the zipper 1" (2.5cm) under your stitching at the bottom edge of the washcloth. The zipper will be sewn into the stitching when the pocket is attached. Be careful not to fully unzip the zipper until the pocket is attached.

Place the washcloth pocket at one of the bottom inside corners of the bath sheet, pin, turn under the bottom edge of the zipper, and stitch the pocket in place with a zigzag stitch. Notice that there are no raw edges to turn under, as you're stitching around the selvage edges of the wash cloth.

If you make the pocket by cutting off part of the hand towel (you may do this when making a child's hooded towel), then do it this way: Cut off at least 4" (10cm) at each end of the hand towel. This should take you past any border on or woven in the towel. If you feel the hood is now too wide for the length, cut off several inches and discard.

Sew the zipper to the raw edges of the pieces you cut from the hand towel, leaving finished outside edges. Stitch the pocket as described in step 3.

Variation:

A plain bath towel is a perfect canvas for your artwork. Appliqué names, animals, or comic book characters so they're visible on the back when the towel is worn.

If you have some bachelors in your life, knit them potholders, coasters, and dishrags (page 27). Christmas ornaments (Chapter 8) are also fine gifts for men who put up their own trees. Check out the Victorian Stockings on page 100. Why not make one shaped like a muscular man's leg and painted with shoes and socks? If you know any fishing enthusiasts, look on page 25 at the plastic bows— One is filled with all sorts of fishing flies. Or, add about 2" (5cm) of stitches and 2" (5cm) of length, and machine knit one of the hats on page 44, if you live where it's cold enough to wear one.

You'll never have to shop for ties or handkerchiefs or games again. And everything you make will be treasured.

Chapter 8

The Christmas Exchange

Projects:

- ♥ *Advent Calendar*
- ♥ *Crocheted Wreath Pin*
- ♥ *Victorian Christmas Stocking*
- ♥ *Cathedral Window Ornament*
- ♥ *Quick Needlepoint Ornaments*
- ♥ *Battenberg Star Ornament*
- ♥ *The Year of the Seminole Ornament*
- ♥ *From Angel to Zebra Ornaments*
- ♥ *Stitched Lace and Wire Ornaments*
- ♥ *Gold Lamé Star Ornaments*
- ♥ *Christmas Tree Skirt*

Fig. 8.1 *Celebrate Christmas!*

Many words have more than one meaning. If we say *exchange*, do you think of the verb "replacing one thing with another" or the noun "a place where stocks and bonds are bought and sold"? We call this chapter the "Christmas Exchange," likening *exchange* to the New York Stock Exchange. This is a chapter to enter when you're looking for Christmas decorations such as ornaments, Advent calendars, and tree skirts—gifts that keep on giving as year after year they're taken out and hung with care.

Ornaments can be your bestsellers at a Christmas boutique or bazaar. The small crocheted wreath can be a tree ornament or a pin or napkin rings for the Christmas table. The Advent calendar is a great Christmas gift (present it on Thanksgiving). The tree skirt and tree top angel (page 62) are different—unusual—for friends, family, or yourself. Make up a bunch of the Battenberg stars and use them for hostess gifts at all the holiday parties you attend.

Here's the chapter where you'll find gifts for aunts, uncles, teachers, scout leaders, co-workers, your most casual and your closest friends, and for the person who has everything. Happy Holidays!

Advent Calendar

Fig. 8.2 Advent calendar

Advent calendars heighten the suspense of Christmas's arrival. When children are toddlers, they can hang a small ornament to a bow each day in December and visualize how long it will take until Christmas Day. No more of that constant question: "When is Santa coming?" As children grow older, the fun comes in not only adding ornaments to the tree each day, but in unwrapping the calendar and ornaments after Thanksgiving in preparation for December 1. Always included on our calendar are ornaments the children made when they were too young to know what they were making as well as others they made and added to the tree in later years. Make this a family project—all the ornaments don't have to be made in one year. If you prefer to buy ornaments, then buy the miniature ones found in Christmas shops.

The only rules for the calendar are that the ornaments must fit in the pockets on the calendar, and that there must be one angel (which goes into pocket 24). When the angel goes on the top of the tree, you celebrate Christmas.

You Will Need:

Felt (comes in 72" [1.8m] widths) (If you have a choice, buy lightweight.)
White: 1/2 yd (46cm) (cut into two 18" x 36" [46cm x .9m] pieces)

Green: 9" x 24" (23cm x 61cm)
Red: 1/8 yd (11.4cm)
Gold: small scrap about 6" (15cm) square
Gold cord: 5-1/2 yds (5m) (gold "Gift Tie" or "Tinsel Cord" is fine)
1-1/4 yds (1.1m) wide cord or braid for the hanger and top bow
2 push pins or thumb tacks
1 dowel (3/8" x 36" [1cm x .9m]) cut in half
Thread to match each felt color (or use nylon monofilament)
Green machine-embroidery thread
Vanishing marker
Rotary cutter and mat
T-square ruler
Glue stick
Adding machine tape or tear-away stabilizer
Aleene's *Stop Fraying*
Ornament hangers

1. Before you begin, press the pieces of felt. Straighten each piece as you measure and cut it. Also, press the felt as you complete each step.

2. Tree: Cut 1" (2.5cm) off the green felt. Place the 9" x 23" (23cm x 58cm) piece of green felt to the right on one of the white felt pieces, 3-1/2" (9cm) from the top. Following the diagram in Figure 8.3A, cut out half a Christmas tree, star, and tub. This is the positive image; the fabric left over is the negative. Flip the positive image to the left side. Cut out another tree shape from the positive tree piece, and flip it back to the right side. Your tree—negative and positive images—will look like the illustration in Figure 8.3A.

Fig. 8.3A. Cut out tree from green felt and flip it to the left. Cut out smaller tree at left, and flip it to the right.

3. Dot the back of the green felt with glue stick to help hold it in place while stitching. Use pins, too, to hold the images in place. Sew with a straight stitch around the green shapes. We used the zipper foot as a guide, placing the foot at the right-hand edge of the fabric and setting the needle position to the right. Cut two 1/4" x 9" (6mm x 23mm) strips from the green felt you have left over. Stitch them in place as a frame at the left top and bottom of the white area.

4. Star: Cut out a star from the gold felt approximately 3" x 3" (7.5cm x 7.5cm), roughly the same as the green tree star. Cut out the left half section of the star and discard, leaving only a frame around that half of the star (Fig. 8.3B). Place the top point over

Fig. 8.3B. Cut out star as shown.

the join in the green felt, pin, and stitch in place. Cut three strips 1/2" x 4" (1.5cm x 10cm) from the rest of the gold felt piece. Use one strip at the top of the tub, another below that, and the third over the join at the bottom (see Color Plate 10). Trim the strips to follow the sides of the container. Pin and stitch in place.

5. Pockets: To make pockets for the ornaments, use the entire width of red felt. Cut a strip 4" (10cm) wide. Mark the strip with a vanishing marker, following the illustration in Figure 8.4, and cut off what is not needed.

The numbers on the pockets can be done in several ways: paint them on with dimensional paints; cut numbers from felt, glue, and stitch down; or embroider the numbers on as we did.

6. Numbers: Back the red strip with adding-machine tape or tear-away stabilizer. Machine baste the lines drawn with the marker. Write numbers from 1 to 24 in the appropriate spaces. Trace them from books or write them freehand as we did. Ours are 1" (2.5cm) high and centered in the 1" x 2" (2.5cm x 5cm) spaces.

Set up your machine for embroidery by lowering or covering the feed dogs, loosening the top tension a bit, and using a darning foot. Set the stitch width on 3mm. Change to green cotton or rayon machine-embroidery thread. Always lock your threads at the beginning and end of each number, and don't sew the stitches too closely together. Move the fabric up, sideways, and down as you embroider the numbers, but don't move your work in a circular motion. First practice on felt backed with the stabilizer.

When you finish embroidering the numbers on the pockets, cut the two strips apart, and carefully pull off the backing paper. Box pleat the strip on the marked lines to form the pockets (Fig. 8.5). Mark one line on the white felt, 3-1/2" (9cm) below the green area, and another line 2-1/2" (6.5cm) below that for pocket placement.

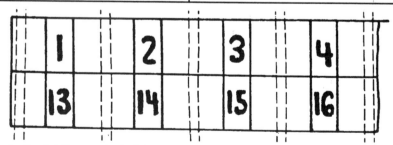

Fig. 8.4 Mark pocket strip for folding and stitching.

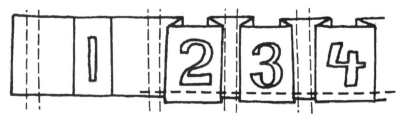

Fig. 8.5 Fold and stitch box pleated compartments to calendar.

Pin the first strip of pockets in place on the top line. Center the section between numbers 6 and 7 at the middle of the calendar, and pull gently until 1 and 12 are at each side. To attach the ornament pockets, pin between each pocket and at the sides. Sew up, across and down on the guide lines you previously marked. Attach both strips the same way.

7. Felt Decorations: Cut out twenty-three circles, 1" (2.5cm) in diameter (use a quarter as a pattern), from the rest of the red fabric and arrange them on your tree. Cut the gold cord into twenty-four pieces, each 8" (20.5cm) long. Dip the ends of the cords into *Stop Fraying,* and let dry. Fold one cord in half and place it near the top of a red circle. Sew back and forth in place to attach the ornament to the calendar. Do all of the cords the same way. Sew the last cord to the top of the star.

Tie each cord into a bow, and place a drop of *Stop Fraying* at the center of each so it stays tied. These are the hangers for your small ornaments.

8. Finishing: Return to the other piece of white felt and back the calendar with it. Pin the back in place, and stitch all around from the front with transparent thread. Trim the edges. Fold the top and bottom edges to the back, forming 2" (5cm) hems.

Stitch above the green felt and below the red pockets to hold the hems (casings) in place. Slip in the dowels. Cut a piece of wide gold cord 24" (61cm) long, and tack the cord ends to the ends of the top dowel to make a hanger (Fig 8.6). With the remaining

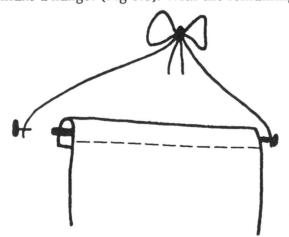

Fig. 8.6 Slip dowel into top casing, then tack cord to ends for hanging.

cord, tie a separate bow for the top. By usi[ng] tacks through the cord and into each end of the dowel, you can easily take the calendar apart after the season, roll it around the dowels and tissue paper and store it until next December.

9. Buying or making special miniature ornaments can be a year-long or years-long project. Your favorite craft store probably has an area devoted to doll houses and miniatures. In these stores, you'll find practically anything you can think of in miniature form—from sleds to sewing machines, gift packages to garden tools, and apple pies to xylophones. Glue a tiny loop to the back of the miniature for attaching to the calendar, and dab with glitter if desired. Inexpensive charms are available through the mail (see "Sources of Supplies"), which would make wonderful ornaments. Cut small medallions from lace and dab them with glitter; purchase tiny embroidered or sequinned appliqués (letters are also available); or take a walk through your hardware store and see what suggests itself—nuts and bolts painted with gold metallic paint for Dad to hang on the calendar. Use purchased ornament hangers (Fig. 8.7) to hang the ornaments on the gold cord bows.

Merry twenty-four days of Christmas!

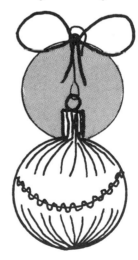

Fig. 8.7 Hang ornaments over bows.

...cheted
...ath Pin

Fig. 8.8 Crocheted wreath pin

While fiddling around with a crochet hook and bias cut rags, using a "crab" ("shrimp" in Great Britain) or backward single crochet, the strip started to curve. Who are we to fight the forces of nature? After clipping the thread and tieing the ends together, there it was—a tiny wreath! If possible, find a fabric that has no right or wrong side. We used cotton madras plaids with a gold mylar thread.

Buy corsage pins, and give away these wreaths to anyone who is around at Christmas.

You Will Need:

70" (1.8m) bias strip (will need to be pieced)
"H" (5.5mm) crochet hook
Hair spray (lacquer-base) in pump bottle
Aleene's *Stop Fraying*
Pin-backs (optional)
Corsage pins (optional)
Hot glue gun (optional)

1. Cut a yard of fabric into 1-1/4" (3cm) bias strips. It will take about 70" (1.8m) to make one wreath. Do not make continuous bias, as the seams are too bulky for this use. Instead, overlap the strips, and stitch with a straight machine stitch (Fig. 8.9).

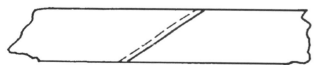

Fig. 8.9 Overlap bias strips, and stitch together.

2. Using an "H" (5.5mm) crochet hook, and leaving a 7" (18cm) length of fabric, *chain (ch) 3, single crochet (sc) in front loop of third chain from hook.**
Repeat from * to ** seven times. End off.

Tie the two lengths into an overhand knot and then into a bow. Trim the ends, and put a drop of *Stop Fraying* on the knot of the bow.

3. Finishing: Use a corsage pin to attach in place, or put on a pin-back with your hot glue gun. Attach a hanger cord for a tree ornament. To stiffen the bow, spray it lightly with a lacquer-base hair spray.

If you use a solid color, dust the finished wreath with an all-purpose glitter spray, which you can find where silk flowers are sold. Be sure to follow the directions on the can; the vapors are harmful and flammable.

Variations:

A. Crochet 1/8" (3mm) ribbon for tiny wreaths to decorate your Christmas placecards.

B. Dip in *Stiffy* after crocheting, but before tying bow. Tie bow and mold to desired shape. Let dry.

C. Use these items as napkin rings.

D. Decorate the wreaths with beads or charms, if desired.

E. Make smaller wreaths by cutting the strips 3/4" (2cm) wide, and using an "F" (4mm) hook.

Production:

Open out a yard of fabric, and fold one corner up (Fig. 8.10), creating the largest

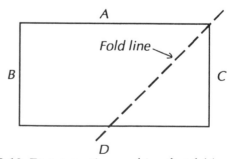

Fig. 8.10 To cut continuous bias, first fold up side C to meet side A.

diagonal possible. Cut along the fold (Fig. 8.11). **Do not open.**

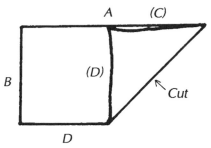

Fig. 8.11 *Cut along fold.*

Bring the top corner of the cut edge to the bottom corner of the same edge (Fig. 8.12 A and B).

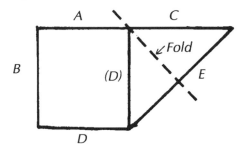

Fig. 8.12A *Fold down from side C on dotted line.*

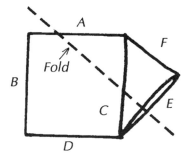

Fig. 8.12B *Fold again on dotted line parallel to side F.*

Fold on dotted line. Fold the leftover single layer of fabric on top of your roll (Fig. 8.13). Using a rotary cutter, ruler, and mat,

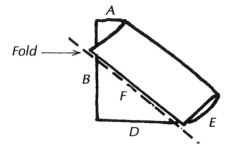

Fig. 8.13 *Again, fold on dotted line at F.*

cut the fabric into 1-1/4" (3cm) bias strips (Fig. 8.14). Overlap the pieces and sew into 70" (1.8m) strips (Fig. 8.9).

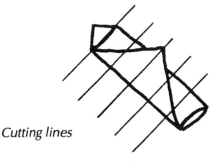

Cutting lines

Fig. 8.14 *Cut out bias strips perpendicular to the last fold line.*

Keep the strips in a bag along with your hook and crochet them whenever you have five minutes. Tie all the bows and spray the wreaths later. You can easily sell these for

> ♥ *You will sell a hundred $2.00 items for every $20 item in your booth at the bazaar. As Mrs. F.L.S. of Michigan pointed out in the January 1920 issue of "Needlecraft": "It is much easier to sell those of lower price than more elaborate pieces. I notice, for example, that the large, expensive yokes are on exhibition much longer than the smaller ones."*

$2.00 each, and you can literally make hundreds in record time. These would be ideal favors for a large Christmas luncheon.

Victorian Christmas Stocking

Fig. 8.15 *Pieced, embroidered, and beaded Christmas stocking*

These sensuous Christmas stockings are holiday favorites. Originally made for friends and family, they are one of Jackie's most popular classes.

This stocking is 24" (61cm) long, fully lined, and covered with sumptuous embellishments. No craft ribbons allowed—only double-faced satin, taffetas, or exquisite velvets and velveteens. (We wanted an heirloom quality to our stocking.) These stockings are never the same when made twice. We've used the traditional red and green, but that isn't as fun as branching out to the unexpected. Many of our inspirations are found in old button boxes, antique braids, and lace.

Originally, we did all the embroidery by hand—and still do sometimes. But sewing machines offer such beautiful stitches today. Even a plain feather stitch done with rayon or metallic threads is wonderful.

First decide what fabrics you'll use. Will you embellish a one-piece stocking of velveteen, or patch together fabrics and sew them to a muslin backing? Find ribbons in three widths, at least 2 yds (1.8m) each for bows. Add 12" (30.5cm) more for each ribbon rose, if you make your own. You'll also need varieties of fine ribbons for the stocking front in different sizes as well as laces, beads, and buttons.

You Will Need:

3/4 yd (69cm) velveteen (enough for front and back)
3/4 yd (69cm) satin or silk-type lining
Sewing thread
Heavy duty carpet thread
Ribbon in three widths
Ribbon roses
Old buttons
Beads
Various laces

1. First cut out the stocking front, using the pattern shown (Fig. 8.16). If the stocking is

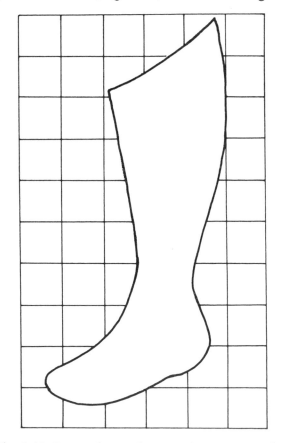

Fig. 8.16 *Pattern for stocking: Each square equals 4" (10cm).*

to be patched, cut it from muslin; if the stocking is in one piece, cut it from velveteen. Cut the back (turn the pattern over) from one piece of velveteen for either type (We've discovered a velveteen called *Matinee* [see "Sources of Supplies"] that has nap, but no direction. When using *Matinee*, you can buy less fabric because you can place the pattern anywhere on the cloth.)

Choose a satin or silk-type lining, and cut out two pattern pieces (front and back).

2. You may first want to sketch the stocking on paper, but usually it's easier to design right on the fabric. The planning takes the longest, but it is also the most fun. Find ideas in books on clothing and costume. Books on military uniforms contain a wealth of ideas for braids, buttons, and pleats. Victorian couture gives ideas for passementerie (visit your library). But no matter how carefully a stocking is planned, it never ends up exactly the way it was first envisioned. These stockings evolve.

To do the patchwork stocking: First overlap the fabric scraps on the muslin, rather than butt them together, when placing one piece next to another. This procedure enables you to decorate, cover, or fold under only one raw edge at a time.

Cover edges with lace or ribbon, or fold under fabric edges and embroider them with decorative stitches. Couch down cords and strings of beads, too. We also like to personalize each stocking with a monogram or name.

At the top of the stocking stitch "Merry Christmas," using an alphabet on your machine or stitching it in freely. When the stocking is finished, perhaps this and other embroidery and beads are hidden under the lace ruffle. The concealment is not a mistake. We do this on purpose because we want the decoration under the ruffle as elegant as the rest of the stocking. No matter who looks at these stockings, the person always lifts the ruffle to see what's underneath. And the peeker is not disappointed! You can also add beads and old buttons by hand or by machine.

3. When the stocking front is completed, stitch all around 1/4" (6mm) from the edge. Next, add the top ruffle. If the lace is not gathered already, zigzag over a cord at the top of the lace and pull up on the cord to gather it. You may want to add another piece of gathered lace at the top for a more finished edge. The lace ruffles are placed directly under the staystitching and basted in place (Fig. 8.17). The sides of the lower

Fig. 8.17 Baste ruffle under the top line of staystitching.

piece of lace are also basted to the sides of the stocking, but the top short ruffle is rolled at the sides and hemmed by hand (Fig. 8.18). Add a strip of ribbon to the top, between the ruffles, by machine or by hand.

Fig. 8.18 If preferred, add a short ruffle above the stocking before you add the ribbon.

4. Pin the front to the back stocking, right sides together, and stitch the foot first on the staystitching line and up the leg to the top. Go back and do the other side. When I sew it together this way, there is less creeping, and the front and back fit together perfectly. Next, turn the stocking right side out and fold down the top at the stitching line.

5. Place the lining pieces, right sides together, and stitch around them except for the top. Staystitch 1/4" (6mm) down from the edge, around the lining top. Fold down at the stitching to the outside (the lining is still wrong side out).

Push the lining down into the stocking (Fig. 8.19). We used the end of a long water-

Fig. 8.19 Push lining down into the stocking.

color brush or dowel. Place the top fold of the lining at the folded edge of the stocking. Whip stitch by hand around the top. We usually handstitch a strip of lace around the top inside of the stocking to give it an elegant finish.

6. Buy or make ribbon roses for the centers of the bows. Also, make a hanging cord either from pearl cotton, a short string of beads, or cord from a drapery or fabric store.

7. Use three different width ribbons to embellish the stocking at the hanger. They can be one to three different colors and widths. Make large loops and tie the loops together with a narrow ribbon or cord, leaving long ends of ribbons to hang at different lengths from below the ruffle of the stocking to right below the calf (Fig. 8.20).

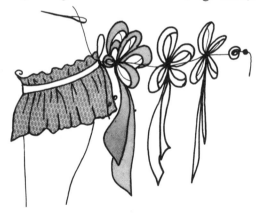

Fig. 8.20 Attach roses and ribbons in this order.

To assemble the ribbons, hanger, and roses, first handstitch the hanging cord loop to the right side seam of the stocking. Leave enough cord below the loop to add color or interest to the ribbons. Tie overhand knots at the ends of the cord. Cut back, and dot the ends with *Stop Fraying*. Or, tie the knots an inch above the ends, and fray out the cord. Next, stitch down the ribbons. The wider ribbon will be the first stitched in place, then any narrower ones in descending order—ending with the narrowest. Three ribbon roses go on next. Stitch them in place in the center of the ribbon loops. Place a pearl in the center of each rose and stitch through it, the rose, ribbon, and the stocking for a strong anchor (Fig. 8.21).

Fig. 8.21 The finished stocking—voilà!

Variation:

Since each stocking is, in effect, a different variation, you're on your own to create the stocking of your dreams.

The Ornament Exchange

As we mentioned at the beginning of this chapter, *exchange* is also a verb. We belong to several guilds and groups whose Christmas tradition is an ornament exchange rather than a gift exchange. You might suggest this practice to your interest group, friends, classroom, family, scout troop, co-workers, or wherever group exchanges take place.

Every Christmas since they were born, we've either made or bought a special tree ornament for each of our children. (We began putting the year and the child's name on the back with a permanent ink pen after the first few Christmases when we had a terrible time remembering which ornament belonged to which child.) As the children grew, putting up the tree became a treasured family time. And each child would search out his or her ornaments to hang on the tree. As our children left home, we sent them on their way with a collection of familiar ornaments so their first tree would be adorned with memories of home and Christmases past.

Christmas ornaments are one of our favorite gifts to give and receive. Decorating our Christmas tree is spending an evening traveling back through time. Thoughts and images of relatives and friends fill the room as their ornaments are hung with care.

Some ornaments symbolize certain craft periods: the year of the Seminole ornaments, the year of the sequinned styrofoam balls, the year of the decorated tuna fish cans, the year of the patchwork wreaths, the year of the crocheted Santas, and so on and on. We have enough ornaments now, even with the loss of our children's, to decorate several trees. As we moved from place to place, friends moved through our lives, but their ornaments remain as a testimony to our special time together. And Christmas has become our time to remember them as we place their ornaments on our tree.

Making and giving Christmas ornaments is a special way to touch people's lives once a year—and you don't have to keep your address book up to date to accomplish this. We gave ornaments that either the children or we had made to their teachers and to their friends' parents. We always noted the child's name and the year inconspicuously on the back or bottom. We have fun fantasizing that as trees go up at Christmas, the teachers and friends' parents will remember a special moment with the child who made the ornament they're holding. The memory is another stitch of the threads that entangle us with each other and that have become part of the weft of our lives.

Cathedral Window Ornament

Fig. 8.22 *Cathedral window ornament*

Over the years we've seen several different cathedral window ornaments, and this small one is our favorite. It's perfect for small trees, as the finished ornament is only about 2-1/2" (6.5cm) in any direction. Use lamé for the small squares, and the ornament will sparkle. There's a great deal of handwork, however, so it would not be cost efficient to make these for sale.

If you spend a lot of time waiting during any given day, do the machine stitching and pressing on the large squares (through step 3), and keep a supply of these ornaments on hand to finish. All you need with you as you wait is a spool of thread, a needle, small scissors, and a thimble.

You Will Need:

Wonder-Under
Two contrasting fabrics (We used red and
    green.)
1 skein stranded floss for tassel (optional)
Needle and thread to match 5" (12.5cm)
    squares
Stuffing
Five 5mm gold beads (optional)

1. Press *Wonder-Under* on fabric from which
small squares will be cut. (A 9" [23cm]
square of *Wonder-Under* will yield 16
squares—enough for five ornaments.) Cut
three 5" (12.5cm) squares from one fabric,
and three 2-1/4" (6cm) squares from contrasting fabric.

2. Press 1/4" (6mm) seam allowance to
wrong side on sides *A* and *C* of the 5"
(12.5cm) square (Fig 8.23A). Fold the square

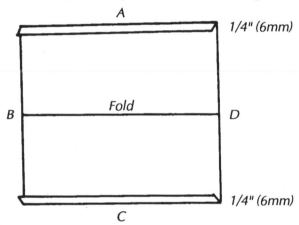

Fig. 8.23A. Fold squares into rectangles.

in half with right sides together bringing *A*
to *C* and stitching 1/4" (6mm) seams in sides
B and *D* (Fig. 8.23B). Turn to right side, and

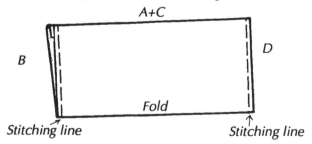

Fig. 8.23B. Stitch up sides B and D.

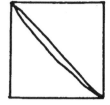

Fig. 8.24 Turn, and bring edges together.

bring sides *A* and *C* together at center (Fig.
8.24). Ladder stitch this seam together, being
careful not to catch the back of the square in
your stitching. Take two small backstitches
to secure. **Do not cut thread.**

3. Place one 2-1/4" (6cm) square on top of
the seamed side of the stitched square,
placing the corners of the small square in the
centers of the sides of the stitched squares
(Fig. 8.25). Bond in place.

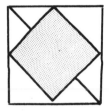

Fig. 8.25 Place square of fabric over the opening.

4. Bring the four corners of the large square
to the center, and tack securely in place.
(Place small gold bead here for variation.)
Beginning at each corner, ladder stitch the
corner closed for about 1/4" (6mm). Take
thread to back and secure with two small
backstitches. **Do not cut.** Return threaded
needle to the right side, fold each side back,
and slip stitch into place (Fig. 8.26). Repeat
with all three squares.

Fig. 8.26 Bring corners over square, and stitch.

5. Place two squares back to back, and ladder stitch together as shown in Fig. 8.27 (*C* to *C*). Then add the third square as shown in Figure 8.27 (*A* to *A*). Fold side back, and

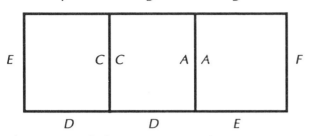

Fig. 8.27 *Stitch three squares together.*

stitch together as in Figure 8.28 (*B* to *B*). Place filling inside and continue stitching

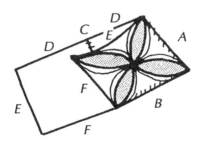

Fig. 8.28 *Fold back one side and stitch B to B. Stitch D to D, E to E. Stuff with batting, and stitch closed F to F.*

sides together (*D* to *D*, *E* to *E*, *F* to *F*). Before stitching the last side, push in more filling, if needed, until the ornament is tight. Stitch shut (Fig. 8.29).

Fig. 8.29 *Cathedral window stitched closed*

Omit the bead at one corner (if you're using them), and attach a hanging cord there. If desired, place a tassel at the bottom point.

Variation:

Cut three 5" (12.5cm) squares from one fabric. Then follow steps in Figures 8.23A and B and 8.24. Embroider on the squares or cover them with lace. Finish the ornament as above.

Quick Needle-point Ornaments

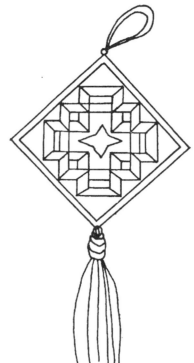

Fig. 8.30 *Needlepoint ornament*

You can interpret quilt designs in canvas embroidery. When Jane couldn't find stitches that worked in the way she wanted, she devised a whole series of Norwich variations, beginning with a Norwich star. Each variation is flexible and lends itself to constant alteration, thus, one variation begat a whole family. Most of the stitches in these ornaments are several generations removed from those first ones, and there are many yet to be discovered.

Work these ornaments on interlock canvas for its ease in finishing with a long-legged cross or binding stitch. Work both sides of the ornament, since they stitch up so quickly. Worked with the new metallic ribbon threads, these ornaments shine and twinkle like stars on the tree. The ornaments are small (2-1/4" [6cm]) in diameter and jewel-like in appearance when worked on 18-mesh canvas.

While it is possible to work these stitches free, Jane suggests stretching yours on a frame when working with the metallic ribbons, floss, or ribbon threads. Cut a 5" x 9" (12.5cm x 23cm) piece of interlock, and stitch three ornaments at a time. When the motifs are stitched, remove the canvas from the frame, and cut the ornaments apart (3" x 5" [7.5cm x 12.5cm]). Now you can finish them at spare moments throughout the day and evening.

What you will find different about these stitches is the fact that they are worked with two fibers at the same time. Alternating first one needle and then the other, a woven or interlaced effect is created. The only trick to this is to always bring the working needle to the front in its next working hole (Fig. 8.31).

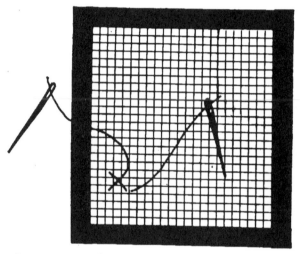

Fig. 8.31 *Two threaded needles are used.*

If the threads are allowed to dangle at the back, they will get into an awful muddle, and the needles will slide off and bury themselves in the carpet.

As with their ancestor, the Norwich stitch, there is almost no thread on the back of the canvas with these variations, so don't hesitate using more expensive fibers.

You Will Need:

3" x 5" (7.5cm x 12.5cm) piece of 18-mesh interlock per ornament
1 skein stranded floss or stranded silk
1 tube (8m of 1/16" [1.5mm] metallic ribbon contrasting with the floss)
Two #24 tapestry needles
2-1/4" x 4-1/2" (6cm x 11.5cm) scrap of quilt batting
Stuffing (optional)

1. Charts for this project are at the back of the book on page 140 – 143. Each side of the ornament uses 40 threads of canvas: 32 x 32 threads for the motif, surrounded by one blank thread, one row of tent stitch, one blank thread, and the thread for the binding stitch (8 threads). Start counting threads about 3/4" (2cm) in from the edge. Mark the center hole (20 threads from the starting point) with a pencil. Don't mark any other lines, however, as so much of the canvas is exposed. Stretch the canvas on the frame.

> ♥ *Fill in the blank canvas with diagonal tent, if you wish. These ornaments can also be put on one of the crocheted cords (page 57 – 58) and worn as a pendant.*

2. Thread both needles with your chosen fibers. Knot one end of both threads, and seal the other end of the metallic ribbon thread with a drop of *Stop Fraying* or nail polish. The thread will splay without this step, although that will not affect the stitching. Begin with a waste knot about 15 threads away from the center, and take a backstitch in the area that will be covered by your first stitching (Fig. 8.32). Since there is

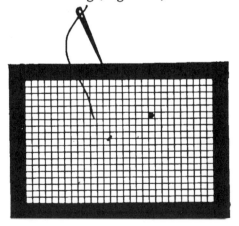

Fig. 8.32 *Start thread by knotting on top, then beginning several threads beyond the knot.*

> ♥ *These stitches are easy for beginning canvas embroiderers, undoubtedly because the novices have no pre-conceived prejudices about where the needle should come up and where it should go down. Follow the numbers, remembering to alternate the needles where indicated, and the designs will quickly appear on your canvas.*

almost no thread on the back of the canvas, you need this backstitch to anchor the working threads. Remember to always bring your working threads to the front in position for their next stitches. On Unit One on the chart on page 140 this would mean that you bring the floss up at 1, down, and to the front at 3. The metallic will come up at 2, down, and to the front at 5.

Continue stitching in this manner, always coming up on the odd numbers and down on the even ones. Whenever possible, end off the threads with two tiny backstitches in an area that will be covered by stitching. And leave a 3/8" (1cm) tail when you cut the thread on the back. If this isn't possible, find some stitches on the back into which you can fix the thread.

3. The charts (pages 140 – 141) are given for one quadrant of the design. Work the center stitching in the upper right quadrant of your canvas, and turn the canvas to the right for the next quadrant. Work all four areas. Leaving eight blank threads, find the center hole of the second side, and work the design in the same manner as before.

4. Remove the canvas from the frame and trim, leaving ten blank threads all around. Fold four threads to the back, leaving two threads on the fold for the binding stitch. Clip out a 3 x 3 thread square at each corner to relieve the bulk. Work the one row of tent through *both* layers of the canvas, except at the side where the ornaments are joined. Here, you will work only through one layer.

5. Begin the binding stitch (a long-legged cross worked by beginning and continuing with a repeat of *ahead four, back two** [repeating between the * and **]) at the

joined edge of the ornament. Work two sides. See chart on page 139.

When you reach the second corner, take one overhand stitch. Then pull out about 3" (7.5cm) of your thread, loop it, and secure with another overhand stitch (hanging loop). Continue to the next corner. Fold the piece of quilt batt in half, and slip inside the ornament.

If you want to stuff the ornament as well, do so now between the layers of batt. Complete the last side. Make a small tassel (about twenty-five wraps over a 3" [7.5cm] piece of cardboard), and stitch it to the corner opposite the hanging loop.

Hang these on the tree with an ornament hanger slipped through the loop. The ribbon is too fragile to slip on and off the branches.

Variations:

A. If you switch the positions of the metallic ribbon and the floss, the designs will look completely different. Substitute *Watercolours* or over-dyed fibers for the floss to obtain a blurred effect. If you aren't into glitz, use the 1/16" (1.5mm) ribbon thread instead of the metallic ribbon.

If you're basically a machine stitcher, and have spools and spools of metallic thread, simply take about five or six strands, thread them through your tapestry needle, and substitute for the metallic ribbon.

Use a fine sparkly knitting thread instead of the metallic ribbon; stitch a small sample to be sure it doesn't shred going through the canvas. Candlelight or a #8 Balger braid are also good substitutes.

B. Work these on 13-mesh canvas with appropriately sized threads for a 3" (7.5cm) ornament or on 10-mesh for a 4" (10cm) ornament. However, we think they're more effective on 18-mesh.

Use the inside squares marked with an asterisk (*) on the ornament charts on pages 140 – 141 (one-quarter shown) as quilt blocks to interpret a quilt on canvas.

Battenberg Star Ornament

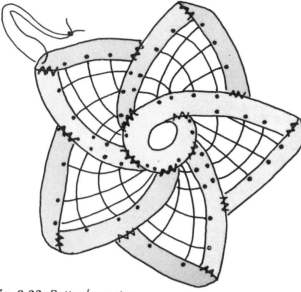

Fig. 8.33 *Battenberg star*

There is a different Battenberg lace project in each book in the *Know Your Sewing Machine* series (see "Bibliography"), any of which can be used as an ornament. We decided to include a new one in this book—a Christmas star.

There are varieties of white, off-white, gold, and silver Battenberg tapes from which to choose. The tape is available by mail order (see "Sources of Supplies") and from some needlework shops.

You Will Need:

Water-soluble stabilizer
Spring hoop
Vanishing marker
Gold Battenberg tape
Gold metallic thread on top and bobbin
Wash-away basting thread
Sewing machine
#70 (#10) sewing machine needle
Glue stick
White permanent marker
Ornament hanger

1. Begin by drawing the design (Fig. 8.33) on a piece of water-soluble stabilizer. Add another piece of stabilizer underneath, and baste the gold tape in place on the pattern.

2. Place a layer of stabilizer on top of the tape, and clip all the layers into the spring hoop you've chosen. Draw in the stitching lines with the white permanent marker.

3. Set your machine for free-machine embroidery: Feed dogs down or covered, presser foot off; or, use a darning or free-machine embroidery foot. With a straight stitch, sew in one of the grid lines. Anchor by stitching into the tape, then return to the other side. Go back and with a narrow zigzag cover the previous stitches. Continue in this manner until all the lines are filled in.

4. Take the stabilizer out of the hoop, and cut around the star to remove most of the stabilizer. Place the star on a clean dish towel, folding part of the towel over it to cover. Press with an iron until the star is almost dry. Remove it, and let dry completely.

Add a gold cord to one point for hanging on the Christmas tree.

The Year of the Seminole Ornament

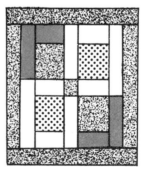
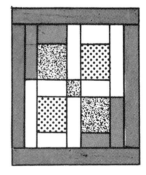

Fig. 8.34 *Seminole ornament examples*

The Seminole Indians of Florida were the pioneers of the quick-piecing methods we use today. Their ingenuity in creating intricate bands of brightly colored patchwork is all the more impressive when we consider that they did it with hand-turned sewing machines and without graph paper, rotary cutters, or heavy plastic rulers clearly marked in 1/8" increments.

Seminole patchwork is simple, but you need to be deadly accurate in your measurements so each little block lines up and creates a crisp design. The good news is that with relatively few strips, you can stitch lots of complicated ornaments in an evening—with time left for stuffing.

Seminole patchwork is traditionally done of cotton broadcloth in solid colors. An opulent, lavish look can be achieved by using silk broadcloth or noil with a touch of tissue lamé, perhaps as color D. If you back the lamé with a woven cotton fusible interfacing, it behaves. The interfacing comes in black or white, and will alter the original color—use both within a given project, and create two colors of lamé from one. The

> ♥ *Fabric is cut into strips, sewn into bands, and cut into segments. If you do the surrounds with Color* D, *you will "lose" this element for a variation of the original design. If the surrounds are made of Color* A, *another design emerges.*

following materials, plus an evening of cutting and sewing and more cutting and sewing and then stuffing, will yield fourteen ornaments—seven with one color backing and surround and seven with another. Not a bad output, considering one evening of handsewing produced only one of the cathedral window ornaments.

You Will Need:

8-1/2" x 45" (22cm x 1.1m) Fabric *A*
11" x 45" (28cm x 1.1m) Fabric *B*
10" x 45" (25.5cm x 1.1m) Fabric *C*
3" x 45" (7.5cm x 1.1m) Fabric *D*
Stuffing
Sewing machine
Rotary cutter, mat, and *Omnigrid* ruler
Hanger cords
1/4" (6mm) seam allowance is included throughout

1. The piecing instructions are on page 144. Cut the strips across the width of the fabric, using the rotary cutter and *Omnigrid* ruler.

Fabric *A*
2-1/2" (6.5cm)
two 1" (2.5cm)
two 2" (5cm)

Fabric *B*
1-1/2" (4cm)
1" (2.5cm)
three 1" (2.5cm)
5-1/2" (14cm)

Fabric *C*
1-1/2" (4cm)
three 1" (2.5cm)
5-1/2" (14cm)

Fabric *D*
2" (5cm)
1" (2.5cm)

2. Sew the strips into the bands described below, setting aside the unused strips for later. Press all the seams in the same direction.

Band One
2" (5cm) *D*
2-1/2"(6.5cm) *A*

Band Two
1" (2.5cm) *D*
1-1/2" (4cm) *C*
1" (2.5cm) *A*
1-1/2" (4cm) *B*
1" (2.5cm) *A*

Band Three
2" (5cm) *A*
1" (2.5cm) *B*
2" (5cm) *A*

3. Then cut the bands into segments.
Band One Segments
Twenty-eight 1" (2.5cm)

Band Two Segments
Twenty-eight 1-1/2" (4cm)

Band Three Segments
Fourteen 1" (2.5cm)

4. Begin sewing the segments into the motifs as shown on page 144. Sew all the first and second segments together in 1/4" (6mm) seams, creating pattern unit *M*. Take half of these, and join them to the third segments, creating pattern unit *N*. Reverse the remaining pattern unit *M*s and sew to the other side of *N*. Press all the seams in the same direction. You now have fourteen motifs.

5. Cut fourteen 4" (10cm) segments and fourteen 5-1/2" (14cm) segments from the remaining 1" (2.5cm) strips of fabric *B*. Stitch the 4" (10cm) segments with 1/4" (6mm) seam allowance on opposite sides of the motifs. Stitch the 5-1/2" (14cm) segments on the remaining two sides. Repeat this step with the rest of the fabric *C* strips and the other seven motifs. You now have fourteen ornament fronts.

6. Cut seven 5-1/2" (14cm) squares from each of the 5-1/2" (14cm) strips of fabrics *B* and *C*. Match the color of the backing square to the surround of the motif and place it on the motif with right sides together. Stitch around in a 1/4" (6mm) seam, leaving a small opening for turning along one side. Turn and stuff. Sew a hanging cord in one corner. You may add a small tassel, if you wish.

Variations:

A. Double the measurements of the strips and segments, and you will have seven 10" (25.5cm) square Seminole potholders.

B. Join four 5-1/2" (14cm) motifs together before adding the surrounds, and you have a purse front.

C. Omit the hanging cord, and you have a pincushion.

D. Omit the surrounds and stuff with shot, rice, or beans and you have pattern weights or bean bags.

From Angel to Zebra Ornaments

Fig. 8.35 Santa Claus

Fig. 8.36 Mrs. Santa Claus

Fig. 8.37 Elf

While almost every project in this book is done with squares, rectangles, circles, or triangles, the following ornament is made with an organic shape. This shape can make all sorts of different characters—from angels to elves, from Santas to reindeer, from cats to dogs, from elephants to zebras. Make the shape from different fabrics, and add the appropriate ears, horns, whiskers, beards, dresses, wings—whatever is needed to create the desired character. Add painted and embroidered faces, depending on how much time you have. Make beards of lace, eyelet, or yarn. Use wings of feathers and felt, purchased crocheted doilies, wide lace, fabric, and lamé. Mixtures of yarn with a strand or two of glitz makes great hair. Add blush to the cheeks—either tinted glitter or some of your own makeup. Make a zillion the same or everyone different—a proven best seller—as Joe Wilson the Cajun cook, would say, "I gar-an-tee it!"

You Will Need

(to make an angel):

Piece of ecru fleece at least 12" x 5" (30.5cm x 12.5cm) for body
Thread to match
4" (10cm) piece of 1" (2.5cm) eyelet with beading
8" (20.5cm) piece of 12" (30.5cm) ribbon
12" (30.5cm) hanging cord
Stuffing
4" (10cm) round crocheted doily for wings
Scraps of mohair-type, glitz, and fingering yarns
16–20" (40.5cm–51cm) piece of heavy covered floral wire for fringe fork
Aleene's *Stop Fraying*

1. Enlarge and trace the pattern (Fig. 8.38).

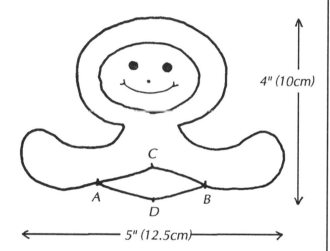

Fig. 8.38 *Angel pattern showing face and gusset placement*

Cut it out of poster board. **No seam allowance is included.** Place the pattern on the wrong side of your fabric, and trace around it with a pencil. This will be your seam line. **Do not cut out.**

Place the traced fabric on top of another piece of body fabric, right sides together. Pin enough to avoid slipping.

2. Stitch around the doll on the traced line with small stitches (18 or more to the inch). Cut out 1/8" (3mm) away from the stitching. Cut a slit in the back (where the wings will be attached). Turn and stuff firmly. Close the opening with a tiny whip stitch.

3. Embroider the eyes, mouth, and nose. (You may also paint or draw on these de-

tails, or substitute beads, sequins or buttons for them.)

4. Make the yarn fringe for the hair as follows:

a. Take several different yarns and threads for the hair and find the ends. To keep the yarns from tangling and running all over the floor, place them in a ziplock bag with the ends extending. Close, leaving a small opening for the yarn to feed through.

b. Get a glass or cup with a diameter around 3" (7.5cm). Place the center of the floral wire at the outside back of the glass, and bend it into a hairpin shape. Bend the rounded end up about 3/4" (2cm) as shown in Figure 8.39. This is a tiny fringe fork.

c. Wrap the yarn around and around the fork for several inches, starting at the open end and coming toward the bent end. **Do not cut out the yarn.** Place the hook under the presser foot on your sewing machine with the bent end toward you. Using a small straight stitch (18 or so to the inch), stitch down the center of the yarn (Fig. 8.39). When you have sewn through most

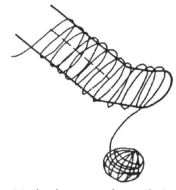

Fig. 8.39 *Stitched yarn on fringe fork*

of the yarn on the pin, ease the rounded edge toward you, and continue winding yarn. Stitch and wind until you have a piece about 10" to 12" (25.5cm to 30.5cm) long. Cut the yarn and remove the fringe fork.

d. Secure this fringe to the head, either with small tacking stitches or glue, twisting the yarn in a spiral direction around the stitching to avoid the flat look. If some areas look sparse when you're finished, cut off a piece of the fringe and stitch or glue it in. You may cut the loops, if you wish, after the hair is on the doll.

5. Place the eyelet around the neck. Turn under 1/8" (3mm) on one edge, then lap and whip stitch together at the back. Run ribbon through the beading on the eyelet, beginning and ending at center front. Tie in bow, and trim ends.

6. Take a large tuck in the center of the doily to form the wings, and stitch in place at back.

7. Thread the hanger cord into a large-eyed needle, and pull through the top of the head, going from front to back and taking at least 1/4" (6mm) onto the needle. Tie a square knot in the cord, and dot with *Stop Fraying.*

Variations:

A. Mrs. Santa: Cut out figure form from red fleece. Cut slit for turning under where the face will go. Enlarge and cut out face (Fig. 8.40) from pink felt and glue in place as shown on pattern (this covers the slit). Cut two 1/2" (1.5cm) strips of *Pellon Fleece* (or anything that looks like fur) long enough to go around the legs and glue in place. White

Fig. 8.40 Enlarge oval shape for face pattern.

lace can be used for the "dress" and white yarns for the hair.

B. Santa: Cut out a face from pink felt, trimming off the bottom edge of the face. A scrap of 1/2" (1.5cm) wide eyelet is used for the beard and glued to the back of the bottom of the felt face. Glue the face in place. Glue a small red pom pom in place for the nose. Cut out a hat (Fig. 8.41A) from the same fabric,

4" (10cm)

1/4 Circle

Fig. 8.41A. Pattern for cone hat

and sew the seam. Glue in place on the head. Cut a piece of fleece, and fit around the base of the hat all around the head. Glue a tiny white pom pom in place at the top. Use glue to arrange the folds in the hat. Glue fleece around the "legs," and a piece of black ribbon around the neck. Attach hanging cord.

C. Elf: Cut out figure from green cotton knit. Cut slit on the head under the hair area. When stuffing the elf, use a needle and thread to form the ears at the side of the head.

Hair is made from "eyelash" yarn tacked in place, and tiny jingle bells are added to the feet. Tie a red ribbon around the neck; make a green cap like Santa's and glue a red pom pom in place. Your elf could have a light green pom pom nose, if desired.

D. Omit the hanger cords and use as ornaments on a wreath. Use as a stocking stuffer or small toy. (**No** buttons, jingle bells, or any other attachments for babies or small children—though you may put the bells or music boxes inside.) String several or more together for a mantle swag or a baby's crib toy.

E. Take the pattern to your local copier, and have it reduced to pin-size or have it blown up several times to make a larger toy. If you do this, draw a diamond-shaped gusset (Fig. 8.41B). The gusset is twice as long (*A* to *B*)

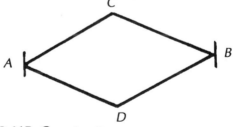

Fig. 8.41B. Gusset pattern

as it is high (*C* to *D*). Add seam allowance. Using your pattern, cut out the gusset, and place between the points under the ornaments (Fig. 8.38). Stitch in place.

F. Black and white striped fabric will make zebras; gray velour or fleece suggests elephants or mice. When making animals with ears or horns (added after stuffing), leave open at the bottom for turning and stuffing. Bond two layers of felt or *Ultrasuede* together before cutting out horns.

Unless making a floppy-eared dog or rabbit, lightly stuff the ears before gluing or stitching in place. Do give whiskers to cats, rabbits, mice, and dogs; long tails and big round ears to monkeys; little pointy ears to pigs; and a single horn for a unicorn—all details available at your local craft store. Have several different sizes of the pattern made at your copier's so you can have Mama, Daddy, and Baby. Most of all, enjoy creating creatures of all kinds—real and imaginary.

> ♥ As Dr. Seuss says, "Think left and think right and think low and think high. Oh, the Thinks you can think up if only you try."

Production:

Using 1/4 to 1/2 yd (23cm to 46cm) of fabric, trace as many body patterns as possible, always leaving two seam allowances between each. Stitch all the ornaments at one time. Make several yards of the yarn fringe for the hair. Rent a favorite movie, sit down, and cut out the dolls one at a time or all at once—it's up to you. Turn, stuff, and toss in a box. Then have everyone finish these at their leisure. Suggest doing the face as soon as the stuffing is finished, since the face establishes the personality. We try to keep a box of these around at Christmas time so we can whip out a quick gift if we need it.

Stitched Lace and Wire Ornaments

Fig. 8.42 Wire ornaments

These ornaments are the result of two visits—one to an after-Christmas sale at a large discount store in January of 1989, and the other to Jane's aunt. These white wire ornaments are perfect frames for hand or machine embroidery.

Aunt Ella showed us one of her latest projects, a gold cross stitched on plastic canvas with most of the canvas exposed. The canvas didn't look like any we'd ever seen; it twinkled as though it were lit. She explained that a sheet of crushed cellophane was sandwiched between the two layers. We had iridescent plastic film on hand and had done some experiments with it: Stitching on it and throwing it in the washing machine. The plastic film didn't dissolve in water; it emerged wrinkled, but whole. Even though the film can be stretched in a frame and stitched without any support, we found it easier to control the stitching when we used water-soluble stabilizer.

Chances are you may not find "empty" wire ornaments, but you can always shape ones out of 16-gauge stem wire (covered with white or green tape) that's available wherever silk flowers are sold. Bend the wire around various jars, dowels, or anything that gives the desired shape. Fine-tune and twist to secure with long-nosed pliers, and clip the ends with wire cutters (Fig. 8.43).

Fig. 8.43 Wire shaped for ornaments

If using "bare" wire, we do a close zigzag stitch over all the wire to completely cover it (step 2 below). These forms, or anything that has open areas can also be used for hand-made needle lace (see "Bibliography").

You Will Need:

Wire ornaments or 16-gauge stem wire
Iridescent plastic wrapping film
Water-soluble stabilizer
Opalescent machine-embroidery thread
Natesh or *Sulky* multicolored rayon
    embroidery thread
4" (10cm) spring machine-embroidery
    frame
Beads, sequins, bits of lace, pearls-by-the-
    yard
#14 sewing machine needle
White pen (optional)

1. Cut a 5" x 10" (12.5cm x 25.5cm) piece of stabilizer. Then cut a 6" (15cm) square of the film, crush it thoroughly with your hands, and smooth it out. Fold the stabilizer in half, and sandwich the wire shape and the film between the two halves. Add any additional embellishments between the layers. Then stretch in the frame.

2. Wind the opalescent thread on the bobbin, and thread the upper machine with the rayon. Lower the upper tension about 1-1/2 to 2 numbers. Set your machine for darning and remove the presser foot. Embroider the interior with straight and/or zigzag stitches, making sure that any embellishments are firmly attached to the film. Be careful not to hit the wire; it will break your needle. If you want to stitch definite patterns, such as florals, draw them on the stabilizer or film with a white pen. When you have completed the fill-in, set your machine for a wide zigzag and stitch closely. Enclose the wire in satin stitches, and at the same time attach the plastic wrapping film all around the edge.

3. Remove from the frame, and trim the excess stabilizer and film right next to the stitching all the way around. Take the ornament to the sink and carefully dissolve all of the stabilizer. If you can't wait for the ornament to dry naturally (about an hour unless your thread is packed extremely tight), dry it with a blow dryer.

Variations:

A. Form the ornaments out of green wire and embroider them with gold metallic thread on both the upper and bobbin areas. Add bits of gold lamé as described below.

B. Use two layers of the film, and trap sequins or beads by stitching all around them.

Gold Lamé Star Ornaments

Fig. 8.44 *Gold lamé star*

Water-soluble stabilizer has revolutionized machine embroidery. A plastic sheet that dissolves in water, water-soluble stabilizer is stitched on as if it were fabric, which enables you to change directions when embroidering "in space." After the plastic is rinsed under water, the threads remain.

The following idea is an easy "get acquainted with water-soluble stabilizer" project as well as a beautiful Christmas ornament. Cover your Christmas tree with lamé stars of all sizes.

You Will Need:

Water-soluble stabilizer
Spring hoop
White opaque marker
Scraps of gold lamé
Gold metallic machine-embroidery thread
Ornament hangers

1. To make the star, you need a double layer of water-soluble stabilizer and a spring hoop large enough to fit in a star or stars. Before you snap the stabilizer into the hoop, draw stars on the bottom layer of stabilizer (use a white opaque marker). Scatter tiny scraps of gold lamé on this layer inside the outline (leave open spaces—they add to the beauty). Cover with another piece of stabilizer. Slip this sandwich of two layers of stabilizer and a middle layer of gold lamé into your spring hoop.

2. Thread your machine with metallic gold thread on top and on the bobbin. Dip the needle down to bring up the bobbin thread, and hold both top and bobbin threads to one side. Lower or cover the feed dogs and loosen the top tension a hair.

First, stitch all around the star on your marker line. Clip the thread ends. Stitch lines back and forth and from one side to another (making some short, others long), and cut across the diagonal with some passes. Be careful not to make too many lines, but try to stitch through as many scraps as possible so it all holds together. Keep stitching out to the outline stitches to anchor the threads. Add a couple of circles of stitches at one point of the star for hanging, or poke a hanger through the stitches when you hang it on the tree.

3. Finishing: Cut all around the star, removing as much stabilizer as possible. Clean up the edges by cutting off any fabric or thread that extends beyond the outline. Hold the star under the faucet and remove most of the stabilizer. Leave a bit of goo to act as a stiffening agent. Place the star on a piece of fabric (we used a dishcloth), and pull it carefully into shape. Cover with another cloth, and press with an iron. Remove before it dries completely or it will stick to the dishcloth. Lift from the cloth, and let it dry completely on a countertop.

Variations:

A. Stitch tiny stars in gold or silver (or combine colors) for Christmas earrings. Slip them on to kidney wire findings (Fig. 6.9).

B. Add a layer of crushed mylar iridescent film between the layers of water-soluble stabilizer, and proceed as above.

Christmas Tree Skirt

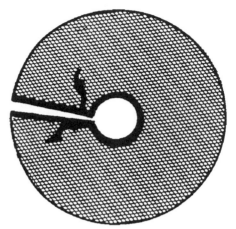

Fig. 8.45 *Christmas tree skirt*

What do you put at the bottom of your Christmas tree to hide the stand? A sheet perhaps, or do you purchase one of those flimsy cotton skirts they sell at the grocery store around Christmas? Have we got a solution for you!

Take yourself down to your discount warehouse, discount store, factory outlet, thrift shop—anywhere that might have round tablecloths for sale! Yes, *round* tablecloths. Buy whatever size you want; some of our friends have skirts that are 60" (1.5m) round. We found the handmade lace cloth we used at a Wal-Mart for less than $10.

You can paint, print, or stencil Christmas designs around the skirt; bond on purchased sequin Christmas appliqués; purchase fabric of Christmas cutouts and bond them to the skirt; put batt behind and quilt; add lace, beads, rick-rack, decorative machine stitching—whatever. We could go on and on. We backed this one with felt because the lace is fragile and we wanted another color behind to show off the lace. Follow the directions below for cutting and binding the back opening so you can slip your tablecloth skirt around the tree.

You Will Need:

36" (.9m) round tablecloth (size is optional)
1-1/4 yd (1.1m) felt
Glue gun
Thread to match lace cloth and bias tape
1 pkg double-fold bias tape to match cloth or felt
Scissors
Vanishing marker

1. Cut a 42" (1m) diameter circle out of the felt. (You may cut scallops by using a glass, cup, or small plate if your lace cloth warrants such a trim.) If your cloth is a different size, buy enough felt to cut a circle, giving you at least a 3" (7.5cm) border of felt showing beyond the lace.

2. Pin the cloth to the felt and stitch it securely in place with narrow zigzag machine stitching. The lace will dictate where this stitching will go to be as unobtrusive as possible.

3. Find a glass, cup, or bowl with about a 3-1/2" (9cm) diameter. Place it on the center of the right side (lace) of the skirt, and draw around with the vanishing marker. Draw a line from the bottom to the inner circle, finding a logical place to cut the tablecloth. **Do not cut.**

4. Open out one side of the bias tape, and starting at the border of the skirt, pin the cut edge of the tape right at the drawn line. Stitch it into position as far as the inner circle. Cut the tape. Repeat for the other side of the line. Cut up the drawn line. Turn the bias tape to the back, and stitch in place.

5. Machine straight stitch (staystitch) on the drawn circular line. Cut out the circle a scant 1/4" (6mm) beyond the staystitching. Cut a piece of bias tape long enough to go around your opening, plus an additional 24" (61cm). Measure 12" (30.5cm) from one end of the tape, and begin applying the bias as before around the opening. Turn to the back. Begin your stitching at one end of the tape, continue around the opening, and stitch to the other end. Tie an overhand knot at each end of the tape.

> ♥ *Surprise, surprise—ties to hold the skirt in place! (We really used ties so we wouldn't have to miter the corners where the back opening joined the circle—but don't tell anybody.)*

You'll find a most unusual tree-top angel under the variations of the angel pin on page 62. We've now given you directions for what you need to complete your Christmas tree from top to bottom, with everything in between. All that remains for us to do is to wish a "Merry Christmas to all and to all a good night."

Chapter 9

Bazaars and Fundraisers

Projects:

- ♥ *Wreaths*
- ♥ *Display*
- ♥ *Displaying Small Items*

Congratulations! If you're reading this chapter, chances are you have either been appointed chairman of a bazaar, asked to head a committee at your organization's next fundraiser, or perhaps taken an auxiliary volunteer's job in the gift shop at your local hospital.

In this chapter we'll show you what to expect after you've assumed any of these jobs. Included are what committees you'll need; how to pick a date for a show; how to get publicity; how to display your wares; and what to do when the last item is purchased, the cleanup committee has done its job, and you all start planning for the next sale.

We've done it all—and enjoyed ourselves in every instance. It always seemed the best of all possible worlds that we would spend so much time doing what we loved best, searching out or designing interesting items that we'd be expected to sew, embroider, knit, or crochet.

Core Committee: After you've agreed to chair the next event, you must form a core committee to decide on the type of fundraiser (bazaar, boutique, fair—whatever) that is to be. Either the core committee or booth chairman prices the crafters' items for the bazaar. If the bazaar benefits a church or a club, crafters donate their time and wares (although the church or club will probably buy the materials).

Crafters price their own products if they pay a fee for their space at the bazaar and will realize the profit from the booth. Sometimes they must give a percentage of their profit to the bazaar, instead of a booth cost. Sometimes they do this in addition to the booth cost.

Time: The core committee chooses a date for the event—hopefully ten to twelve months hence. Perhaps your organization has a traditionally established time (the first weekend in May, Halloween, the first weekend in December, etc.). If not, you will need to consider the following: (1) The weather in your area will affect attendance—whether it's an indoor or an outdoor event. (2) Other organizations in your area may have yearly events that weekend. Plan yours at least a month away if at all possible. If there is any big yearly event in your general area (such as Houston's annual Quilt Festival or California's Marin County Needlework Show that will diminish your attendance, plan around it.

Many cities have annual listings of the bazaars, boutiques, and fundraisers within their area; smaller townships often have calendars that list the major events during the coming year. You will not only want to be sure your date is as clear as possible, but you'll also want to list your event.

Restrictions and Liabilities: Having picked a date, the next step will be for the core committee to find out what state, county, or city restrictions may exist.

Ask questions such as, "Can we hold a raffle?", "Is a Bingo booth allowed?", "Must we collect sales tax?," "Do we need any special permits?", "Are there any restrictions about serving or selling food?".

Also, find out about the extent of the liability you will be assuming in your state. (We're not trying to scare you, but it is better to know the answers to these questions going in, rather than being surprised with problems the day before an event.)

Committees: You will need the following committees: Site, Publicity, Treasurer/Cashier, Scheduling, Set-up and Take-Down, Cleanup, Raffle (if being held), Food (if being served), Baby-Sitting, Telephone, and Parking. You may need other committees such as Games and Prizes or White Elephant, depending on the type of fundraising event. You should also have an assistant chairman who, hopefully, will chair the event next year.

A special word is needed about the Treasurer/Cashier and her committee because it is of key importance. This committee is responsible for all the monies, paying the bills, reimbursing chairmen for their expenses, seeing that any necessary taxes are collected and paid, and developing the procedures for handling and guarding the money during the show itself. Since bazaars and boutiques are well-publicized events, they can be particular targets for unscrupulous individuals. The committee can check to make sure the cash boxes are not sitting out within reach of the general public during the event.

The monetary committee should have an adequate supply of change on hand, sales slips, and a cash box with key for each booth. The cash boxes (with adequate change) can be handed out each day before the doors are opened and collected at the end of each day, when the receipts are removed and counted.

Develop a questionnaire for the people in your organization to determine the various talents available. Don't be like the army and have the engineers cook, the cooks build bridges, and the computer experts dig trenches. We won't tell you that it's easy to get people to serve as chairmen of the various committees, but you do need those, too.

Involve as many people as possible. If you are doing a school benefit, a Sunday School fair, or anything raising funds for children's benefit, then involve the children. Meet with art teachers to see what things the children can make; perhaps they can design and paint the posters. (What's going to attract more attention, another slickly designed announcement stuck in store windows along with all the others, or a child's drawing?)

You might print the posters with the appropriate information, and let the children add the artwork. They'll have fun, feel involved, and the teachers will bless you (it takes countless tasks to keep the children interested and involved day after day). High school art students can silk-screen posters, T-shirts, and totes for your fair.

Site: Your site committee will need to decide where the event will be held. This is also an important question as regards to liability. A school fair on school grounds would probably be covered; yet, a school fair on private grounds might not be. Is there adequate parking available or will you have to make special arrangements? Is there access for the handicapped? Is there a kitchen available?

Are there any restrictions about what can and cannot be sold? Are there enough tables and chairs of the proper size available for the event, or will you have to rent them?

Does the place require a custodian of its own on the premises; and if so, who pays his fee? If there is no custodian present, who will know where everything is kept?

How much does the place charge, and what does the rent include? Is there a public address system available if you need it (for announcing winners or locating lost children)? Who is responsible and what kind of cleanup is expected? What kind of security will you need? (If it is more than a one-day event, you may need overnight protection.) How early can you have access to the facility, and how soon after the end of the event must you be out? If a wedding reception is planned for the evening of your day event, find another spot.

You probably don't realize it, but you're at least a quarter of the way home when you've answered all of the above questions. We're going to take you another quarter in three little words: *Pick a theme.*

Theme: Pick a theme and subsequent decisions will be made within narrow limits. For example, choose a geographical location, like the Mediterranean. Because we enjoy the sound of alliteration (the use of the same consonant or vowel at the beginning of each or most words), we'd suggest you name your event the "Mediterranean Market."

If your boutique is a Christmas one, you can have a Nutcracker theme with the booths named for the various characters, a nutcracker on the tickets and posters, etc.

If you're responsible for a church bazaar, choose a story in the Bible as your theme. Other suggested themes are: musical (New Orleans' jazz, early rock and roll, Country Western, or Broadway musicals), literary (poetry or poets, novels, or authors), color or colors (the Black and White Bazaar), and time (1920s, 1930s, 1940s, etc.).

Consider a "Turn of the Century" bazaar, either looking back to 1890-1900, or forward to the twenty-first century. If your event is to benefit a school, run a contest among the students to select a theme or to develop an image to use with the theme you've chosen.

Art supply stores and large bookstores have graphic art departments where you will find many "clip-art" booklets on various themes. Purchase one that relates to yours. Have the appropriate committee prepare the tickets and posters, and plan the decorations and publicity using some of the images.

Young Helpers: Perhaps your fundraiser has nothing to do with children, but you have a swarm of your own you need to entertain over endless summer months, rainy days, school vacations. Get them involved; put them to work. Children are wonderful to work with; they're full of fresh ideas and unique approaches. Plus, they'll be much more understanding of your need to work on your items if they feel involved.

If children really can't help with what you're doing, then let them help free up your time. Young people don't mind doing dishes, helping with dinner, or whatever, if they know it has a purpose. (Also, paying children a salary or per-task compensation can turn even the most recalcitrant into a willing worker.) We remember when we were children how much we wanted to be included in what was going on, and how much we hated being told to run along and play while the grownups got on with whatever. Today we love to hear our adult children reminisce about our crafting days in the studio and about helping in various booths at assorted fairs.

You can also give children a wonderful sense of their own usefulness when items they've made are sold to make money for their school or church. They'll be a lot more help in cleaning up if they've been a part of making the mess in the first place. And what grandparent could possibly fail to buy the special towel that Johnny printed or the tote bag with the pocket design that Katie drew? Sure, you probably could do it better and faster, but what's the message you want to give your children? Ours was that we chose to use our talents to their benefit, that we could do what we loved to do best of all, that we could all have fun, and that the by-product was money for their library, playground, field-trip fund, or whatever. What might have looked like unselfishness to some was pure selfishness on our part.

Publicity: Most of the signs you need can be done on various desktop computer programs from *Print Shop* to *First Publisher,* from *Printmaster* to *MacPaint.* Find the computer-literate among your membership and put them to work. If anyone has a laser printer as well (or if your school or organization has one), your signs will be everything you could want. We print ours on an inexpensive dot matrix printer and use a copier to copy them to card stock, cover stock, or Bristol board. If anyone has a labels program, he or she can design and print the camera-ready work for tickets and raffles. All you will need is to have them printed or copied (whichever is cheaper), and to cut them on someone's paper cutter.

> ♥ *If you want tickets perforated for free, such as between the body of a raffle ticket and the name and address, you simply run them through your sewing machine without any thread.*

Organization: You will need to hold committee meetings, but keep them to the barest minimum. Have chairmen report directly to you on a bi-weekly basis for the first few months, then weekly as you near the event. When you do have meetings, draw up an agenda and stick to it. If a chairman can't attend, have him or her send you a written report.

Set up a time path and checklist, noting the dates by which certain decisions will be made: Site will be chosen by ___, newspaper notices go out by ___, food to be ordered on ___, ticket sales begin on ___, etc. The more organized you are, the fewer headaches you'll have, and the fewer surprises with which you will have to deal.

Probably one of the biggest fears when running a bazaar is that there won't be enough merchandise for sale. One way to overcome this is to hold "Making Days," when everyone gathers and works together to produce in an afternoon what would take several weeks if working alone. Let's take a look at the following project to see how this can be accomplished.

Set a day and time for a wreath-making afternoon. We don't know if this is a part of the Peter Principle or Murphy's Law, but we do know that small groups produce more than large ones. We'd suggest six to eight people, and no more than ten.

Sample wreaths are made to determine the supplies needed. Then one or two people purchase the wreaths, ribbon, embellishments, and bags of glue sticks for glue guns. Other workers are given a list of what they need to bring (glue guns, extension cords, rulers, and scissors).

The day of the workshop, stations are set up for each step. With the wreaths that follow, two people work together on the first step: One winding the ribbon and another wielding the glue gun. Other steps can be divided and assigned as you wish.

Wreaths

Fig. 9.1 *Sewing wreath*

Fig. 9.2 *Scout wreath*

Fig. 9.3 *Cheerleader wreath*

Small wreaths are often sold in craft stores at give-away prices. When you can find them on sale, buy them! They are not only best-sellers at bazaars, but they can be made and sold as fundraisers at schools, churches—wherever. Since generic wreaths sell so well, imagine what something more original will do. Imagine making wreaths for golfers, tennis buffs, and new babies, or for holidays, birthdays, or graduations. Choose a wreath committee, have everyone don thinking caps, and dream up wreath ideas.

> ♥ *Den Mothers, have the boys and girls make them to display their Cub, Webelo, Brownie, Bluebird, Girl Scout, or Boy Scout pins and awards.*

Find the best buys for the embellishments you'll glue or hang on the wreaths. Party stores are gold mines; discount stores, at the least, silver. Fabric chains are ideal for inexpensive ribbons, lace, and buttons. Watch for sales at your favorite craft stores. And do hit all the after-Christmas sales any place and everywhere that carry ornaments, cards, or gift wrappings. Scour thrift stores and find mail-order sources for large quantities.

We've made three wreaths to get you started. One is for sewing friends, another for den mothers, and the third for cheerleaders and football fans.

You Will Need:

4" (10cm) grapevine wreaths
4" (10cm) piece of wire to hang wreath
Decorations for your chosen theme
Glue gun

1. Sewing Wreath: We found all the sewing implements in an inexpensive sewing kit purchased at a discount store. Everything is attached with a glue gun. Wrap the wreath in wide rick-rack and glue the ends down. Wrap the paper tape measure, clip off, and reserve the rest for later. Glue down the ends of that, too. With the glue gun, attach the small scissors, emery strawberry with color-ful glass-head pins, needle threaders, and buttons. String tiny spools of thread onto cord, and drip glue into the center of the spools to hold them in place. Loop the remainder of the tape measure, and glue to the wreath.

Make a bow of lace, and glue on top of the loops of the tape measure. Pull a colorful cord through the holes of a large button, knot it, and glue the button down in the center of the lace bow.

2. Scout Wreath: The Cub and Webelo's wreath is wrapped with a 3"-wide (7.5cm) piece of Webelo's scarf cut on the bias (you can get several wreaths out of one scarf). As you wind it around the wreath, tuck the raw edges underneath, and glue down the join ends at the top of the wreath.

Next, get out badges and pins, take off the clasps, and squirt a glob of glue on the back of each before embedding it into the wreath (some of the pin will go through the scarf wrapping, too).

At the top of the wreath, glue a slightly flattened scarf slide. Cut lengths of grosgrain ribbons in green, red, blue, and yellow to match the scarf and loop them in the middle, pulling the loops through the slide. These are glued inside the scarf slide (if you have too many pins for the wreath, you can also pin them to the ribbons).

3. Cheer Leader Wreath: You need acetate ribbon, 1/2" (1.5cm) wide, in the school colors. Glue them together at the front where the mum goes, and wind them around the wreath and back to the starting point, again gluing them in place. Then string purchased football ornaments around the wreath as you did the ribbon—except touch the ornaments with the hot glue to further hold them in place.

After cutting a circle with a diameter of 1-1/2" (4cm) out of poster board, cut twelve 3" (7.5cm) pieces of the maroon ribbon, and glue them around the edge of the poster board as shown in Figure 9.4. Cut several

Fig. 9.4 Make a pom pom

different short lengths (4" to 6" [10cm to 15cm]) of both ribbons, and glue them together on the poster board circle. Then glue a silk mum in place at the center of the circle. Using small gummed letters, put the year on the mum and the team name on one of the ribbons. Add a small megaphone. (Our local craft stores are full of football charms in all sizes.)

To personalize, and as a finishing touch, add a boyfriend's name and jersey number on one of the ribbons.

4. Finishing: At the top back of the wreath, slip the piece of wire under and around several of the vines. Twist the ends of the wire to make a hanging loop.

Let us add a few further thoughts on workshops. Begin a series of workshops with a simple project like the wreaths. Make a prototype or several of the product that will be assembled in the workshop. Gather everything needed for the item—down to the last, least thing. Either mark or cut out whatever will be sewn. When everyone arrives, set up an assembly line. If someone says there isn't anything he or she can do, let this person be a gofer who can go for coffee, thread, needles, run items between different workers—anything that helps the workers work. In just one afternoon you and everyone else will be amazed at what is accomplished. Build in as much success as possible to keep them all coming back.

You'll progress to the more difficult items, but by then everyone will have a lot of experience working together. And do let these be brainstorming sessions. As people are working, ideas will occur to them. Encourage them to share their ideas.

If there is any pre-work to be done on the next project, you can assign that now. You will need about 15% more projects if they are going home with people. This isn't a judgment or a condemnation. People's lives change everyday. A new grandchild is born and grandmother is needed elsewhere. Someone comes for a visit, children get sick, life happens. And while the project, the boutique, the commitment is important, people have to keep their priorities straight, and whether you like it or not, sick family members, new grandchildren, husbands, and children come first.

The big day has finally arrived: the culmination of all the plans. Everything has been gathered, purchased, and produced. Your next step is to set up the hall.

Display

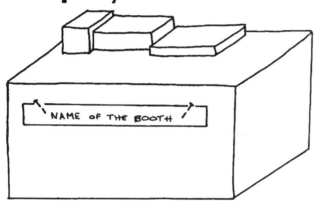

Fig. 9.5 *Table showing boxes on different display levels*

Have you ever walked into a large hall before it's been transformed into a bazaar, needlework show, or festival? Usually there are any number of bare tables spread around the room, and the whole area looks pretty dismal. Not to worry; we're here to show you how to transform your booth or show into a colorful, welcoming display that will attract customers like the proverbial moth to flame.

The first step will be to cover the tables. The color choice will depend on the products to be displayed and on the general theme of the show. If the show is a Christmas festival and most of the wares are red and green, we suggest black, navy, or a very dark black-green for table covers. We use dark colors all the time, as do most jewel merchants in their displays. Red and green would look festive, but the goods you're trying to sell would virtually disappear. It's the merchandise you want everyone to see,

not the tables. White or off-white table covers are boring and look like sheets even if they're not, and conversely, dark sheets look like table covers, not sheets (one of those psychological truths that probably earned someone a Ph.D.).

Most tables supplied by craft shows or used in schools and churches are 30" x 8' x 30" (76cm x 2.4m x 76cm), which means that a cloth 90" x 156" (2.3m x 3.9m) will cover the table and drape to the floor. (You can rent one for about $16 a night.)

Today, as this book is written, 90" (2.3m) wide sheeting is available at the fabric chain stores. We've found it on the sale table for as little as $2.50 a yard; the better grade runs around $5 a yard. This means that you can purchase 4-1/2 yards (4.1m) and have a cloth with 3" (7.5cm) hems at each end for anywhere from $12 to $23. Two uses, and you've saved $20 in rentals.

Linen factory stores are another source. If the tables are smaller, it's an easy task to fold the cloths to fit. We'd suggest that you or your group invest in table covers if you have booths from year to year at different shows. Not only will your booth appear more professional and your merchandise sparkle with a dark floor-length table cover, but the cover will hide all your additional merchandise, sales slips, purse, comfortable shoes, old clothes you wear when setting up and tearing down the booth, and the food and drink you're not allowed to have in the hall. And friends who visit the show always ask if they can leave their assorteds under your table.

The champion of champions when it comes to transporting goods and transforming tables into booths is Dawsie Crain, owner of Chaparral (a needlework shop in Houston, TX). Dawsie has a large old station wagon, and she knows where everything goes when she starts loading up. She also has any number of open file boxes with handles (cutouts in the sides). These are easily carried into and out of the car (but we don't put books in them). Many of the goods are put in large shallow open baskets in which they'll be displayed.

Dawsie has a small dolly that saves on trips to and from the car. We take "Wheels" (portable suitcase carrier) along, too, for transporting items such as thirty-five-pound sewing machines from the parking lot to the show site.

When we arrive at the show, we unload the file boxes, cover the tables, unpack the boxes, turn them upside down on the top of the table, and cover them with a cloth (purchase an additional 1-1/2 yards (1.4m) of the sheeting for this use). Voilà! We now have two levels on which to display. Customers can more easily see the various products, and the merchandise is more attractively displayed.

Dawsie's major contribution to the art of display, however, is possibly the most ingenious we've ever seen. Since she's not only smart but also very giving, she's allowing us to share the requirements for this rigging with all of you (Fig. 9.6).

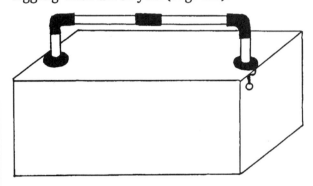

Fig. 9.6 Clamp pipe across table to hang crafts.

You Will Need:

Four 4' (1.2m) lengths of 2" (5cm) PVC pipe with threading on one end of two pieces
Two flanges
Two large C-clamps
Two bent fittings ("L")
One straight fitting
3/4 yd (69cm) sheeting

1. Screw the two threaded ends into the flanges, and clamp them to the table. Fit the other two pieces of pipe into the straight fitting. Put the bent fittings on the other ends of the long pipe you constructed, and fit these onto the pipes that are attached to the table.

2. Buy an additional 3/4 yd (69cm) of sheeting, and make the shirring to cover the pipe (Fig. 9.7). Now you have an area from which you may hang items that aren't too heavy:

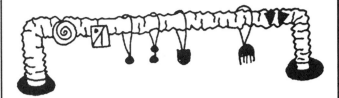

Fig. 9.7 Shirr fabric to cover pipe.

necklaces, some decorated T-shirts, Christmas ornaments, garlands, or small wreaths. Make several 8" (20.5cm), 10" (25.5cm), and 12" (30.5cm) circles of fishing line, and slip them on the long pipe before you place it in the bent fittings. You can use these to hang items at different lengths. Use safety pins to pin necklaces directly into the shirring, which cuts down on mysterious disappearances. Perhaps you've figured out the real beauty of this contraption: It breaks down into a small 4'-long (1.2m) bundle, which is easily carried in a car or shipped in a trunk or carried in a garment bag.

Displaying Small Items

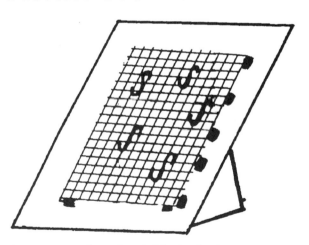

Fig. 9.8 Foamboard with black plastic canvas cover and hooks

Foamboard is another useful display tool, especially for necklaces and small items. It comes in many colors, including white and black (as does the plastic canvas), and is available at your local art supply and craft stores. These boards are inexpensive, quick to make, and are ideal for displaying the angel pins on page 60.

You Will Need:

- 20" x 30" (51cm x 76cm) sheet black foamboard
- 4 sheets 7-mesh black plastic canvas 10-1/2" x 13-1/2" (27cm x 34.5cm)
- 80 black pony beads
- Two scraps of white foamboard at least 8" x 10" (20.5cm x 25.5cm)
- *Household Goop*
- Wide black marker
- 4 pkgs (14 per) pin-on drapery hooks

1. Foamboard cuts easily with a craft knife. Don't try to make the cut in one move. Rather, stroke a score mark with a light touch three or four times until the cut is complete. When scoring, draw the knife through two times and check. Continue until the piece easily opens, but do not cut through the poster board on the back. If you're not thoroughly intimidated, take your knife in hand, place the board on your cutting mat, place your large ruler in place, and cut the black foamboard in half (two 15" x 20" pieces [38cm x 51cm]).

2. Cut 10 mesh off the long side of each piece of plastic canvas, reducing both to 9" x 13-1/2" (23cm x 34.5cm). Hold the plastic canvas in place on the left of the foamboard with a margin of board on three sides. With a pencil, mark four evenly spaced marks through the mesh across the top and five down the side. Mark across and down until the area is completely marked (Fig. 9.9). Repeat for the second piece of canvas.

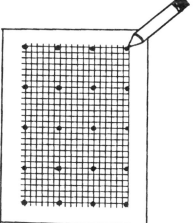

Fig. 9.9 *Marking board for pony bead spacers*

Put a glob of *Household Goop* at each mark, and place a black pony bead on top of the glue. When all the beads are glued in

place, put another glob of *Goop* on the top of each bead and place the pieces of canvas on top of these. Allow to dry at least overnight, preferably longer.

3. **Supports:** Cut the white foamboard into two rectangles, each measuring 8" x 10" (20.5cm x 25.5cm). With your pencil, draw a light line 3/4" (2cm) in on each long side. With your ruler and knife, cut this rectangle into two triangles by cutting between the pencil marks (Fig. 9.10). Make a mark 2"

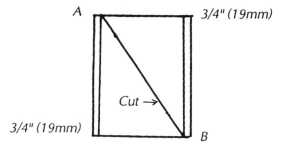

Fig. 9.10 *Score foamboard 3/4" (2cm) from each side; cut on diagonal from A to B.*

(5cm) up from the bottom on the slanted edge. Cut straight across from the 3/4" (2cm) line to the mark (Fig. 9.11). Score the board

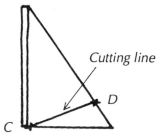

Fig. 9.11 *Make mark 2" (5cm) up from bottom of diagonal (D); cut on line CD and remove lower triangle.*

along the pencil mark on the side of one triangle. Turn the other triangle over, mark, and score a line 3/4" (2cm) from the edge. Glue in place 4" (10cm) in from both sides on the back.

4. **Finishing:** Take the wide black marker and color all around the white cut edge. (Okay, maybe you can skip this step, but it looks more professional done this way.)

5. Use the pin-on drapery hooks to hang your wares. Bend the hooks open slightly

Fig. 9.12 *Bend out drapery hooks at back to use in plastic canvas display boards.*

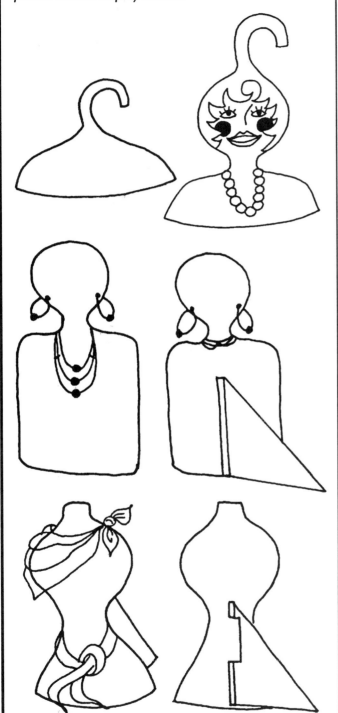

Fig. 9.13 *Cut foamboard into other shapes, and paint some of them for display purposes.*

(Fig. 9.12), and don't push the hooks all the way down onto the canvas. Only place them as far as necessary to hold them in place.

Foamboard can be cut to any shape with supports cut and scored as above. You may want torsos with a neck for displaying necklaces, head and shoulders shapes for the knitted caps, and hanger shapes on which to display garments (Figs. 9.13A–F).

The board comes in many colors, but you also can paint on any color or desired design. Construction of shelves for lightweight articles is easy and inexpensive.

Cover boxes with fabric by folding and pinning the fabric into place underneath the boxes (you can use the fabric later in a project). Turning the boxes right side up and using them to gain one or more layers, stack several at angles to each other (Fig. 9.14), gaining different heights. Make several small cloths to match or contrast with your large cloth and use to drape over the boxes.

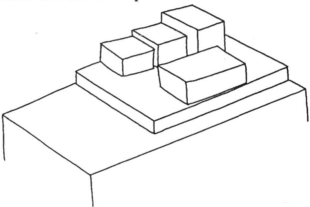

Fig. 9.14 *Boxes stacked at different heights can be covered with fabric for an attractive bazaar table.*

Keep your eyes open for inexpensive display material, perhaps wire baskets that can be turned upside down. You can place items on the top and hang others from the wire mesh with drapery or steel shower hooks.

Use small ladders (especially the wooden ones that you can paint) to display items like the small sewing bags on page 69 or the fanny packs on page 12. Make some bird pins (page 62), and place them on an interesting piece of driftwood. Pin the Victorian stockings on page 100 all around the edge of your table for a festive Christmas booth.

Borrow as many artificial trees as you need to display the Christmas ornaments. If yours is a Christmas fair, decorate the trees with tiny lights, hang on the ornaments you're selling, and place the trees around the hall. Many small trees will enhance the entire area.

Inexpensive fold-out corrugated cardboard display boards are available at office supply stores. Ours are 36" x 48" (.9m x 1.2m). We bonded fabric to them with *Wonder-Under* and use map or push pins to secure our wares.

Another possibility is to cover them with colored fishnet, and hang items on the net with the drapery hooks. These should be placed on the floor at the side of your booth, as they are too high to use on top of the table. Cut one in half (18" x 48" [46cm x 1.2m]) to use for tabletop display.

Deb Bergum from Glen Ellyn, IL, showed Jackie her interesting way to display post and french ear hook earrings. Here are her directions: Cut a piece of plastic window screen, 9" (23cm) x 24" (61cm), and bind the long edges with narrow, double-fold bias tape. After stitching down the binding, fold under the short sides 1-1/2" (4cm), and stitch across at the raw edge to make casings.

Cut two 1/2" (1.5cm) dowels into 9" (23cm) lengths, and sandpaper the ends to smooth them. Drill a hole at each end of one dowel, then slip the dowels into the casings.

To hang the display screen, cut a piece of heavy cord at least 12" (30.5cm), and slip the two cord ends into the dowel holes. Pull the cord down through the holes, and tie knots to keep the cord from slipping out. (Make many of these and sell them at your booth, too.)

Another screen idea: Buy two small window screens, wire the two frames together at the sides, and set up in a corner of your booth for a larger earring display.

Don't forget pegboards. Spray paint them ahead of time to make them more attractive. For the bazaar, set them up easel-style; they can show off everything from stationery to photographs. Or, wire two pegboards together through holes at the sides, and set in place on the table or floor, depending on their size.

The main idea is not to have a flat tabletop with items laid out row by row. Flat tops are boring, and they make it difficult to see the merchandise.

Look for ideas in magazines and shops. Keep decorations around the hall to a minimum, letting your booths tell the story. (This also keeps your costs down while speeding up cleanup.) Even if you don't have a holiday theme, consider using artificial Christmas trees to hang jewelry and small items or simply for their decorative value.

Whether you have a preview night or not is up to you and your audience. Selling hours can be as long or as short as you can staff. There is only one hard and fast rule we would caution you against breaking, unless you are intending to move out of the country when you complete your chairduties: *Do not discount* any item during or at the end of the show. We know all the reasons for doing this: "I never want to see this stuff again." "Any dollar is good, and isn't that the bottom line?" **No, No,** and **No.**

If you're unfortunate enough to chair a boutique where the policy is to discount everything at the end of the show, then no one wants to buy until then. You can't blame customers; why should they spend $5 if tomorrow at 8 PM they can buy the same object for $2? Consider those supporters who come the first day or opening night, and spend a great deal of money, paying the going price for each item. Don't you think they would be a little put out if they found out that their friend had paid only $2 for something that cost them $5—simply because the friend knew what would happen and they didn't? Wouldn't you be a little put out if the same happened to you? So place large signs around everywhere that inform, **"There will be no discounts at the end of the show."** Then take the leftover items and hold a garage sale several months later, adding the proceeds to the final count. All of us hate being taken advantage of by people standing around checking us out, intending to return at the end to buy at bargain prices. So please, don't insult the people who pay the prices you've set by letting others buy for less.

You don't want to hold a garage sale? You want the last day of the fair to be the **last day?** You never want to see another tote bag, another angel, another baby blanket as long as you live? That's even easier. Give away whatever's left to your nearest shelter for abused and battered wives and children, the area hospital, the county halfway or recovery homes, the community nursing home, or agencies that deal with the homeless. Check your Yellow Pages if you don't know of some place in the community that would benefit from the leftovers. In this scenario, everyone wins.

Cleanup is simply that. Muster all the bodies you can. Leave the place better than you found it, so next year's committee won't have to deal with fallout from this year's oversights. Have the cashier count and bank the money. Then go home and see if your family still recognizes you.

All that's left is the wrap-up done about a month hence, when all the bills have come in and been paid. Have each of your committee chairmen write a one-page report, including what they did, suppliers they used if applicable, what worked and what didn't, and recommendations for next year's committee. You, as chairman, write your report and then, bind all the reports together in a small folder labeled with the current year. Pass this folder on to the next chairman. Then prepare to hear, "Congratulations. You did a super job!"

Afterword

Writing this book has brought back many wonderful memories of days and months spent working on fundraisers of one kind or another—from the sale of pansy plants in high school through elementary school Christmas boutiques to celebrity baseball games. When people visit my home, they're always surprised not to find many hand-made items around. First, I'd need a mansion to house everything I've made through the years. Second, and more importantly, for me the joy has always been in the making and the giving.

Jane Warnick

I hope we've achieved our goals in writing this book—that you found appealing projects to make and new ideas to use so you'll feel confident about chairing the Christmas bazaar or making favors for a Christmas dinner. But, especially, I hope you'll make gifts instead of buying them—just for the joy of it.

Jackie Dodson

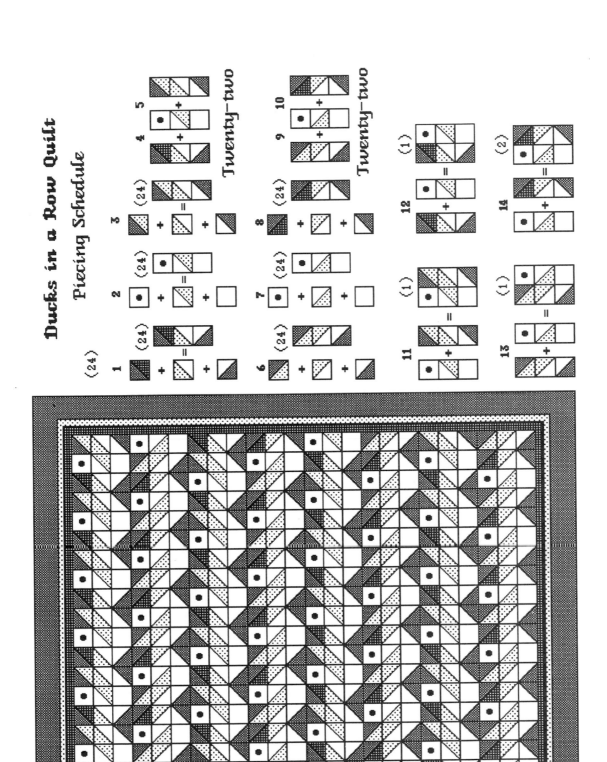

Machine-Knitted Fair Isle Hat

Repeat

Pattern Repeat

14 stitches × 15 rows

■ = Contrast yarn

I Promised You a Flower Garden

Pink
Light Pink
Green
Yellow
Light Green

Bands

A B C D

Piecing Schedule

Segments

1 2 3 4
1r 2r 3r 4r

1 + 2   3 + 4   1-2 + 3-4 = (16)
1r + 2r   3r + 4r   1r-2r + 3r-4r = (8)

Needlepoint Earring #1

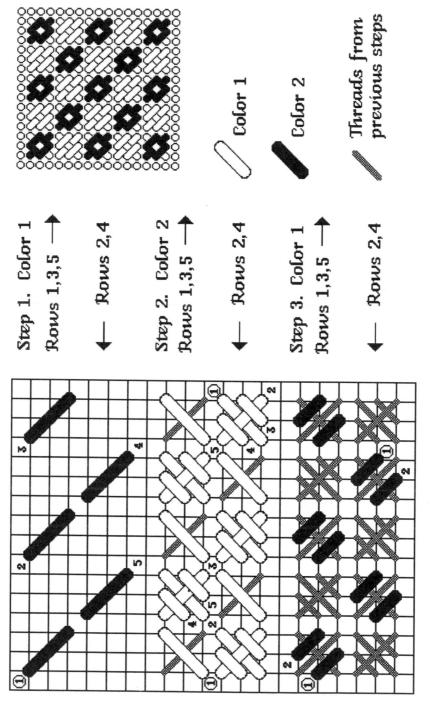

Step 1. Color 1
Rows 1,3,5 →

← Rows 2, 4

Step 2. Color 2
Rows 1,3,5 →

← Rows 2, 4

Step 3. Color 1
Rows 1,3,5 →

← Rows 2, 4

Color 1

Color 2

Threads from previous steps

The needle comes from the back to the front of the canvas at the numbers.

Needlepoint Earring #2

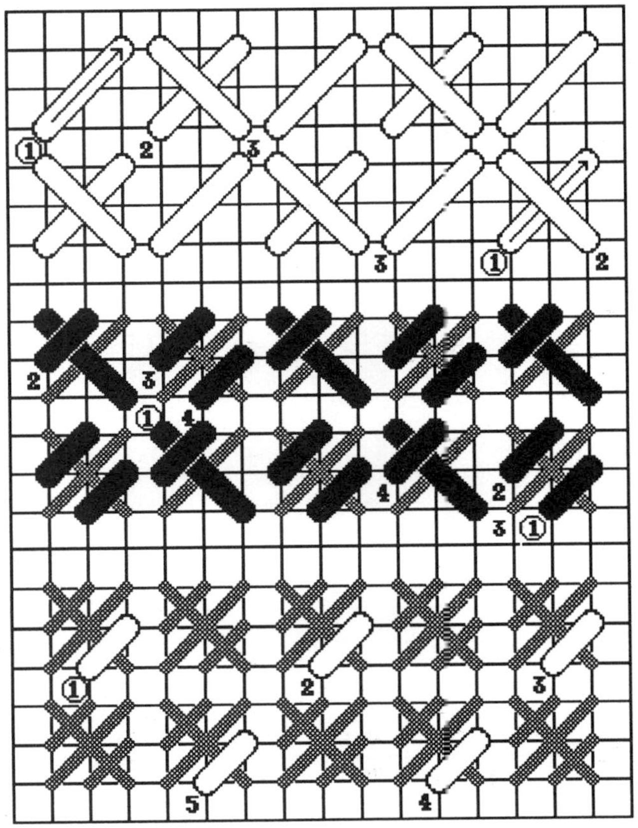

Step 1. Color 1
Rows 1,3,5 →

← Rows 2,4

Step 2. Color 2
Rows 1,3,5 →

← Rows 2,4

Step 3. Color 1
Rows 1,3,5 →

← Rows 2,4

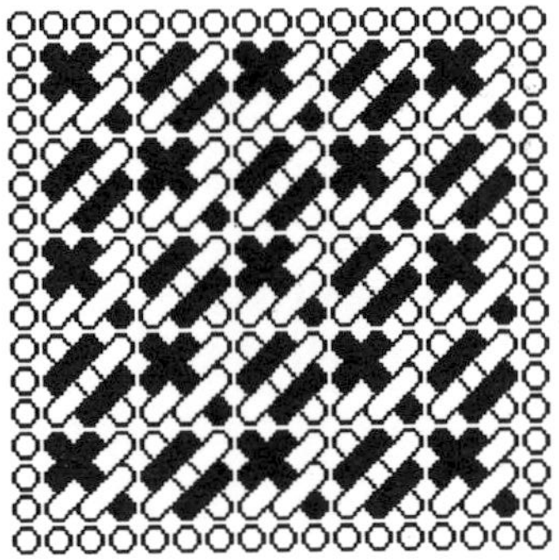

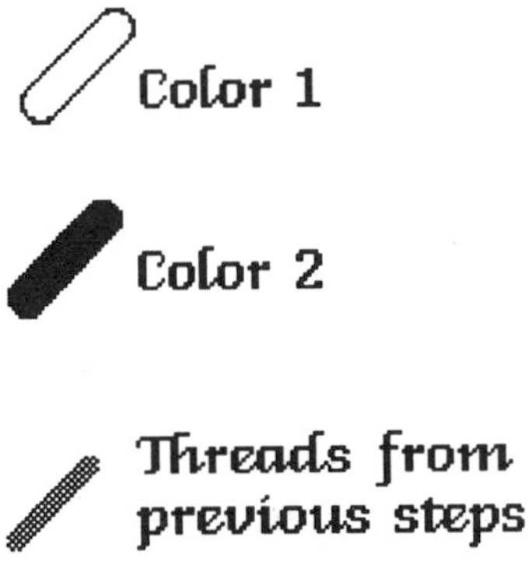

Color 1

Color 2

Threads from previous steps

The needle comes from the back to the front of the canvas at the numbers.

Needlepoint Needlecase

DMC Color Chart

- ▫ 310 Black
- ▪ 732 Olive Green
- ◭ 934 Black Avocado Grn.
- ▯ 739 Tan Ultra Vy. Lt.
- ◉ 734 Olive Grn. Light
- ◲ 309 Rose Deep
- ◪ 3733 Rose Pink
- Ⅎ 815 Garnet Medium

Work the back in tent stitch with #310 Black, working the scroll stitch border (chart on following page) in the same area as on the front.

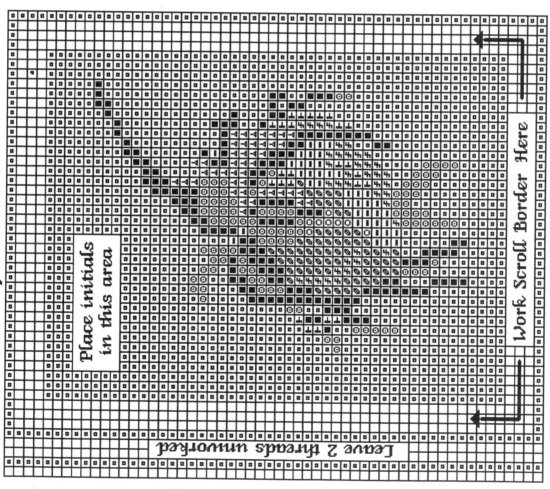

Place initials in this area

Work Scroll Border Here

Leave 2 threads unworked

Scroll Border.
Needlecase

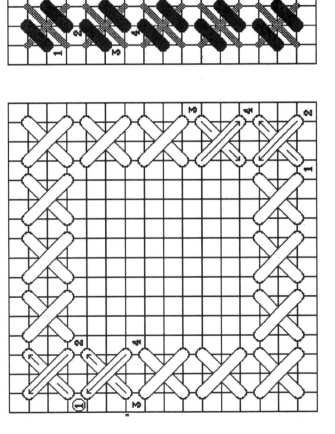

Step 1. Color 1 – DMC #739
Work twelve cross stitches across the top and bottom and sixteen on the sides between the corner stitches.

Step 2. Color 2 – DMC #310
The scroll will become apparent when you add the final row of tent stitch around the border.

The needle comes from the back to the front of the canvas at the numbers.

Needlepoint Needlecase Alphabet

Each block represents *either* a cross stitch or tent stitch.

Phone Home

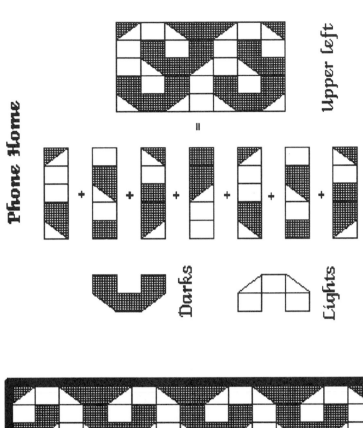

Darks

Lights

Upper left

Piece the triangles into rectangles and the rectangles into blocks of five by seven. Sew the blocks into strips and join the strips to complete the top.

Phone Home

You must be careful to make sure that phones of a color join together across and down.

For example, there is a light colored phone that is found in the lower right of block 2, the lower left of block 3, the upper right of block 6, and the upper left of block 7 as shown by the pattern.

Edge Stitch for Ornaments and Needlecase

1. Fold the canvas to the back leaving two threads exposed and work a long-legged cross stitch across these threads as shown on the chart below.

2. When you reach a corner, shorten your stitches if necessary and take one or two whip stitches in the corner threads to reinforce.

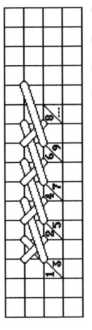

The needle comes from the back of the canvas to the front at the numbers.

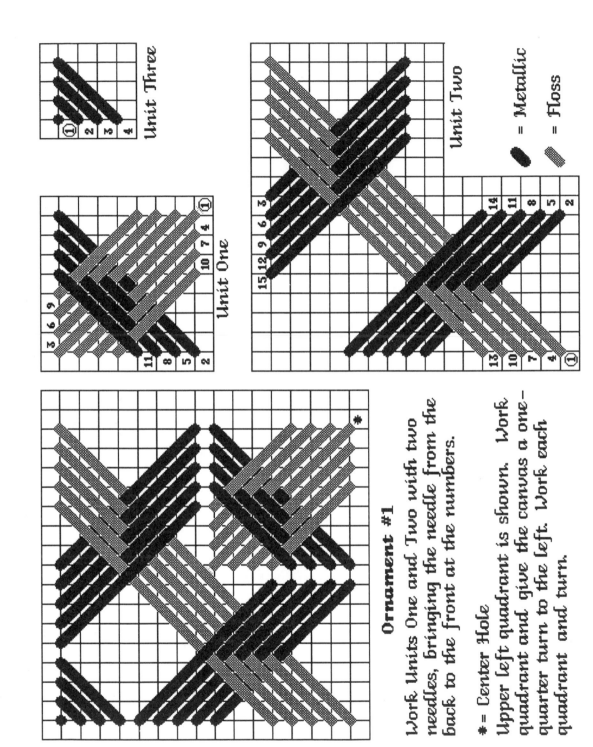

Unit Three

Unit One

Unit Two

= Metallic

= Floss

Ornament #1

Work Units One and Two with two needles, bringing the needle from the back to the front at the numbers.

* = Center Hole

Upper left quadrant is shown. Work quadrant and give the canvas a one-quarter turn to the left. Work each quadrant and turn.

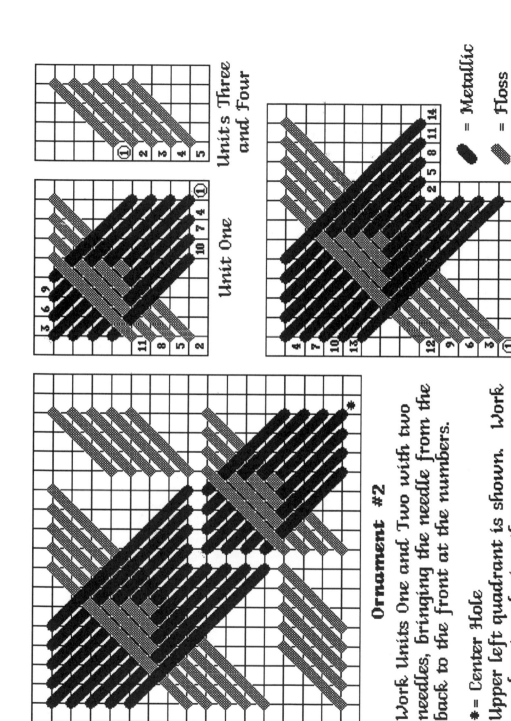

Units Three and Four

Unit One

Unit Two

= Metallic

= Floss

Ornament #2

Work Units One and Two with two needles, bringing the needle from the back to the front at the numbers.

* = Center Hole

Upper left quadrant is shown. Work quadrant and give the canvas a one-quarter turn to the left. Work each quadrant and turn.

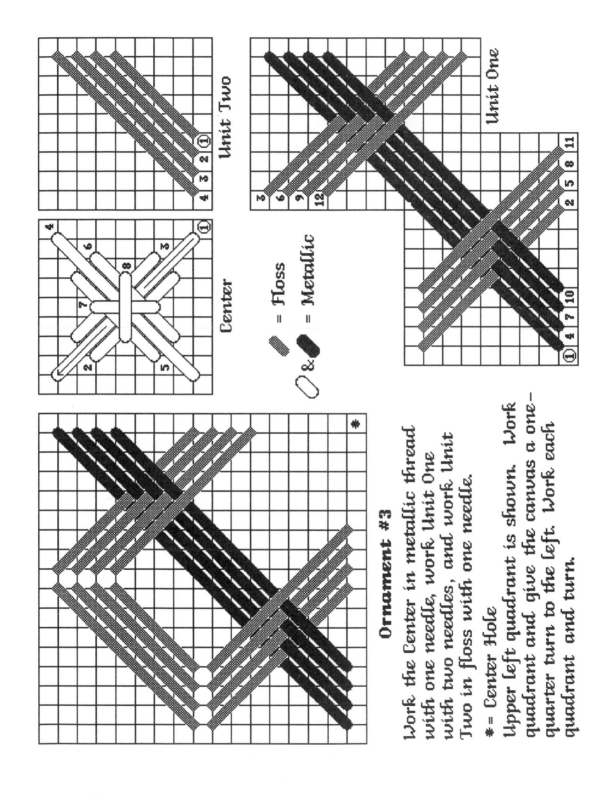

Unit Two

Unit One

Center

⬮ = Floss

⬮ & ⬛ = Metallic

Ornament #3

Work the Center in metallic thread with one needle, work Unit One with two needles, and work Unit Two in floss with one needle.

＊ = Center Hole

Upper left quadrant is shown. Work quadrant and give the canvas a one-quarter turn to the left. Work each quadrant and turn.

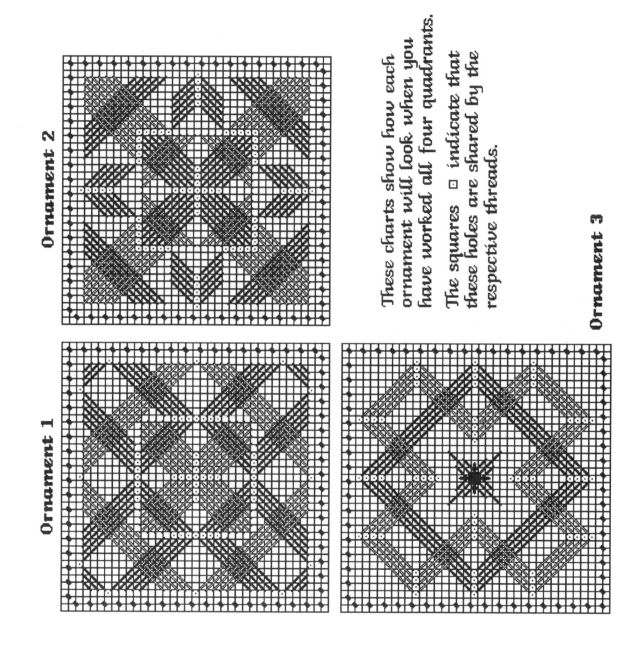

Ornament 2

Ornament 1

These charts show how each ornament will look when you have worked all four quadrants.

The squares ⊡ indicate that these holes are shared by the respective threads.

Ornament 3

Seminole Patchwork Ornament

Fabric A ☐
Fabric B ▪
Fabric C ▨
Fabric D ▨

Segments

1 2 2r 3 3r

Bands

One   Two   Three

Variations

A   B   C   D

Add Borders

Pattern Units

M + N =

Bibliography

You will find a list of the books in Chilton's Creative Machine Arts series inside the first page of this book.

Bradkin, Cheryl Greider. *Basic Seminole Patchwork.* Leone Publications. Mountain View, CA. 1990.

Britton, Dorothea S. *The Complete Book of Bazaars.* Coward, McCann & Geoghegan, Inc. New York. 1973.

Burdett, Rosalind, and Annette Claxton. *Gift Wrapping and Greeting Cards.* Gallery Books. New York. 1990.

Campbell-Harding, Valerie, and Pamela Watts. *Machine Embroidery: Stitch Techniques.* B. T. Batsford, Ltd. London, England. 1989.

Christensen, Jo Ippolito. *Teach Yourself Needlepoint.* Prentice-Hall, Inc. Englewood Cliffs, NJ. 1978.

Dobie, Jeanne. *Making Color Sing.* Watson-Guptill Publications. New York. 1986

Enthoven, Jacqueline. *The Stitches of Creative Embroidery.* Schiffer Publishing Co. West Chester, PA. 1987.

Fanning, Tony and Robbie. *Get It All Done and Still Be Human.* Kali House. Menlo Park, CA. 1990.

Hoover, Doris, and Nancy Welch. *Tassels.* Apple Tree Lane. Palo Alto, CA. 1978.

Howard, Constance. *Embroidery and Color.* B. T. Batsford, Ltd. London, England. 1976. (Paperback edition 1986.)

—*Inspiration for Embroidery.* B. T. Batsford, Ltd. London, England. 1966. (Paperback edition l985.)

—*The Constance Howard Book of Stitches.* B. T. Batsford, Ltd. London, England. 1979.

Jansen, Packo. *Wrapping Gifts Beautifully.* Sterling Publishing Co. New York. 1991.

Johannah, Barbara. *Half-Square Triangles.* Self-published. Navarro, CA. 1987.

—*The Quick Quiltmaking Handbook.* Pride of the Forest. Menlo Park, CA. 1979.

Kitagawa, Yoshiko. *Creative Cards.* Kodansha International. New York. 1987.

Lazar, Shelley Faye. *Pictures in Needlework.* Macmillan Publishing Company. New York. 1990.

Montano, Judith. *Crazy Quilt Odyssey.* C & T Publishing. Martinez, CA. 1991.

Nordfors, Jill. *Needle Lace and Needleweaving.* Van Nostrand Reinhold Co. New York. 1974.

Ollard, Caroline (introduced by). *The Complete Book of Needlecrafts.* Chilton Book Company. Radnor, PA. 1990.

Pearson, Anna. *The Complete Needlepoint Course.* Chilton Book Company, Radnor, PA. 1991.

Reader's Digest. *Complete Guide to Needlework.* The Reader's Digest Association, Inc., Pleasantville, NY. 1979.

Rhodes, Mary. *Dictionary of Canvas Work Stitches.* Charles Scribner's Sons. New York. 1980.

Righetti, Maggie. *Crocheting in Plain English.* St. Martin's Press. New York. 1988.

—*Knitting in Plain English.* St. Martin's Press. New York. 1986.

—*Universal Yarn Finder.* Prentice-Hall Press. New York. 1987.

Roche, Nan. *The New Clay.* Flower Valley Press. Rockville, MD. 1991.

Rush, Beverly, with Lassie Wittman. *The Complete Book of Seminole Patchwork.* Madrona Publishers. Seattle, WA. 1982.

Svennas, Elsie. *Advanced Quilting.* Charles Scribner's Sons. New York. 1980.

Walker, Michele. *The Complete Book of Quiltmaking.* Alfred A. Knopf. New York. 1986.

Walters, James. *Crochet Workshop.* Sidgwick & Jackson. London, England. 1979. (Reprinted 1983.)

Wittman, Lassie. *Seminole Patchwork Patterns.* Self-Published. (P.O. Box 774. Rochester, WA. 98579.) 1979.

Zimmerman, Elizabeth. *Knitting Without Tears.* Charles Scribner's Sons. New York. 1971.

Sources of Supplies

Aardvark Adventures in Handicrafts
P.O. Box 2449
Livermore, CA 94551-2449
1-800-388-ANTS
Machine embroidery thread, shisha

All Night Media, Inc.
Box 10607
San Rafael, CA 94901
"Postcard" rubber stamp, stamping accessories

Beadworks
139 Washington Street
South Norwalk, CT 06854
Jewelry findings, beads, threads

The Bee Lee Co.
P.O. Box 36108
Dallas, TX 75235-1108
Sewing supplies, buttons, rick-rack, ribbon

Chaparral
3701 West Alabama, Suite 370
Houston, TX 77027
Needlepoint canvas, Watercolour, metallic ribbon, thread, needlepoint and knitting supplies

Clotilde Inc.
Box 22312
Fort Lauderdale, FL 33335
Sewing notions, machine embroidery supplies, ribbon floss, rotary cutters, mats

Compucrafts
R.F.D. 2, Box 216
Lincoln, MA 91773
The Stitch Grapher program for IBM, Apple, and Macintosh computers

Enterprise Art
P.O. Box 2918
Largo, FL 34649
Fimo, Sculpey, craft supplies, jewelry findings, dimensional paints

Fabulous-Furs
700 Madison Avenue
Covington, KY 41011
1-800-848-1650
Faux fur remnants

Flynn Quilt Frame Company
1000 Shiloh Overpass Road
Billings, MT 59106
1-800-745-3596
Half-square quilt templates, quilt frames

Hill Country Weavers
918 W. 12th Street
Austin, TX 78703
Parisian cotton yarn and rayon chenille

Home-Sew
Bethlehem, PA 18018
Lace, rick-rack, buttons

Keepsake Quilting
Dover Street, P.O. Box 1459
Meredith, NH 03253
Quilting supplies, themed fabric assortments, books

Knit King
1128 Crenshaw Boulevard
Los Angeles, CA 90019
1-800-962-6446
Knitting machines, books, cone yarns

Mary Jane's Cross 'N Stitch, Inc.
5120 Belmont Road Suite R
Downer's Grove, IL 60515-4334
1-800-334-6819
Cross-stitch fabrics, threads, books, charts, hang towels, ready-to-stitch items

Nancy's Notions
P.O. Box 683
Beaver Dam, WI 53916-0683
1-800-765-0690
Sewing notions, video rental club, embroidery supplies

Newark Dressmaker Supply
6473 Ruch Road, P.O. Box 2448
Lehigh Valley, PA 18001
Bulk metal eyelets, sewing notions, Lily cotton yarns, cone yarns, cross-stitch supplies, fabric paints

Only the Best
P.O. Box 160232
Cupertino, CA 95016
Rubber stamps, pads, stamping accessories

Open Chain Publishing
P.O. Box 2634-GG
Menlo Park, CA 94026
Creative Machine *newsletter, Chilton and Open Chain books*

Ornamental Resources, Inc.
P.O. Box 3010
Idaho Springs, CO 80452
Charms, beads, jewelry findings

Quilters' Resources
Box 148850
Chicago, IL 60614
Lamés, old buttons, braids, trinkets, books

Quilts and Other Comforts
Box 394-237
Wheatridge, CO 80034-03494
Fabric assortments, quilting supplies, books

Sax Arts and Crafts
P.O. Box 51710
New Berlin, WI 53153
Art supplies, jewelry findings, metallic confetti

Sew Fit Co.
P.O. Box 565
LaGrange, IL 60525
Rotary cutters, mats, presser feet

Marinda Stewart
P.O. Box 402
Walnut Creek, CA 94596-0402
Fanny pack pattern

Sulky of America
3112 Broadpoint Drive
Harbor Heights, FL 33983
Rayon and metallic machine-embroidery threads

Western Trading Post
P.O. Box 9070
Denver, CO 80290-0070
Porcupine quills, fur, beads

Index